HOLOCAUST DENIAL

HOLOCAUST
DENIAL

Kenneth S. Stern

The American Jewish Committee
New York

Kenneth S. Stern is program specialist on anti-Semitism and extremism for the American Jewish Committee.

The American Jewish Committee protects the rights and freedoms of Jews the world over; combats bigotry and anti-Semitism and promotes human rights for all; works for the security of Israel and deepened understanding between Americans and Israelis; advocates public policy positions rooted in American democratic values and the perspectives of the Jewish heritage; and enhances the creative vitality of the Jewish people. Founded in 1906, it is the pioneer human-relations agency in the United States.

First printing April 1993
Second printing June 1993

DEDICATION

This publication is dedicated to the memory of Zachariah Shuster, who gave 40 years of extraordinary service to the cause of world Jewry, human rights, and Jewish-Christian understanding. He opened AJC's European office in 1948, helping thousands of Holocaust survivors, and, later, North African Jews fleeing anti-Semitism, rebuild their lives. On behalf of the AJC, he had a hand in establishing the Conference on Jewish Material Claims Against Germany, the passage of *Nostra Aetate*—which marked a turning point in Catholic attitudes toward Jews—and the publication of German textbooks containing accurate information about Jews, Judaism, anti-Semitism, and the Holocaust. In the early 1950s, Zachariah Shuster was one of the first to speak out about the plight of Soviet Jewry. It is appropriate that this book—one of the first to target Holocaust denial—be dedicated to him.

CONTENTS

PREFACE

I became interested in Holocaust denial when I saw history repeating itself. Whenever I asked friends what they thought of those who claim the Holocaust was a hoax, they'd laugh. "Who believes these nut cases?" they'd ask. "There's so much evidence about the Holocaust, why worry?"

I remembered similar reactions to the United Nations' equation of Zionism with racism in 1975. "No one will take this seriously," many said. They were wrong. In only a few years, the Zionism = racism canard found its way into dictionaries, law books, even placards in parades. Jews were told on many college campuses, including some U.S. campuses, that because they were Jews they were Zionists, and because they were Zionists they were racists. Even after the UN repealed the resolution in 1991, this slander remains a justification for anti-Semitism in many parts of the world.

The history of anti-Semitism emblazons one truth above all others: lies that promote Jew-hatred must never be ignored. Holocaust denial, though ridiculed today, has the attributes to become a potent form of anti-Semitism.

This book is divided into five parts. The introduction traces what denial is, and who is behind it. The first chapter examines denial in the United States; the second looks at denial worldwide. The third chapter debunks the deniers' specific claims. The last chapter offers a framework for combating denial and anti-Semitism in the generations to come.

I hope this book persuades the reader of two things: one, that Holocaust denial must be taken seriously; two, that combating it cannot be a matter of Holocaust education alone. Holocaust denial is not about historical truth. It is about anti-Jewish hatred as part of a political agenda—and must be confronted as such.

This book's release coincides with the opening of the Holocaust Memorial Museum in Washington, D.C. The Memorial may become a focus for the deniers, who will now have a symbolic address to target their neo-Nazi views. This publication is intended not only to suggest how to combat Holocaust denial, but also to increase awareness of the Museum's lesson: that genocide is always possible if people are complacent about hatred.

Kenneth S. Stern
Program Specialist, Anti-Semitism and Extremism
American Jewish Committee

HOLOCAUST DENIAL

INTRODUCTION

"How many Jews were gassed?" the protestors repeated over and over, as they marched in front of NBC headquarters in New York. "None!" they yelled. "Stop the hoax!"

Reporters interviewed the demonstrators.

"Why are you opposed to NBC showing the film *Holocaust?*" one reporter asked.

"Because," a protestor explained, the movie is "a Zionist attempt to further instill a guilt complex in the minds of the American people so that we will fail to analyze our Middle East policy objectively, and thus not question the billions of American tax dollars squandered on Israeli military supplies."

"But didn't the Nuremberg trials prove the existence of the Holocaust?" the reporter asked.

"No," the protestor explained, "no responsible historian today considers the Nuremberg trials as anything but a 'kangaroo court' conducted by the victors."

"But weren't Jews persecuted in Germany?" the reporter challenged.

"While discrimination against Jews did exist in Germany," the demonstrator admitted, "the official objective of the German government was to encourage the emigration of Jews, not extermination."

This bizarre protest occurred on September 9, 1979.[1] Thirteen

1

years later, it was Jews who had to demonstrate in front of another media giant. In 1992 the *Sunday Times* of London hired one of the world's leading Holocaust deniers, David Irving, to translate the diaries of Joseph Goebbels—for a fee of $150,000.[2]

The 1990s are witnessing a steady growth of Holocaust denial worldwide. Who believes such nonsense—that the Holocaust never occurred? Today, one in ten Italians do.[3] Fifteen years ago, Holocaust denial was the stuff of cut-and-paste hate literature and neo-Nazi catalogs. Today, it is promoted in the political process, the media, and the university, even in the United States. In 1986 the Institute for Historical Review (an anti-Semitic organization created to promote Holocaust denial) testified before Congress about Holocaust curricula in public schools.[4] In 1992, two Republican presidential candidates endorsed Holocaust denial, one (David Duke) fully, one (Patrick Buchanan) partially. Throughout the 1980s and into the 1990s deniers have been invited guests on scores of radio and television programs. Holocaust-denying ads have been printed in many college newspapers.

Denial, or "revisionism,"[5] as the deniers cynically call it, plays on classical anti-Semitic stereotypes: Jewish conspiracy and Jewish control of the media. It is unabashedly anti-Israel. It is well organized. And it exploits a true historical phenomenon: history is always reexamined by later generations, especially histories of wars, since the victors do indeed put their "spin" on events.

What "spin" do the Holocaust deniers put on World War II? One that, like any crazy dogma, is internally consistent, entirely self-supporting, and rejects any challenge as conspiratorially inspired. Its adherents are zealous because they believe they have discovered a societally suppressed "truth." Root such a dogma in a well-financed pro-Nazi and anti-Jewish ideology and anything becomes possible, especially as Holocaust denial is presented as noble intellectual inquiry, not as attack on Jews or as the "spin" modern-day Nazis would prefer.

"What proof exists that the Nazis practiced genocide or deliberately killed six million Jews?" the Institute for Historical Review asks in a widely circulated question-and-answer leaflet about the Holocaust (now translated into German, Italian and Spanish).[6] "None," the sheet proclaims. "The only evidence is the testimony of individual 'survivors.' This testimony is contradictory, and few 'survivors' claim to have witnessed any gassing. There is no hard evidence whatsoever: no mounds of ashes, no crematoria capable of doing the job, no piles of clothes, no human soap, no lamp shades made of human skin, no records, no credible demographic statistics."

"Why did the Germans intern Jews in concentration camps?" the leaflet asks. It answers: "Because the Germans considered Jews a direct threat to their national sovereignty and survival, and because Jews were overwhelmingly represented in Communist subversion."

Question: "How many Jews died in the concentration camps?" Answer: "About 300,000."

Question: "How did they die?" Answer: "Mainly from recurring typhus epidemics that ravaged war-torn Europe during the period. Also from starvation and lack of medical attention toward the end of the war when virtually all road and rail transportation had been bombed out by the Allies."

Since no extermination camps were on German soil (which is true), the deniers paint Dachau, a concentration camp in Germany, as a relatively pleasurable place.[7]

What was Auschwitz then, located in Poland? Answer: "A large-scale manufacturing complex . . . and its inmates were used as a work force."

What about gas chambers? There weren't any, the sheet says: "Auschwitz, captured by the Soviets, was extensively modified after the war and a mortuary was reconstructed to look like a large 'gas chamber.' After America's leading expert on gas chamber construction and design, Fred Leuchter, examined this and other alleged Auschwitz gassing facilities, he stated that it was an 'absurdity' to claim that they were . . . used for executions."

Deniers argue that all the confessions at Nuremberg were false, the result of torture; that gassing was only for delousing; that if gassing had been the policy, a gas other than Zyklon-B[8] would have been used; that the crematoria could not have operated quickly enough to account for all the dead; that pictures of the dead were of people who had died of typhus, or, as the IHR's question-and-answer sheet proclaims, "piles of German women and children killed in Allied bombing raids who have been passed off as dead Jews."

3

Deniers, of course, argue that Nazi Germany in general, and Hitler in particular, weren't so bad. Question: "What was the main provision of the German 'Nuremberg laws of 1935'? " Answer: "Laws against intermarriage and sexual relations between Germans and Jews, similar to laws existing in Israel today." Question: "Were there any American precedents for the Nuremberg Laws?" Answer: "Many states in the U.S.A. had laws preventing intermarriage and sexual relations between persons of different races long before the Nazis." Question: "What evidence is there that Hitler knew of the ongoing Jewish extermination." Answer: "None."

Through lies, distortions, and half-truths, hard-core deniers repaint a world where Nazis are the victims and Jews are the villains. It is, literally, history turned on its head. And it is a revised history that is very attractive: it rejects any need to feel bad about genocide—in fact, if you feel bad about genocide, you're a sap.

That's why, when Josef Schwammberger, a Nazi war criminal responsible for the deaths of hundreds of Jews, was sentenced to life imprisonment in Germany on May 18, 1992, protestors not only demanded Schwammberger's release, but also decried "the lie that only one country was guilty for the war."

The danger of denial is that one need not be a neo-Nazi to imbibe the anti-Semitism of this poisonous nectar. This is especially true for young people, for whom the 1930s and 1940s are the stale history of their grandparents' youth. Put yourself into an eighteen-year-old's frame of mind. Who is to say Nazism was so bad? After all, it wasn't a fringe movement. In one of the greatest industrial powers of all time, millions followed this doctrine. And, of course, maybe some Jews were exterminated, but who is to say that Jews haven't exaggerated the details for their own purposes? This alleged Holocaust occurred during a war. Civilians always die during wars. It wasn't only Jews that were killed. Who knows what happened anyway? It's old history, so why does it matter?

In the United States during the 1991–92 academic year, a denier named Bradley Smith offered Holocaust-denying ads to college newspapers. A few ran them. Most didn't. Holocaust "revisionism," as Smith called it, was roundly ridiculed, as if someone wanted to recast the experience of slavery as a myth, stating with a straight face that the slave ships were actually pleasure boats.[9] But the slavery-Holocaust comparison is not valid. People may diminish the horror of slavery, but no one would deny it—the institution was even written into the U.S. Constitution (slaves were to be counted as three-fifths of a human being). Nor does one need to know the names of the slave ships, or the ports of entry, or the points of origin, or the names of the plantation owners, or the diaries of the times, or the horrors of the Middle Passage, to know that slavery occurred. Holocaust deniers exploit the fact that the Holocaust occurred during a war, and that German leadership tried to hide evidence of its guilt. Like defense lawyers freed from any rule of evidence, deniers distort or invent or ignore "facts" to "prove" their thesis (that the Holocaust never occurred) or to create the impression that the Holocaust is a topic to be debated. There are "revisionists" and "exterminationists." Two sides to every story. You don't want to debate? That's suppression of free speech, they say—as well as evidence that you have something to hide.

With years of practice, millions of dollars to spend, and an increasingly large collection of material, the deniers are here to stay. They are especially targeting the young with anti-Semitic hate cloaked—as William McPherson, writing in the *Washington Post,* correctly calls it—"in the garb of reason." And make no mistake about it—to the unknowing, the minutiae of Holocaust denial appear reasonable. It is anti-Semitism masquerading as objective scholarly inquiry.

Who is behind it? Where did it start? What is its agenda? How does it differ in the United States, Canada, Western Europe, Eastern Europe? Why does it have support from both the Left and the Right? How does it relate to classical anti-Semitism? How does it fit into anti-Israel propaganda? Why have some seen this as legitimate debate rather than hate or fiction? In the United States, what are the First Amendment implications? How have institutions (media, talk radio, colleges, politicians) dealt with denial? How should they? What will happen when there are no more survivors and liberators, when new generations are further removed from the Holocaust? How are genocides remembered or misremembered anyway? Are there historical lessons to suggest how to combat denial? What do these lessons say about community interaction, about the ability of groups with "competing genocides" to work together? How successful has education been as an antidote for Holocaust denial? Can hateful fiction be fought with historical truth? Or should hate be the primary target?

If those questions are troubling and difficult to answer, consider this one: What if the post-World War II decline in anti-Semitism—as proved by attitudinal surveys, polls, and the opening of previously barred doors to Jews—is partly a reaction to the Holocaust? If this theory is true, then does the passage of time, let alone the attempt to deny the Holocaust, mean that our children and grandchildren will live in a more anti-Semitic world?

The Beginnings of Holocaust Denial

Holocaust denial began before the Holocaust ended.

"In 1944," explains Gerry Gable,[10] editor of the London-based antifascist monthly *Searchlight,* "people who were SS, who were propagandists, who were involved in the camp system, knew they lost the war, and left Germany. Sweden was one of the places they went. Some went to the Arab states, and into some South American countries. There they began to work for the readjustment of history. Holocaust denial material first appeared very very early after the war."

One of the earliest European Holocaust deniers was Paul Rassinier, a French concentration camp survivor. A former socialist and anarchist, he first blamed the *kapos* for the suffering in the camps, then used every inconsistency he could find in statements about the Holocaust to cast doubt on both the Nazi intention to kill Jews and the numbers of Jews killed. His book, published in French as *Le Monsonge d'Ulysse* in 1949, was translated into English after his death in 1967. It is still widely promoted by neo-Nazis around the world.

Americans added to the early denial literature. Harry Elmer Barnes, an isolationist, was best known for his writings whitewashing the German role in World War I. In 1962, in a pamphlet called *Blasting the Historical Blackout,* Barnes claimed that Germans who were expelled from Poland and Czechoslovakia after World War II suffered a fate "obviously far more hideous and prolonged than those of the Jews said to have been exterminated in great numbers by the Nazis." According to Holocaust scholar Lucy Dawidowicz, Barnes had "already doubted that the Third Reich had committed any atrocities or murder" by 1962.[11] In 1966, he published "Revisionism: A Key to Peace," in which he claimed that "it is almost alarmingly easy to demonstrate that the atrocities of the Allies in the same period were more numerous as to victims and were carried out for the most part by methods more brutal and painful than alleged extermination in gas ovens."[12]

By the late 1960s, both Barnes and Rassinier had died. A new crop of deniers replaced them. David Hoggan wrote *The Myth of the Six Million*,[13] published by Noontide Press, part of the network of anti-Semitic enterprises associated with America's leading anti-Semite, Willis Carto[14] and his Liberty Lobby.[15] This work attempted to disprove the German eyewitness reports of the Holocaust, and otherwise rebut the evidence of the murder of European Jewry.[16]

Denial literature was first noticed outside the neo-Nazi crowd in 1976, when Dr. Arthur R. Butz, an American professor at Northwestern University (who still teaches electrical engineering there), wrote *The Hoax of the Twentieth Century*. Butz admitted that Jews were persecuted, but denied they were exterminated. Any chambers were for delousing, he charged. "Jews," he insisted, "should be elated to discover that large numbers of their people were not deliberately destroyed." People who had never heard of Holocaust denial learned of it through the controversy surrounding Butz, whose right of academic freedom was supported by Northwestern's faculty.[17]

Holocaust denial was launched as a serious enterprise by professional anti-Semites in 1979. Willis Carto, apparently not satisfied to promote denial through his other anti-Semitic outlets, opened the Institute for Historical Review.

Carto, according to Gerry Gable, is "a life-long anti-Semite." Carto and his colleagues "got a bit of money from the Middle East, and elsewhere, and started to recreate history. They give themselves spectacular titles. The Institute of This. The Institute of That. Professor this. Professor that. And you look at some of their professorships, and they've got nothing to do with the subjects they're writing about."

In 1979 the Institute had its first annual conference. Deniers from around the world attended, and exposed American white supremacists and neo-Nazis to this new idea. David Duke, then a Ku Klux Klan leader, attended an IHR meeting. He was apparently so enthralled that a 1980 edition of his Klan paper, the *Crusader,* was dubbed a "Special Holocaust Edition." "Germans and Southerners are invariably portrayed unfavorably by the Jewish-dominated media . . . Photographs . . . of alleged gas chamber victims were fakes," he wrote. Another Nazi leader, Frank Colin, head of the National Socialist Party of America, also enthusiastically embraced this further ideological justification for his anti-Semitism. "There was no Holocaust," Colin said, "but they deserve one—and will get it."[18]

Holocaust denial was attractive to the far right anti-Semitic crowd because it validated their belief that Jews were evil and conspiratorial. By ignoring all the facts and witnesses that belie denial, Holocaust denial can be given an air of truth, especially if this "truth" is written by people with Ph.D.'s. That is why Carto's lie-tank collected professors and began publishing the *Journal of Historical Review,* designed to look like any other academic journal. Today, the IHR churns out not only scholarly looking journals, but also audio and videotapes of its conferences.[19] IHR material—including books and pamphlets—is sent all over the world. The IHR is the spine of the international Holocaust denial movement, and, according to Leonard Zeskind,[20] research director of the Center for Democratic Renewal, the IHR's influence now is only a fraction of what it will be. "It is getting a $10 million bequest from one of the heirs of Thomas Edison," Zeskind notes, "solely for the purpose of promoting Holocaust denial."[21]

What Do They Say to Deny the Holocaust?

The worst mistake any rational person can make is to think that since Holocaust denial is so irrational, it must appear irrational to others. It doesn't.[22] Read any Holocaust denial article that avoids overt Jew-hatred, and the arguments appear logical, internally consistent, and reasonable. French professor Robert Faurisson, for example, denies the existence of gas chambers at Auschwitz by writing about the characteristics of the gas used to kill Jews—Zyklon-B. He argues that Zyklon-B is an effective killer that sticks to surfaces. How, he asks, could such a powerful, combustible, and explosive gas have been used, when the testimony about the camp suggests that no special equipment was used to take the dead bodies out, that there would have been poisoned air pockets between corpses, that the people who removed the bodies smoked while doing so, and that the removal of corpses was said to be immediate when, even with the best technology, it would have required nearly a day to ventilate a gas chamber?

Fred Leuchter, a self-proclaimed and self-taught "expert" on gas chambers, is the newest darling of the denial clan. He says he examined buildings in Auschwitz-Birkenau and Maidanek which would have contained chemical residue from the gas chambers if any Zyklon-B had been used, and found none.[23]

Others point to statistics of Jewish population before and after the war. For example, in a booklet titled *Auschwitz: Truth or Lie,* by Thies Christophersen, the number of Jews in 1938 is given as 15,688,259—source, the American Jewish Committee; and 18,700,-000 in 1948—source, a *New York Times* article. How could there have been a Holocaust if there were 3 million more Jews after the war than before?

Each professional denier has developed an "expertise." For the British David Irving, for example, it is the rehabilitation of Hitler. Regardless of their prime focus, however, most deniers come back to a central theme: that the indictment of Nazism as an unequivocally evil episode in human history is simplistic and in error. There are, after all, two sides to every story. After wars, the victors always write the history. Certainly, there must have been atrocities by both sides. Why are the Germans the only ones talked about? What about Allied bombing of German cities—Dresden, for example?

To those who did not live through the events, the recasting of World War II may seem reasonable, especially if it is punctuated with stories that paint Churchill and Roosevelt as conspirators secretly plotting to pull poor Germany into a war it did not want. Evil becomes diluted in relativity. If one believes in a relativized history, then anyone who points to an aspect of the same history, such as Nazi anti-Semitism, as unabashed evil becomes suspect. Jews, then, who knew nothing but unabashed evil during World War II, are double victims of the Holocaust.

Chapter 1

HOLOCAUST DENIAL IN THE UNITED STATES

Holocaust denial, although widely ridiculed, has appeared in many American institutions. In the classroom. On the campus. In politics. In libraries. On computers. On radio and television. It has not always been responded to well. The Institute for Historical Review and its fellow deniers know that if they target their message wisely and widely, they will have some success; and where they don't, the controversy they create will be success enough.

In the Classroom, on the Campus

In 1987, in Aurora, Colorado, public high school teacher Dorothy Groteluschen told her students that the Holocaust was really a "holohoax,"[1] and distributed copies of an article entitled "Swindlers of the Crematoria."[2] She was disciplined. She sued. The school district settled, paying her $3,850.[3]

In 1990, in Winnetka, Illinois, a couple removed their daughter from her junior high school classes when the Holocaust was studied. Holocaust study was mandated by Illinois law. The parents complained that the curriculum was the product of a "demented mind," namely Jewish propagandists who wanted the world to learn "gross distortions and myths" about the Holocaust. In support of their decision, the girl's parents quoted *The Hoax of the Twentieth Century* by Arthur Butz.[4]

In 1990, Donald Hiner taught a Western Civilization 101 class at Indiana-Purdue University. He said the Holocaust was a "myth"; that "the worst thing about Hitler is that without him, there would not be an Israel"; and that "If the Holocaust really occurred, you wouldn't have 2.5 million in Israel getting reparations." Considered a "good" teacher by students and administration alike, Hiner's Holocaust denial went unnoticed for more than half the academic year, until one student taped a lecture and brought it to a dean's attention.[5]

Other teachers have also used Holocaust-denying material. Some have been caught. Richard Countess, for example, was stopped from teaching a course using Arthur Butz's work at the University of Alabama. But others claim to be using the material without objection. One teacher from South Carolina, signing only his initials, wrote in the Institute for Historical Review (IHR) *Newsletter* that his students were "captivated" by Holocaust denial. "Many students in my class have asked if I will meet them away from school during the summer just to talk," he wrote, "and I have agreed."[6]

Certainly, there are no school districts in the United States mandating or encouraging the teaching of Holocaust denial. But some teachers are, in fact, teaching it, others are writing it, and the issue, once discovered, becomes one with which academics have trouble. The deniers intentionally cloak the controversy they create in the garb of academic freedom and the discovery of knowledge through debate.

Consider the controversy surrounding Arthur Butz's publication of *The Hoax of the Twentieth Century* in 1976. Butz's claim of academic freedom was supported by the Northwestern faculty. Butz had tenure, which was held to be inviolate regardless of what crazy, hateful theories he believed. (Butz, of course, was an associate professor of electrical engineering and computer science, not of history.) The faculty was on one side. On the other were Jewish alumni and contributors, outraged that their funds went partly to pay Butz's salary. They threatened to withhold their contributions.

Although the administration disapproved of Butz's views—and urged the history department to hold a series of lectures to tell the truth about the 6 million Jews who had been murdered—it "just didn't get it" about Holocaust denial. Holocaust scholar Lucy Dawidowicz, who was asked to give one of the lectures, wrote that she "argued in private with some members of the faculty and the administration that the university's response was inadequate, for it seemed to me that they regarded the affair merely as an unfortunate incident affecting Jewish sensibilities. In fact, in their public statements the university's president and provost had treated the Butz scandal as a Jewish family sorrow. . . . No one at this great center of learning seemed to regard Butz's absurdities as an offense against historical truth, a matter supposedly of concern to an intellectual and academic community."[7]

When Holocaust denial appears in an academic institution, Jews invariably are the most concerned and most visible in response to the outrage. Rarely has either the hate inherent in Holocaust denial or its intellectual dishonesty been fully appreciated by non-Jews. Old adages like "there are two sides to every story," or demands to "debate the facts," are everywhere to be heard. By demanding "open debate," the deniers obscure the truth that scholars debate the Holocaust's facts and lessons all the time—just not with neo-Nazis. The deniers want to poison that debate with their carefully crafted fiction, knowing that their charges of coverup and conspiracy are so farfetched that, by their very nature, they cannot easily be refuted.

Making Holocaust denial seem not so outrageous is the self-appointed task of Bradley Smith, who is both the media project director for the Institute for Historical Review, and the head of something he calls the Committee for Open Debate about the Holocaust. In the early 1990s, he submitted Holocaust-denying ads (see appendix A) to college and university newspapers, with some degree of success.[8] For many, he was able to confuse the issue with one of free speech. Why, after all, should his point of view be rejected? Didn't newspapers have a responsibility to present all sides? What is it, he asked, about the Holocaust alone that gets people so upset if questions are raised? No other aspect of human history, he argued, is "off limits" for debate.[9]

His approach, appealing to the First Amendment, confused the naive by disguising his design. Every aspect of human experience should be studied—and perhaps none more so than the history of human indulgence in hate and genocide. There have been thousands of books written about the Holocaust. Scholars worldwide are studying it. Some "truths" about the Holocaust have been challenged. Many believed gas chambers had been used at Dachau—they were not. Many believed Jews had been made into soap—historians now refute that claim.[10] But these revisions of history were made by scholars—people who have real credentials, no anti-Semitic agenda, and who look at piles of dead bodies and human hair and children's shoes, mounds of documents and confessions and eyewitness accounts, and ask "What does this all mean?" rather than "How can I twist this evidence to cast doubt about the Holocaust?" Scholars are not people whose works are promoted with ads asking readers to look "at the guilt, and the gelt,"[11] or whose material—like Bradley Smith's or David Irving's—can be purchased from the same catalogs that market Hitler's best speeches of 1933, the marching songs of the Waffen SS, the *Protocols of the Elders of Zion,* and books on eugenics (which try to prove that blacks are biologically inferior to whites). Just as no newspaper that pretends to know the difference between fact and fiction would print an ad for the "true" black experience in the American South printed by the Ku Klux Klan, no self-respecting newspaper should print Holocaust-denying ads. (In fact, the American Historical Association issued a statement deploring "the publicly reported attempts to deny the fact of the Holocaust. No serious historian questions that the Holocaust took place."[12])

Many who do not recognize Holocaust denial as neatly dressed anti-Semitism also miscomprehend the First Amendment. If Smith were promoting the "virtues" of child molestation, no student newspaper would accept his advertisement, or give credence to his argument that the question was not being fairly "debated."

When Smith first offered his ads, the American Jewish Committee wrote to every college and university president in the United States, documenting Smith's relationship with the anti-Semitic Institute for Historical Review (see appendix B) and pointing out that "the First Amendment does not require a newspaper to accept every ad any more than the right of Americans accused of crime to a lawyer obligates all lawyers to take every client."

Smith, and others like him, will continue pushing Holocaust denial and picking First Amendment fights to draw attention to themselves and to paint their agenda as a reasonable one. How institutions such as universities and the media react is critical—as well as whether real historians speak out to denounce these neo-Nazi impostors.[13]

Institutional leadership must debunk the deniers' First Amendment claims. University presidents, chairs of departments, members of the boards of trustees and others must stress that while deniers unquestionably have the right to speak, to print their own newspapers, and to produce their own radio shows, the First Amendment does not obligate anyone else to give them a forum. These leaders must also denounce the hatred, bigotry, and historical pollution that is the handiwork of deniers who pose as historians. An institution amplifies and legitimizes anti-Semitism either by accepting an ad (thereby saying that Holocaust denial is worthy of some respect), or by appearing indifferent to this injection of hatred. Either way, people are hurt. AJC encouraged university leaders to use their own free speech rights to denounce this form of anti-Semitism.[14]

Radio and Television

Before Bradley Smith offered ads to college newspapers, he targeted talk radio,[15] both directly and through deceit. For example, during the Persian Gulf War in 1991, he sent circulars to radio stations advertising himself as an expert on war-crimes trials—an issue concerning Iraqi dictator Saddam Hussein. A few minutes into an interview, however, Smith mentioned how the Nuremberg trial actually didn't work. From there, he was off on his agenda of Holocaust denial.

Various talk-show hosts, most prominently Barry Farber, refused to give Smith air time. Smith retaliated with nasty cards about Farber sent to people in the medium. Other talk show hosts, sensing a controversial topic, accepted Smith's request to appear.

In the spring of 1990, the American Jewish Committee published a report, *Hate on Talk Radio,* that exposed the Liberty Lobby, the Institute for Historical Review, and Bradley Smith's attempts to promote Holocaust denial through talk radio. By Smith's own account, after the release of the AJC report only nine of 900 invitations he sent to stations resulted in on-air interviews.[16] Nonetheless, Smith knows that radio and television want spicy topics to drive up ratings, and Holocaust denial will certainly generate heat.

14

Smith also knows that he and his cohorts have a reservoir of facts, half-facts, quarter-facts, and outright lies to counter any talk-show host—for what radio personality can spend hundreds of hours researching the deniers' reasonable-sounding lies? Smith also knows that the people who can expose him are in a quandary: If they do not appear with him, his lies are unchallenged; and, worse, if they confront him, Smith's credibility is enhanced—there is now a "debate" between "opposing theories," something he craves.

Programs where the "fact" of the Holocaust is debated are macabre things. Deniers appear reasonable with their minutiae, while survivors who try to debunk the hate are abused for the emotion in their voices. Listening to one of these programs makes one wonder what an eighteen-year-old might think—Is there something to this debate? Does this old history really matter? Either way, the deniers win.

Most major Jewish organizations will not debate a Nazi or a member of the Ku Klux Klan, nor will they debate whether the Holocaust was fact or fiction—any more than a black leader would dignify a KKK member with a debate about whether slavery existed, and if it did, whether it was a good thing. As Michael Harrison, one of the nation's leading talk-show hosts and publisher of the trade journal *Talkers,* notes, most people in the industry are of "goodwill." Once they understand the pernicious motive of Holocaust deniers—that these folks are not just quirky members of another "flat-earth society"—they will not provide them a forum. Of course, there are still opportunists. And the deniers know that even people of goodwill may not understand their hateful agenda until after a program is aired—if then. For example, in 1992, on Yom HaShoah, the day of Holocaust remembrance, the Montel Williams television talk show devoted an hour to the claims of Holocaust deniers, who were debated by survivors and an author. (See appendix C.)

Libraries and Courts

In 1984, the California Library Association planned to provide an exhibition booth to David McCalden, a Holocaust denier. The American Jewish Committee and the Simon Wiesenthal Center objected, as did other groups and individuals. McCalden was disinvited. He sued, claiming that his civil rights were violated. After years of litigation, the U.S. Court of Appeals for the Ninth Circuit granted McCalden's widow (McCalden died, and his widow was given the right to press his case) the opportunity to have a trial on his claims. The Supreme Court declined to review that decision in 1992. AJC and the Wiesenthal Center insisted that they did not violate McCalden's rights, and were prepared to fight the case. Fortunately, McCalden's widow withdrew the suit. However, one wonders what chilling effect such litigation would have had on other groups or individuals that don't see fighting bigotry as their mission. Holocaust deniers may continue to sue those who oppose their message, since litigation also attracts the media attention they covet.

It has not only been through orchestrated media events and litigation that libraries are encountering Holocaust denial. In Wichita, Kansas, a lawyer asked the public library to buy Arthur Butz's *The Hoax of the Twentieth Century* and Wilhelm Staeglich's *Auschwitz Myth*. By a vote of 7–4, the library board refused.[17]

Deniers in New Jersey, California, and elsewhere repeatedly place Holocaust-denying literature into books about the Holocaust. And many libraries, not knowing the bigoted nature of some books with titles referring to the Holocaust, have put denial literature on their shelves and in bibliographies alongside credible scholarship. For example, in 1981, the public library in Cherry Hill, New Jersey, took part in a community project to construct a "living monument" to the victims of the Holocaust. The library submitted a list of books it wanted to buy. Among them were Arthur Butz's *The Hoax of the Twentieth Century* and David Hoggan's *The Myth of the Six Million.*

One of IHR's earliest self-confessed "gimmicks" was a crass $50,000 award for "proving" the Holocaust. Most of the Jewish community declined to dignify the offer with a response, for good reason. First, the IHR would have control over the "judges," who could all be deniers. Second, legally, an offeror of a reward would have the right to structure his or her offer in any way he or she liked, thereby making a court challenge difficult. Third, the IHR would get the free publicity and credibility its offer was designed to attract. And, fourth, the Holocaust was a proven fact, at Nuremberg and elsewhere, through overwhelming evidence. There was no need to

16

enter the trap of what the IHR termed its "#1 gimmick."[18] (Simon Wiesenthal staked a claim to the IHR's corollary offer of $25,000 for proof that the *Diary of Anne Frank* was legitimate. The IHR, however, refused Wiesenthal's request that both sides find and accept a former California Supreme Court justice to review the evidence. Wiesenthal withdrew his claim.)

Mel Mermelstein, a survivor whose family had been killed in the Holocaust, took up the challenge. He submitted eyewitness accounts, documents, photographs, and histories to the IHR. When he heard nothing in response, he sued—and was tormented by the deniers for his efforts. (David McCalden, IHR director at the time, wrote to Mermelstein: "I notice that you go under two names, Mermelstein and Memmelstein. Having two names would indicate to me you have been gassed at least twice, possibly also receiving [*sic*] double pensions for your execution."[19])

On October 9, 1981, Los Angeles County Superior Court Judge Thomas T. Johnson ruled that the Holocaust "is not reasonably subject to dispute. . . . The court does take judicial notice that Jews were gassed to death in Poland in Auschwitz in the summer of 1944 [when Mermelstein's family was there]." Mermelstein was awarded damages of $90,000, and the IHR was ordered to apologize.[20]

Mermelstein, quoted in the *Washington Post*,[21] said, "I feel relieved. But I wonder why I should feel that way, because it is an established fact."[22]

Mermelstein's principled and courageous action against the IHR, and the AJC's defense against David McCalden, are not the only times Holocaust denial has entered American courts. When White Aryan Resistance leader Tom Metzger was tried in California for burning a cross, his defense attorney submitted a question for potential jurors: "A belief held by some people in this country is that there was no deliberate and systematic killing of Jews by the Nazis during the 1930s and World War II. Do you agree or disagree with this belief, and why?"[23] Courtrooms, in some ways the best place to debunk the deniers because rules of evidence require proof of facts, are also troublesome venues. Legal cases will turn on issues beyond the facts of the Holocaust; and the deniers will gain the publicity they crave.

The Political Process

In 1991, over 700,000 Louisianians voted for former KKK wizard David Duke as governor, despite his full-fledged Holocaust denial. He won a majority of the white vote on his agenda designed to make whites feel good about hating minorities. Duke not only was caught selling *Mein Kampf* and Holocaust denial material right before the campaign, he made no secret of his belief that the Holocaust was fiction. Would so many have voted for him if he proudly proclaimed that the earth was flat?

Patrick Buchanan, like Duke, was also a Republican presidential candidate in 1992. Buchanan had challenged the fact that Jews were gassed at Treblinka, basing his view on a 1987 story about trapped children who survived a Washington, D.C., tunnel partially contaminated with diesel fumes.[24] Buchanan, a nationally known columnist, is trying to become a major Republican party power, and future presidential nominee. His views, flirting around the edges of Holocaust denial (he also wrote of the "so-called Holocaust Survivor Syndrome," and the "group fantasies of martyrdom and heroics"), have not disqualified him. In fact, he was a highlighted speaker at the 1992 Republican National Convention.

That candidates who are known for their anti-Semitic expressions should find Holocaust denial attractive is not surprising. The troubling thing is that when Holocaust denial has appeared in national politics, it has been seen as quirkiness, not hatred—and not even quirkiness sufficient to disqualify someone from office. (President Bush castigated Duke for denying the Holocaust, but not Buchanan.) While no one from a major party has campaigned on a platform of Holocaust denial,[25] the votes of millions of Americans say that this form of anti-Semitism is no big deal. If a candidate is attractive for other reasons, denial of a recent major historical tragedy involving Jews will be overlooked rather than seen as an irreparable character defect. One wonders if Duke would have been equally attractive had he believed that Elvis was alive, that the moon landing had been staged, or that he had been Shirley MacLaine in a prior life.

Elizabeth Rickey,[26] a college instructor and a former member of the Republican State Committee in Louisiana who has devoted years to combating David Duke, said: "When I learned about

David Duke's views on the Holocaust, my first reaction was to be stunned that there was this school of thought that says there's different historical perspectives on the Holocaust. What I found from reading Duke's writings is that David Duke believes that the 'Jewish press,' as he calls it, and Hollywood created this myth of the Holocaust. So we have someone who was a very serious candidate for public office believing this. How seriously should we take this? I found that there's not much of an immune system among young people today, they don't have any historical background. So when someone comes along and says this, that appeals to a certain prejudice that may be existing in them anyway, they tend to pick it up and go with it. I saw what the insidious effect of David Duke's candidacy was. People that followed him got introduced to this concept, and believed it, because they believed in David Duke. And they had no real education in the Holocaust to counter that."

The fact that hundreds of thousands of people voted for David Duke and Patrick Buchanan, despite the two men's dabbling in Holocaust denial, proves that a candidate can be viable in the 1990s in America despite his or her anti-Semitism.

Holocaust Denial in the Separationist American Black Community

Holocaust denial is not the stuff of white supremacists alone. In 1992, a Los Angeles conference was scheduled by a black activist named Robert Brock. Speakers were to include Leonard Jeffries, the former chair of the Afro-American Studies Department at the City College of New York, known for his anti-Semitism,[27] and representatives of the Institute for Historical Review. Jeffries did not appear and later said that he did not subscribe to Holocaust denial, pointing out that black soldiers had been among the liberators of concentration camps.[28] However, other notable figures on the anti-Semitic fringe of the black community have been spreading out-and-out Holocaust denial.

The Final Call is the newspaper of Louis Farrakhan and the Nation of Islam.[29] It regularly features anti-Semitic tirades, some focusing on the Holocaust. For example, Abdul Allah Muhammad wrote in the June 1991 edition that a memorial at Auschwitz had been removed because "the four million extermination victims cited on the stone was a blatant lie. The Auschwitz Museum now puts the number of Jews executed there at 950,000, at least three million less than previously cited. But the most astute Jewish mathematicians will ignore plain facts, continue to bellow the six-million holocaust lie and to condemn anyone who insists upon being intelligent enough to subtract three from six."

Farrakhan, who once called Hitler a "great man," also claimed that "The Zionists made a deal with Adolf Hitler."[30] Denier Arthur Butz was an invited speaker at the Nation of Islam's Saviour's Day celebration in 1985.

Followers of Farrakhan have used the Holocaust as a way to vent their anti-Semitism. Not only is the Holocaust diminished as an historical event in order to claim greater victimization for slavery and the slave trade; slavery is blamed on Jews,[31] and the history of the Holocaust twisted beyond recognition. The Nation of Islam's Khallid Abdul Muhammad, the keynote speaker at a program entitled "The African Holocaust" at P.S. 258 in Brooklyn in 1991, said, "Nobody wants to talk about what the Jews did. They are always talking about what Hitler did to the Jews, but what did the Jews do to Hitler?"[32]

Even though it is used in the fringes of the African-American community, Jew-hatred has been an effective tool of demagogues such as Louis Farrakhan. Other haters, including Jeffries and the Reverend Al Sharpton (who called Jews "diamond merchants" in the midst of the Crown Heights riots) have not adopted Holocaust denial. Jeffries has stressed the black role in liberating concentration camps; Sharpton, recalling Jesse Owens, notes what Hitler would have done to blacks if he had had the opportunity. What happened to Jews during the World War II is understandably not the greatest concern to a community that has its own painful experience with genocide. Nevertheless, the possibility that Holocaust denial could take root in part of the black community exists. The IHR folks would like nothing better than to see Holocaust denial spread anywhere it can. Sooner or later the IHR will point out to a Leonard Jeffries that one can still believe black soldiers bearing witness to the human skeletons of Dachau while believing that there were no gas chambers—the concentration camps liberated by Americans were on German soil; the extermination camps, on Polish soil, were liberated by the Russians.

20

Religious Groups

Holocaust denial fits neatly within the classical anti-Semitism of some fringe religious groups. Since the IHR promoters also traffic in general anti-Semitica, it is to be expected that they would share their pet idea with others similarly predisposed. For example, in May 1990, a thirty-two-page edition of the tabloid *Christian News*—referred to by IHR as a publication "which exercises great influence among Americans true to the traditional Lutheran faith"—was entirely devoted to Holocaust denial, complete with reprints of IHR material.

That some see religious justification for this newest form of anti-Semitism should not be surprising. Much of the old-line anti-Semitic, pro-Nazi propaganda had a religious tinge. It was the Catholic priest Father Coughlin in the 1930s who preached Jew hatred on radio with religious fervor. That strain of Jew hatred has its contemporary followers. In the 1990s, David Duke refitted his anti-Semitic, antiminority beliefs into the cloak of a "born-again" convert. Patrick Buchanan—who liked the values of the "old church," (i.e., before it had taken strides to cleanse the anti-Semitism from its liturgy)—preaches about a "religious war" in America.

Many hard-line hate group members today identify with one of the Identity churches, which preach that Jews are the offspring of Satan, and that blacks are biologically inferior to whites. A part of their gospel is that the Holocaust did not happen.

While these are fringe beliefs, we should not forget that anti-Semitism has a religious grounding. As Elizabeth Rickey noted while watching hundreds of thousands of religious Louisianans gravitate toward David Duke, "there was a certain animosity toward Jewish people that I didn't realize was there. So if I would confront someone who is considering voting for Duke, and say, but look, he believes all this kookie stuff about the Holocaust, they'd dismiss my objection because they associate Jews with being behind big government, liberalism, the media. There's animosity there—in fact, flat out prejudice."

Relativism

Closely related to the dangers of outright Holocaust denial is Holocaust relativism. Relativists acknowledge that the Holocaust occurred, but trivialize what can be learned from it by obscuring its unique universal importance.

For example, when the U.S. Holocaust Memorial in Washington, D.C. was being established in 1983, the national president of the German American National Congress wrote that the "Capitol of the United States should not be utilized to memorialize events that happened elsewhere involving other people. If such a Holocaust Memorial is to be built, let it be done in Israel with the tax money of their citizens." (In fact, even though some public funds will support the Memorial's operation, the museum and its contents are funded privately.)

It is inevitable that a German American group might fear how Germany would be portrayed at a Holocaust Memorial. But ethnic pride and concern are not the only motivation for relativism.

In April 1992, in Spartanburg, South Carolina, Mayor Bob Rowell "downplayed" a proclamation remembering the victims of the Holocaust, according to the *Washington Post,* because the city was attempting to attract a BMW plant. Rowell, who had two uncles who died fighting in World War II, said that the proclamation had been adopted at the urging of the U.S. Holocaust Memorial Council "well before BMW surfaced. . . . I feel the timing was not appropriate to publicize it because it might be misunderstood." His decision was supported by the rabbi of the only temple in Spartanburg. "We want BMW to come here, and we wouldn't want to hurt the chances for the sake of the whole community," the rabbi said.

Even Pope John Paul II, who has worked to improve Catholic-Jewish relations, unwittingly relativized the Holocaust when he linked it to his opposition on abortion in Poland. Others, with more pernicious intent, have diminished the term as well. In 1991, the New York State Education Department's plan for teaching history included a revision of the word "holocaust" into a generic term, one that should no longer apply solely to the Nazi extermination.

The Holocaust has also been relativized through symbols from leaders. When President Reagan went to Bitburg, and laid a wreath at a cemetery that included SS men, he diminished the horror of what the SS was and did. The generation that survived the Holocaust believes two things: that the Nazi genocide represents the quintessential horror of what humans can do to each other, and that the human family must learn the lessons of the Holocaust if people are to survive in a nuclear age. The lessons are not learned if the Holocaust is denied. Neither are they learned if the Holocaust is seen as unimportant, something that we can put behind us, forget, see excuses for, give lip service to, or compromise for temporary political considerations.

Nationalism is a relativizing factor too. Recent history—and perhaps most especially German history in this century—has been driven in large part by the ideology of nationalism. The nation-state is the identity framework that keeps modern society together. The French believe it is something special, or better, to be French; Americans believe it is something special, or better, to be American; and Germans believe—sometimes with a vengeance—that it is special, or better, to be German.

A strong nationalist feeling and feelings of national shame for acts of genocide are sentiments that can coexist, but the natural tendency is for one to repel the other. To Germans, which is the more comfortable image: Chancellor Willy Brandt, in 1970, on his knees before the Warsaw Ghetto Memorial, or Chancellor Kohl with President Reagan fifteen years later, laying a wreath at Bitburg? The former image says *mea culpa*. The latter says, time to get beyond the past and focus on today.

The need to get beyond the past creates a climate open to Holocaust denial and its cousin, Holocaust relativism. Nazism loses its unique evil. It is easier to feel good about being German if the German experience with Nazism was only a chapter in a larger, longer, more general human horror, rather than the quintessential political evil. Sure Hitler killed, but so did Stalin. Sure the Nazis organized political power to exterminate those they did not like. So did the Khmer Rouge in Cambodia.

Holocaust education might provide some brake on the outright denial of the Holocaust, but it cannot dissolve the inevitable historical tendency to diminish it. Today's diminution can become the next generation's denial, or if not denial, at least irrelevancy.

Immediately after World War II in North America, Western

Europe, and elsewhere in the democratic world, the attitudinal levels of anti-Semitism dropped, and doors previously barred to Jews were opened. This change was partly a reaction to the Holocaust, the logical endpoint of anti-Semitism. If the Holocaust is denied, relativized, recedes from memory with the passing of generations, or simply becomes more of an academic phenomenon than an emotional one, the result may be the same: a braking force against the two-thousand-year world tradition of anti-Semitism will be diminished. To be effective in combating Holocaust denial and anti-Semitism, the question, then, is not only what we can do about neo-Nazi deniers, but also how we can insure that the Holocaust's braking force is strengthened, or at least replaced with other societal forces that will check tomorrow's anti-Semitism? Is the answer historical or political? And is the answer the same in the United States as it is elsewhere? Holocaust denial, Holocaust relativism, and the effects of the passage of time on the memory of the Holocaust are not an American phenomenon alone—they are becoming a worldwide problem, even in areas that have no Jews.

Chapter 2

HOLOCAUST DENIAL AROUND THE WORLD

Europe

1979 was a banner year for deniers in the United States. The Institute for Historical Review was launched, and held its first conference.

In 1979 a Holocaust denial conference was also held in Kassel Germany, organized by the European Society for Free Speech. It helped promote Holocaust denial into a growth industry. In little more than a decade since, denial has become what Gerry Gable, editor of the British magazine *Searchlight,* calls the "ideological glue" that keeps the newly emerging neo-Nazi and fascist movements throughout Europe together.

Historian Deborah Lipstadt notes: "As you're getting more right-wing groups, it is going to get even worse. You'll have more and more groups looking for someone to blame as the economy gets worse. So you blame the foreigners, you blame the Turks, eventually, you're going to get to the Jews. And eventually you're going to have to deal with the Holocaust, because the Holocaust is the reason the Jews get 'special dispensation.' "[1]

It is too early to tell how Holocaust denial will fit into the changing patterns of postcommunist Europe. As Leonard Zeskind of the Center for Democratic Renewal points out, "You're going to have the confluence of all sorts of forces. In Poland, for example, you have Polish nationalism, which was opposed to Nazism. You have Polish anti-Semitism, which collaborated with Nazism. You have all those tendencies which were alive 50 years ago reemerge and contend for influence today. That's different in each country."[2]

As the 1990s witness the first great political realignment of Europe following the cold war, the postwar communist era will be reexamined by the newly emerging countries. But the revision of history will not stop there: World War II will be looked at anew. Recasting the war years will not be a matter of abstract academic inquiry alone. World War II was the last era before the communist domination of Eastern Europe. It will be mined by politicians for ideological images of national identity and sovereignty, images that reject the official history imposed by the communists, images that will treat the fascist governments of many of these states as the last true patriotic regimes.[3]

Part of this historical reorientation will focus on the Holocaust and Jews, and even if unaided by the professional Holocaust deniers, the prospects are troubling. Generations of Eastern Europeans were never taught the truth about the Nazi genocide of Jews. They have little way to know, or reason to care, that the symbols of sovereignty reclaimed from a precommunist era drip Jewish blood. In this crucible of skewed history and social upheaval, the potential exists for what Zeskind calls "the reemergence of the demonization of the Jews. And if the Jews are demons, then they must have made up this hoax about the Holocaust."

The IHR understands its market well, and is targeting Europe—including Eastern Europe—knowing that it is easier to make fascists look good if the Holocaust is seen as hoax, especially in societies with a tradition of anti-Semitism. As Mark Weber, the editor of the *Journal of Historical Review,* recently said, "Anyone who does not understand the importance of historical revisionism, or the relationship between political freedom and historical awareness, should look to the full-scale historical revisionism that has swept across eastern Europe. . . ."[4] It is easy to replace one lie with another, especially when, as Leonard Zeskind points out, the IHR is planning to spend millions of dollars spreading Holocaust denial in Europe.

The sad irony is that while the deniers till fertile soil in the former communist countries of Eastern Europe, scholars are digging through the archives, finding that the number of Jews killed may need revising upward. Newly released documents suggest that the Nazis herded more Soviet Jews into ghettos than previously thought—in Homel, Byelorussia, for example, experts previously thought there had been only one Jewish ghetto; new documents show there were four separate ghettos. Once collected, the Jews were killed by local police hired for that purpose.[5]

Germany

The greatest irony of Holocaust denial is in Germany. While the German government is tracking down and prosecuting the last Nazi war criminals, some Germans born two generations after the war are protesting these proceedings, claiming that they are based on "lies" about the Holocaust.

For many years the Institute for Historical Review has been translating denial material and sending it to Germany.[6] Today the IHR has an eager market: there are thousands of neo-Nazi skinheads in Germany who are making the political structure respond to their antiforeigner xenophobic agenda—an agenda that includes Holocaust denial as an ideological cornerstone.[7]

The deniers' interest in Germany[8] is not accidental. Most professional deniers are fascinated with things German, especially Nazis. David Irving reportedly visited Hitler's mountain retreat in Bavaria over thirty years ago, considering it a shrine. Willis Carto has published and promoted mounds of material glorifying Hitler and the Nazis. Building on this fascination, deniers want to remake the history of the Nazis into something positive. They seek to relativize the evil—to say, "Sure the Germans did some bad things in World War II, but so did everyone else." Knowing human nature, and the power of national pride in modern ideology, the deniers believe their message will resonate with new generations of Germans who want to shed guilt feelings over a depressing past. It is no coincidence that *Spotlight* (the weekly newspaper of Carto's Liberty Lobby) writes, "There is now talk of erecting a monument in Dresden, Germany, to the hundreds of thousands of civilians mass murdered there by Royal Air Force and U.S. carpet bombing attacks on the undefended city during the last days of World War II."[9] What greater relief than to learn that the past was not as dismal as was believed, or that the myth of a shameful past was created by people to whom you are still paying reparations?

The deniers are very effective at targeting, and excising, German guilt. Imagine yourself an eighteen-year-old German reading a snippet from *Dealing in Hate: The Development of Anti-German Propaganda,* by Dr. Michael F. Connors, published by the Institute for Historical Review. It is history as one would want it to be:

> At the heart of the conviction that German World War II atrocities were quantitatively and qualitatively without parallel in the annals of human experience is the as yet unverified allegation that, in the pursuit of a macabre "Final Solution," 6,000,000 Jews were cold-bloodedly murdered in gas chambers and before Einsatzkommando firing squads. The "evidence" presented in support of this charge to date has not been more persuasive than that used to substantiate the gruesome stories of German atrocity horrors spelled out in the long since discredited Bryce Report of 1915.
>
> Neither the proceedings at Nuremberg in 1946 nor those associated with the . . . trial of Adolf Eichmann were such as to inspire the confidence of the impartial investigator. Likewise, the frenetic efforts of some academic scholars to prove the charge have fallen quite flat. But even if one should assume the worst to be true and, from the welter of conflicting numerical estimates as to the number of Jewish fatalities, accept the largest, 6,000,000, as undoubtedly correct, the number of victims of these German atrocities would still fall far short of the number of German, Japanese, and Italian non-combatants who perished at Allied hands as the result of mass population expulsions, saturation bombing of civilian centers, post-war deprivation, and Soviet massacres and political liquidations.
>
> The simple fact then is that there is every reason to believe that a final accounting must exculpate Germany of any unique inhumanity in the waging of World War II, just as revisionist scholarship has exonerated her of sole or even primary guilt for the war itself.

The American Ku Klux Klan—which also promotes Holocaust denial—is active in Germany. Having established three chapters by mid-1992,[10] the KKK is working with other foreign groups that also see neo-Nazism as the wave of the German future. These groups are not spreading hatred in Germany on a lark: as of August 1992, there were over 40,000 Germans belonging to neo-Nazi groups. These groups believe in Holocaust denial.

As part of their plan to help bring about a Fourth Reich, KKK organizers, Canadian skinheads, and British far-right extremists are working to make the memory of the Third Reich more "politically correct." In 1991 they marched in the German town of Bayreuth to honor the memory of the late Nazi, Rudolf Hess. The march "drew people from at least seven European countries," the *New York Times* reported.[11] A 1992 rally in Bonn on the anniversary of Hess's death drew 2,000, despite the illegality of the gathering. Anti-Semitic banners and illegal Nazi emblems and salutes were all prominently on view.[12] On August 31, 1992, in the midst of violent rampages in Germany against immigrants, a Holocaust memorial in Bonn was bombed.[13] Attacks on other Jewish sites followed. Concentration camps at Ravensbrück and Sachsenhausen were firebombed. Swastikas were painted on a memorial for Nazi death camp victims.[14]

Holocaust-denying material is increasingly visible in Germany. An ad from a German Holocaust-denying group, the JG Burg Society, as well as an interview with an Arab denier, appeared on April 30, 1991 in two advertising weeklies, *Münchner Anzeiger* and *Trabant Anzeiger*.

In addition to the outright deniers, there are those who relativize the Nazi genocide. After the documentary *Shoah* was shown, MP Dr. A. Dregger suggested that a common commemoration be built—for *both* the victims and the perpetrators. German historian Ernst Nolte wrote: "The SS personnel in the death camps (the most ruthless among the sadistic murderers) could also in a way be considered the victims of the Nazi crimes."[15]

It is no surprise that David Irving's book *Hitler's War* became a best-seller in Germany. According to Gill Seidel in *The Holocaust Denial: Antisemitism, Racism and the New Right,* "It is not difficult to explain its appeal. The argument of the book may be summed up as: 'If only the Führer had known about the murder of the Jews, he would have stopped it.' For . . . Germans who do not want to face up to the past, it was easy to be persuaded that if Hitler did not know, then neither did the person in the street."[16]

To make matters worse, the newest German editions of Irving's *The War Path* and *Hitler's War (Führer and Reichskanzler: Adolf Hitler 1933–1945)* lack his previous references to Auschwitz and Treblinka as "extermination camps."[17] Irving's works are still available despite his conviction and fine of $6,000 in May 1992 for "disparaging the memory of the dead."[18]

According to an American Jewish Committee poll, 58 percent of Germans agree that "it is time to put the memory of the Holocaust behind us," and 39 percent agree that "Jews are exploiting the Holocaust for their own purposes."[19] That is fertile ground for Holocaust denial, especially in a country where young neo-Nazi Holocaust deniers have become a serious terror force.[20]

For many years, the American Jewish Committee has worked with the German government and many German foundations to include Holocaust education in schools. And while these educational efforts must continue and be expanded, they are certainly no panacea. Arthur Fischer, a psychologist from Frankfurt, studied German youth who were taken to former concentration camps to increase their awareness of the Holocaust. If students were not prepared properly, he concluded, the visit could be counterproductive. Some derived "pleasure from the horrors." Others were "disappointed" because they didn't see "real gas chambers."[21]

The German government has also been accused of "indifference" to the memorials at camps in the former East Germany. A plaque at the slave-labor camp at Dora-Nordhausen, for example, still makes no mention of the thousands of Jews who died there, but notes the "victims from Arab states." Dora had only one known inmate of Arab origin—a French soldier whose roots were from Morocco.[22]

Britain

Britain has had a long history of coping with Holocaust denial. In the 1970s Richard Harwood wrote *Did Six Million Really Die?* Harwood was later revealed to be Richard Verrall, once deputy chairman of the right-wing National Front.[23] But Britain's main contributor to Holocaust denial has been David Irving, who, despite his lack of a college degree, is both prolific and polished. Irving, who described himself as a "mild fascist" as early as the

1950s, has made a career out of writing books rehabilitating Hitler and the Nazis at the expense of the Allies and the Jews.

Irving's works, unlike those of many other deniers, have been published by major houses. Viking Press in the United States published his *Hitler's War*. Irving has written books about many aspects of World War II, including a history of the Luftwaffe. His *The Destruction of Dresden* fits well into the deniers' attempt to relativize what they haven't yet figured out how to deny. Irving, like other deniers, claims that Allied war crimes were of the same magnitude as Germany's.[24]

In *Hitler's War* Irving claims that Hitler did not order, and did not know about, any extermination of Jews until 1943 or 1944, and that the "incontrovertible evidence is that Hitler ordered on November 30, 1941, that there was to be 'no liquidation' of the Jews." According to Irving, it was Heinrich Himmler who was responsible for the extermination of Jews; Hitler only wanted Jews relocated, once the war was over.[25]

For nearly four decades, Irving has been what Gerry Gable of *Searchlight* terms the "soft-core" promoter of Holocaust denial. "In that stage he was smart," Gable notes, "because what he was trying to do was to say to the new generation 'Hitler was no worse than Napoleon. Everybody gave Napoleon a bad write-up, but when you put it into perspective, the man forged a modern Europe, and forged certain democratic legal systems, Code Napoleon and all these things. Well,' Irving says, 'give it another 30 years and people will view Hitler in the same way.' And this is what he does with the book. So he says Roosevelt was a political cuckold. That Eisenhower was a womanizer. That Churchill was a drunk. That they were all corrupt. That Stalin was a mass murderer—which is true. So what made Hitler the exception? And this is what they try to sell to people."[26]

Irving is now active in the hard-core world of neo-Nazis, speaking to rallies of deniers in Europe and North America. He claims to have been converted[27] to hard-core Holocaust denial by Fred Leuchter, a man with a B.A. in history masquerading as an engineer, whose ridiculed "report" on gas chambers is a major component of the contemporary Holocaust deniers' arsenal.

Despite his efforts to paint himself as a respectable historian, Irving has never been a serious scholar, and has always flirted with hard-core denial. As Phillip Rubenstein notes, well before Irving embraced Leuchter, "he was happy to state that Anne Frank's diary was a fake. He withdrew only after a successful lawsuit by Otto Frank—Anne's father—forced him to do so."[28]

In 1989 Irving printed *The Leuchter Report* through his Focal Point Publications. Subtitled with hateful "wit," *Auschwitz: The End of the Line,* Irving wrote, on the inside cover:

> The lid cannot be kept on the facts for much longer as copies of this edition of "The Leuchter Report" are being distributed free, not just to all media newsdesks, Members of Parliament and the like, but to the heads of the History, Chemistry, Physics, and Engineering departments, the libraries and junior common rooms of every university in the United Kingdom.

In a House of Commons motion on June 20, 1989, Members of Parliament said:

> This House . . . is appalled by the allegation by Nazi propagandist and longtime Hitler apologist, David Irving, that "the infamous gas chambers of Auschwitz, Treblinka[29] and Maidanek did not exist. . . ."

Among like-minded listeners, Irving airs his anti-Semitism with full venom, while claiming that "There is a whole string of documents showing Hitler putting out his hand to protect the Jews."[30] Irving has spoken regularly in Germany, despite being fined 10,000 deutsch marks for his comments in Munich right after Hitler's birthday in 1990, where he informed 800 listeners that Auschwitz's gas chambers "were erected by the Poles after the Second World War." In court on these charges, Irving told the judge that the Holocaust was "a blood lie which has been told against Germany for 50 years."[31]

Interviewed in Italy in 1992, from where he was deported before he could speak at a neo-Nazi rally, Irving not only denied the gas chambers, but also spoke kindly of Goering and Goebbels, who "did everything they could before the war so that the Jews themselves would leave Germany."[32]

Speaking in Atlanta in 1986, Irving said that "historians have a blindness when it comes to the Holocaust" because, like Tay-Sachs disease,[33] it is a "Jewish disease which causes blindness." Irving also bemoaned the "powerful forces in the media [which] are subverting the traditional values of white men," and gleefully mispronounced the name of Nobel Prize winner Elie Wiesel as "weasel," whom he called a "media celebrity" and a "professional survivor."

"The Jews," Irving says, "are very foolish not to abandon the gas chamber theory while they still have time." He predicts an increase in anti-Semitism because Jews "have exploited people with the gas chamber legend."[34] Irving is also vehemently anti-Israel. "In ten years," he says, "Israel will cease to exist and the Jews will have to return to Europe."

Despite Irving's Holocaust denial, in 1992 the *Sunday Times* of London contracted with him to translate Goebbels's diary. Irving's works are still available in libraries and bookstores, and are used in academe along with credible scholarship, even though he is now barred (because of his Holocaust denial) in Canada, Germany, Austria and Italy.

France

France has had a growth industry in Holocaust denial since the end of World War II. Paul Rassinier, an early denier, insisted that "The drama of the European Jews consists not in the fact that six million of them were annihilated, but rather in the fact that the Jews claim that this happened."[35]

His mantle was admirably adopted by Robert Faurisson, a former associate professor of contemporary literature at the University of Lyon. Faurisson has published prolifically, claiming that the Holocaust was a "lie" and that the gas chambers did not exist.

"This is my conclusion:" Faurisson wrote in 1979, in the French paper *Le Monde*, "the number of Jews destroyed by the Nazis is zero. The genocide against the Jews never happened."[36]

"The heart of Faurisson's argument," writes Werner Cohn, professor emeritus of sociology at the University of British Columbia, "is based on his assertion that Jewish witnesses to the Holocaust are simply liars and that they are liars because they are Jews."[37]

Faurisson is not the only Frenchman promoting Holocaust denial. In 1985 Henri Roques received a doctorate from the University of Nantes for his thesis, which argued that Auschwitz had no gas chambers. In 1986 the French minister of higher education invalidated the thesis. Like Faurisson, Roques is now associated with IHR.

French printing houses also churn out Holocaust-denying material. One, known as La Vieille Taupe (The Old Mole), a left-wing[38] enterprise, sends literature across Europe.[39] A right-wing publication firm named Ogmios (which is said to have financial support from Iran[40]) also prints Holocaust-denial literature. These two presses, which agree on little else, have collaborated on a new publication called *Annales d'histoire revisionniste.*[41] Both presses have printed Faurisson.[42]

In 1990, France passed a law against "criminal revisionism." Faurisson was charged under that provision after a September 1990 magazine interview[43] in which he said the Nazis had no extermination plan, and that there were no gas chambers. Tried in Paris in late March 1991, Faurisson again proclaimed the Holocaust "a lie of history." He was convicted. The court fined him the equivalent of $20,000, but it also "denounced the very law under which he was found guilty of a misdemeanor." According to the Jewish Telegraphic Agency,[44] "the Paris Court of Justice further astounded observers by offering a gratuitous critique of the Nuremberg war crimes court."

Holocaust denial in France has also been aided by Bernard Notin, an instructor at Lyon University. In a prestigious scientific magazine he wrote that "[the gas chambers are] a figment of popular imagination without any historic basis."[45] His suspension for Holocaust denial was later overturned by the Ministry of National Education.[46] However, another denier's sentence was upheld. Alain Guionnet, editor of the monthly *Revision,* was sentenced to three months in jail and fined approximately $13,500. His publication had referred to the "hoax or myth of genocide against the Jews." (It has also reprinted excerpts from *The Protocols of the Elders of Zion.*)[47]

Holocaust denial has received its largest boost from the leader of the right-wing, xenophobic, racist National Party, Jean-Marie Le Pen.[48] In a 1987 interview, Le Pen was asked about Roques and Faurisson. He replied: "I do not say the gas chambers did not exist. I could not see them . . . But I think this is a minute detail of Second World War history." Later, when challenged about these remarks,

Le Pen said, "Yes, it is a minute detail of the war. Are you telling me that this is the revealed truth everyone has to believe? I say that there are historians debating those issues."

In 1988, Le Pen further derided the Holocaust when he made a pun on the name of a minister, Michel Durafour, calling him "Durafour Crematorie," meaning crematorium oven. According to Robert Wistrich, "The journals and newspapers of [Le Pen's] Front National and the radical Right like *Présent, National Hedo, Minute* or *Choc du Mois* support [Holocaust denial]."[49]

French students are being exposed to Holocaust denial. Two young neo-Nazi college graduates—Fabrice Robert and Pier Gaüzerre—were tried in Paris in 1991 after they had pasted posters stating "Faurisson is right: Gas chambers = rubbish" in schools in Nice. Their civil rights were suspended for five years, and they were fined $6,000. The court, however, denied the prosecutor's request that the sentence be posted in the locations where the students had pasted their material.[50]

On April 10, 1992, a French appellate court upheld convictions of two engineers, Vincent Reynouard and Remi Pontier, for distributing literature denying the existence of gas chambers. Reynouard was convicted again on June 11, 1992 for distributing a leaflet entitled *In Prison for Telling the Truth,* and fined for sending Holocaust-denying leaflets to secondary school students.[51]

Meanwhile, a new quarterly, *Revue d'histoirie revisionniste,* has appeared. Directed by Henri Roques, with editorial assistance from Robert Faurisson, the journal also translates IHR material into French.

Austria

Since World War II, Austria's "official version" of history was that it was a victim of Hitler's Germany, not an active partner with the Nazis.

Jennifer Golub, an expert on anti-Semitism at the American Jewish Committee, wrote[52] that the Austrians "mythologized" their World War II experience, and that "until 1986 that denial of guilt corresponded with a taboo against public expressions of anti-Semitism."

The myth and the taboo were shattered that year, when Kurt

Waldheim's role in war crimes came to light, and public expressions of anti-Semitism became commonplace. Despite the revelations (or perhaps because of them and the feeling that a national hero was being attacked by outsiders), Waldheim was elected president.[53]

Austria also has its own homegrown Holocaust-denying publishers. A "notorious" Nazi named Walter Ochensberger printed a magazine entitled *Sieg* (Victory) which claimed that the gas chambers never existed. Ochensberger was tried and acquitted. He boasted that henceforth "nobody can be convicted for questioning the existence of gas chambers for the mass extermination of human beings in German concentration camps and for declaring this view publicly."[54] Two other publications, *Halt!* and *Gack,* also deny the Holocaust. These target school children.[55]

According to a 1991 survey conducted by the Gallup organization for the American Jewish Committee, 39 percent of Austrians believed that "Jews have caused much harm in the course of history." Thirty-seven percent agreed that "Jews exert too much influence on world events." Nineteen percent believed "it would be better for Austria not to have Jews in the country."

These answers demonstrate that 20 to 40 percent of Austrians hold hard-core anti-Semitic beliefs. But between one-third and one-half expressed negative attitudes on the Holocaust, attitudes that make them ripe for the propaganda of Holocaust deniers. According to the AJC survey, 43 percent of Austrians believe that "the Israelis basically treat the Palestinians no differently than the Germans treated the Jews"; 48 percent maintain that, "We, Austrians, too, lost the war in 1945"; 32 percent believed that "Jews are exploiting the National Socialist Holocaust for their own purposes"; and 53 percent agree "it is time to put the memory of the Holocaust behind us."[56]

Belgium, Sweden, Switzerland, Italy, Spain

Holocaust denial has appeared in other parts of western Europe as well.

Revisionistische Biblotheek (Revisionist Library), a Flemish-language revisionist quarterly, frequently uses translated material from the *Journal of Historical Review.*[57] The Beligium far-right also spouts Holocaust denial as a propaganda theme. In March 1991, a deniers' conference was held in Brussels.[58]

A radio station in Sweden called Radio Islam (headed by Ahmed Rami) has broadcast Holocaust denial since the 1980s.[59] Pamphlets by Ditleib Felderer, made to appear as if written by a young girl, were widely distributed in Sweden. They "contained sketches of children surrounding the text. It asked Auschwitz museum authorities to explain why they are trying to convince children that their displays are true. A flyer invited readers to send a lock of human or animal hair to the camp museum so that it would have some authentic hair for its displays."[60]

A Swiss history teacher and university lecturer, Mariette Paschoud—who is also a captain in the women's auxiliary of the Swiss army and a Swiss military judge—has spoken on behalf of Henri Roques, the Frenchman whose doctoral thesis denied the existence of gas chambers. According to the *New York Times*, "Mrs. Paschoud has declared that although she does not deny the existence of Nazi camps, she believes there is no proof that their victims were killed by the use of gas."[61]

Swiss leaflets denying the Holocaust appear regularly. *Eidgenoss* (Swiss Citizen) is a monthly frequently sporting articles excoriating "Jewish propaganda lies" regarding the Holocaust. *Memopress,* a press service, also spouts Holocaust denial. It has a run of 40,000 copies.[62]

Ditlieb Felderer's *The Diary of Anne Frank: A Hoax?* has been translated into Italian, and published by Edizioni All'Insegna del Veltro, which *L'Espresso* has dubbed "a neo-Nazi publishing house."[63] Not only David Irving's work, but David Irving himself has been in Rome. Although he was deported, he was interviewed in the magazine section of *La Repubblica,* during which he denied the existence of the gas chambers, claiming that "the Germans were extremely precise" and thus documents proving the chambers should exist. Asked about the documents showing huge orders of Zyklon-B for Auschwitz, Irving commented: "We cannot exclude that this was used in the crematoria where bodies were incinerated. Not for gas chambers."[64]

Italy has a plethora of outlets printing Holocaust denial, among them Edizioni All'Insegna del Veltro, *La Sfinge, La Sentinella d'I-*

talia, Orion, Il Candido, and *Avanguardia.*[65] According to a 1992 poll, 9.5 percent of Italians believe that the Holocaust never occurred and 42 percent said Jews "should stop posing as victims of the Holocaust."[66]

An ultra-right-wing Spanish group named Cedade has distributed stickers in Barcelona, claiming that "The Holocaust is a lie."[67] A bulletin entitled *Revi-Info* is published by Centro de Estudios Revisionista "Orientaciones" (C.E.R.O).[68] David Irving and Ernst Zündel have traveled to Spain, promoting Holocaust denial.[69]

Holocaust-denying literature and material have also appeared in Denmark, Greece, The Irish Republic, the Netherlands, and Norway.[70]

Romania

On July 2, 1991, Romanian-born Nobel Peace Prize winner Elie Wiesel spoke in Iasi, Romania, at a commemoration of a 1941 pogrom by the Romanian Army that killed 8,000 Jews. The Jews had been rounded up, then machine gunned and bayoneted.

Wiesel's speech was interrupted by a woman in the front row who shouted "It's a lie! The Jews didn't die. We won't allow Romanians to be insulted by foreigners in their own country."[71]

Romania has rehabilitated Marshal Ion Antonescu, its leader during World War II, an ally of Hitler, who was executed as a war criminal.

Before the end of communism, it had been a crime in Romania to possess Western books about the Holocaust.[72]

Ukraine

The Institute for Historical Review *Newsletter* #87, May 1992, noted, under the heading "REVISIONISM IN UKRAINE":

Along with the collapse of Communism in the former Soviet Union has come a drastic reassessment of twentieth century history. Nowhere has this process been more profound than in [the] newly free republic of Ukraine, where Soviet tyranny claimed millions of lives. One remarkable expression of the new Revisionist outlook has been the erection of monuments and plaques honoring the memory of tens of thousands of Ukrainian volunteers who fought against Soviet Communism during the Second World War in the ranks of the Waffen SS, the German-led pan-European combat force. Such memorials have already been erected in the Ukrainian cities of Lvov, Tarnopol and Ivana Frankovska. . . .

Meanwhile, more than 50,000 Ukrainians who were unjustly convicted of crimes under the Communist regime have been granted "rehabilitations" on the basis of the Ukrainian republic's April 1991 Amnesty Law. . . . Some of these rehabilitations may have been granted to Ukrainians who were convicted of mistreating Jews during the Second World War.

Former Yugoslavia

As Leonard Zeskind, research director of the Center for Democratic Renewal, notes: "In Croatia, the Tudjman regime has rehabilitated Nazism. Croatia was a Nazi puppet state. Croatian nationalism was primarily a creature of the Nazis. Germany was the first country to rush to recognize Croatia. And, significantly, that was the first independent foreign policy venture that Germany undertook outside of the NATO consensus."

The postcommunist leader of Croatia, Franjo Tudjman, is a Holocaust denier. In his 500-page *Bespuca—Povjesne Zbiljnosti* (*Wastelands—Historical Truth*), he wrote:

The estimated loss of up to six million [Jewish] dead is founded too much on both emotional, biased testimonies and on exaggerated data in the postwar reckonings of war crimes and squaring of accounts with the defeated. . . . In the mid-'80s, world Jewry still has the need to recall its "holocaust" by trying to prevent the election of the former U.N. Secretary General Kurt Waldheim as president of Austria!

Tudjman, who at least acknowledges that the Jews were persecuted during World War II, suggests that Jews would have been better off if Germany had won, thus allowing what he termed a "territorial solution" to the problem, making eastern Poland a "reservation." He has also said, "The Jewish people soon afterward became so brutal and conducted a genocidal policy towards the Palestinians that they can rightly be defined as Judeo-Nazis.'"[73]

Hungary

According to the Institute of Jewish Affair's 1992 *World Report* on anti-Semitism, Holocaust denial in Hungary is "a regular theme of the anti-Semitic press, with other right-wing journals justifying [denial literature] as part of a 'scholarly discussion.' "[74]

Poland

As in other parts of Eastern Europe, the official history according to the communist regime in Poland highlighted the Nazis as villains but ignored the Jews as victims. That perspective on Jews did not end with the fall of communism.

The 1992 *World Report* notes "insensitivity to the uniqueness of the Jewish fate under Nazi occupation is widespread. . .There has also been a tendency to minimize references to the Jewishness of the victims of the Holocaust and to put a Polish and Catholic mark on the commemoration of the victims of Nazism."

Slovakia

Former President Havel of Czechoslovakia was one of the most articulate voices against anti-Semitism to emerge from the post-communist alignments in Eastern Europe. With the breakup of the country into two, other voices will be better heard.[76] Leonard Zeskind noted, "When Slovakia exerts its drive toward sovereignty, Tiso (the head of the Nazi puppet state) becomes resurrected. In order for Tiso to be resurrected, there has to be a rewrite of the role of that regime."[77]

Russia

Russia has had a lengthy tradition of anti-Semitism. From the pogroms under the czars to Stalin's doctors' plot to masterminding of the "Zionism-equals-racism" resolution, to the anti-Semitic threats of Pamyat, Jew-hatred has been a part of Russian culture.

It is too early to tell whether Holocaust denial will take root there, however.

In Russia, as well as in the countries that became Soviet satellites after World War II, history was dictated by the official party line. Nazism was the fault of the capitalist West. The greatest horror of the war was the massive number of Russians killed by the fascists. That Jews were targeted as the special victims of the Nazis was not mentioned. In fact, when Jews were mentioned, they were frequently called "Zionists" and accused of collaborating with the Nazis.

Holocaust denial existed under the former Soviet system. According to scholar Randolph L. Braham, "the leading Soviet 'historical revisionist,' Lev Korneyev . . . not only questioned the number of Jewish victims, but also suggested, in the vein of his Western neo-Nazi colleagues, that the Holocaust, itself, was a 'myth of Zionist propaganda.' "[78]

Holocaust denial is also part of the post-Soviet landscape. Author Robert Wistrich notes that Konstantin Smirnov-Ostashvili, the Pamyat leader who disrupted a Moscow Writers' Club meeting with anti-Semitic shouts, "holds Jews 'responsible for the mass genocide of the Russian people,' [and] denies that the Jewish Holocaust took place."[79]

With the collapse of communism, right-wing anti-Semitic groups such as Pamyat are a fact of life. Like their neo-Nazi cousins in the West, they berate Jews for all the evils of history, from the killing of Christ to the horrors of Bolshevism. Pointing to the number of Jews in the development of communism (Marx, Trotsky, etc.), they conclude that the fascists weren't so bad. After all, they opposed the "Communistic Jews" and tried to protect their own nationals. Braham notes that "leaders such as Marshal Ion Antonescu, Miklos Horthy, Ante Pavelic and Josef Tiso [are being rehabilitated]."

In this view, the fascists are not so evil, and the Jewish Holocaust not so significant. That does not bode well, especially in a part of the world where there have been few statements of leaders, and few monuments, books, or other memorials that depict Jews as the primary target of the Nazis.

Gerry Gable, editor of *Searchlight,* has "monitored a publication of what used to be the Soviet Writers Union, which is I think now the All-Russian Writers Union. From time to time there's been anti-Semitism on their pages. But there's also been, from time to time, a strong antifascist line. But now there are interviews with British, French, and Belgian fascists. There are interviews with ayatollahs from Iran. And there are lengthy quotes from the *Protocols.* And this sells 100,000 copies per issue. It's extremely well written. There are crude, prewar, *Der Stürmer*-type drawings to go with the text. And the line is being trundled out that the czar was murdered by Steckloff, who was a Jew, on the order of the Bolsheviks, who were, in the main, Jews. And these people have destroyed Mother Russia, and destroyed the church—and we have to restore this."

There is also a problem in leaping from unvarnished Jew-hatred to unbridled Holocaust denial in Russia. As Gable notes, "We're back into the argument, what do we do about the collaborators in the Second World War? Because the Nazis not only killed a lot of Jews, they killed a lot of Russians as well, and a lot of Byelorussians, and Ukrainians, and people in the Baltic states. So they're in a bit of a jam, because even some people that are anti-Semitic will say, 'But yeah, hang on a moment. My family, and the whole village, were butchered by collaborators working with the SS. Are you asking us to accept that as being okay?' But in some of this stuff, it goes as far as saying, 'Oh nobody collaborated. These were Jewish agents working to destroy the nation.' I mean some of this is really paranoid, crazy, crazy stuff. It's paranoia with a huge 'P.' "

The slaughter of so many Russians by the Nazis may make Holocaust denial harder to digest today. But what about in future generations, for whom the horrors of World War II will be more remote?

South America: Argentina, Brazil, Chile, Venezuela, Mexico, Peru

One of the earliest pieces of Holocaust denial was *Mit Goebbels bis zun Ende,* published in Buenos Aires, Argentina, in 1949/1950. According to Yehuda Bauer, author Wilhelm von Oven—an SS officer who worked with Goebbels—"denies any knowledge of crematoria or the murder of Jews, in spite of the unequivocal references by Goebbels himself in his diaries to the crimes being perpetrated against the Jews."[80] (In 1976, the book was republished in Germany under the title *Finale Furioso*.[81])

A book, author unknown, appeared on newstands in some Argentine cities in the early 1970s. Its title was *The Just Fight of the Nazis Against Communism and Judaism*. Heinz Roth published a book in Argentina in 1974: *Porque nos mienten? O acaso Hitler tenia Razón?* (Why Do They Lie to Us? Perhaps Hitler Was Right?) And in July 1991, the far-right paper *Patria Argentina* printed an article by Walter Beveraggi Allende that claimed "the 'holocaust' is a fib for the stupid and credulous."[82]

Holocaust-denying material was an early industry in Brazil as well. Yehuda Bauer notes that "from 1965, cheap publications appeared in German, claiming, for example, that the number of Jewish victims totaled 200,000."[83] Today most Brazilian denial literature is authored by Siegried Ellwanger, a wealthy industrialist, who writes under the name S. E. Castan. Ellwanger's press, Editora Revisao, has given Holocaust-denying books to politicians as gifts.[84]

Chilean Miguel Serrano is a former ambassador to India. He is also an author of many anti-Semitic and Holocaust-denying books. In 1989 he wrote the introduction for *Fin de Una Mentira: Camaras de Gas: Holocaust-Informe Leuchter*—a translation of Leuchter's report.[85]

In Venezuela, the use of the swastika and other Nazi symbols has become widespread as fashion accessories. Neo-Nazi groups are more active than in the past. And, as part of this new activity, "revisionist magazines and books have appeared, as well as Adolf Hitler's *Mein Kampf*," according to the Jewish Telegraphic Agency.[86]

The Institute for Historical Review began distribution of Holocaust-denying literature in selected Mexican venues in November 1991. One target was the German School in Mexico City.[87]

Holocaust-denying literature has also been printed in Peru by a predominantly young neo-Nazi group: the Tercios Nacional Socialists de la Nueva Castilla (National Socialist Corps of the New Castille). The group is apparently made up of "wealthy youngsters" who "operate on a small scale within institutions of higher education."[88]

South Africa

According to Yehuda Bauer, "In South Africa, the deniers of the Holocaust were sued for libel, and the court ruled against the renewed allegations denying the Holocaust."[89]

On February 25, 1992, Dr. C. Zaverdinos, a member of the Faculty of Science at the University of Natal, published a letter in the newspaper *Natal Witness,* lauding the work of Irving, Roques, Leuchter, Faurisson, Verrall and others, and complaining that "the public [is] kept in perpetual ignorance of the fact that there is a debate on the Holocaust."[90]

Both pro-Arab Muslim publications and *Die Afrikaner,* the organ of the far-right Reconstituted National Party, publish Holocaust-denying articles.[91]

Even a government official has apparently embraced Holocaust denial. Louis F. Strofberg, identified as a member of the House of Assembly in Cape Town, had a letter published in the IHR *Newsletter,* in which he lauds IHR as a "hero of the truth unsurpassed in our times," and proclaims that "victory will be ours."[92]

Australia and New Zealand

As long ago as 1980, Lucy Dawidowicz commented on the effect of Holocaust-denying literature in Australia:

> In Australia Butz's book had a profound and unhinging effect on John Bennett, a Melbourne lawyer, for many years secretary of the regional Council for Civil Liberties. Converted by Butz, Bennett distributed about 200 copies of the book and thousands of copies of Faurisson's articles to persons in Australian public life. Early in 1979, Bennett began to speak of the murder of the European Jews as a "gigantic lie" created by "Zionist Holocaust propaganda" to make people support Israel. Several of his sensational letters-to-the-editor were published in leading Australian papers. The subsequent uproar soon brought about his dismissal from the Council for Civil Liberties.[93]

In February 1990, Howard Sattler, a top-rated radio broadcaster in Perth, interviewed American Fred Leuchter. Leuchter told the radio audience that Jews died from "malnutrition," and that Zyklon-B gas was used only for "disinfecting bed linens, delousing." Sattler commented that Leuchter had "been over there and had a look" at the extermination camps and determined that they "could not have been used as gas chambers. . . . The story we just covered relates to the so-called Holocaust."[94]

According to Jeremy Jones, the honorary secretary of the Executive Council of Australian Jewry, in the months before Sattler interviewed Leuchter, "virtually every Australian journalist concentrating on political, cultural, legal or historical affairs has reported receiving unsolicited copies of a 16-page version of 'The Leuchter Report,' with a cover letter from John Bennett, Australia's only prominent 'Holocaust Revisionist.' "[95]

In October 1990, the far-right anti-Semitic group Australian League of Rights held its annual convention in Sydney. Nigel Jackson, a teacher at a well respected Melbourne high school, gave the keynote address. Jackson called the Holocaust "a Jewish myth perpetrated to extort money and sympathy from the West."[96]

Holocaust-denying books and speakers are making their way through Australia and New Zealand with increased frequency. David Irving has spoken in both countries. And belief that the Holocaust is "hoax" does not disqualify one for public service.

Dr. Anice Morsey, a leader of the Australian Arab community, wrote:

> . . . Zionism fabricated and convinced the world with [a story] that there was mass killing of the Jews in furnaces and gas chambers, and even convinced the world that Germany alone killed six million Jews, while the truth is that those Jews who were killed numbered only 600,000 and they were not killed in the gas chambers as was suggested, but they were killed in the conquest's battles or because they participated in the fifth column and they worked as spies in Germany, Poland and France. . . . Zionism convinced the whole world of a disaster that did not occur, and sought to gain the sympathy of the world . . . they placed the world in a position of self-defence and feeling of guilt to such an extent that the Israeli state drains off[97] from the new Germany materialistically.[98]

After this article appeared, Dr. Morsey was appointed an ethnic affairs commissioner by the Victoria government.

Canada

Canada has had two dramatic trials involving Holocaust denial which have raised awareness about denial, as well as questions about the wisdom of providing deniers a trial's free publicity.

Ernst Christof Friedrick Zündel is a one-man neo-Nazi propaganda machine. He markets material flattering to the Third Reich and to Hitler. Co-author of *The Hitler We Loved and Why,* Zündel has referred to Hitler as the "Abraham Lincoln of Germany. . . . This humble, totally dedicated savior. . . . We still love him."

Zündel mailed his wares—including crass racist and anti-Semitic pamphlets and publications denying the Holocaust—throughout Canada, United States, and Germany. His operation was stopped in 1985, when he was charged and later convicted for publishing "false news." His sentence was fifteen months incarceration and probation for three years.

Zündel's conviction was overturned in 1987, and he was retried. A veritable "who's who" of Holocaust deniers testified on his behalf, including David Irving, Bradley Smith, Ditlieb Felderer, and Fred Leuchter. It was on behalf of Zündel's defense that Leuchter had gone to Europe and concocted his "Leuchter Report." (The judge ruled that Leuchter lacked credentials or training to make conclusions about Auschwitz's gas chambers.)

The Canadian prosecutor put the case in perspective when he asked the jury: "What is the major stumbling block to the rehabilitation of the Nazis?" The prosecutor answered: "[I]t is the Holocaust. So long as the greatest inhumanity man has ever done to man exists as a historically accepted fact in the minds of men, the Nazis can never be rehabilitated. He must get rid of it. So he published a pamphlet replete with lies."[99]

Zündel was convicted, and sentenced to nine months in jail.

Another celebrated case involved James Keegstra, the mayor of the small town of Eckville, Alberta. Keegstra was also a popular school teacher. His social studies classes offered classic anti-Semitism of the historic Jewish-conspiracy type, updated with Holocaust denial.

After years of teaching anti-Semitism as truth, Keegstra was removed from his post, prosecuted, and convicted of "promoting hate," an offense under section 281 of the Criminal Code.[100] The appellate courts upheld the constitutionality of this statute, but returned the case to the court below to resolve other issues, involving jury selection. Keegstra was tried again, convicted, and sentenced to a $3,000 fine in the summer of 1992.[101]

Also in the summer of 1992, the Canadian Supreme Court overturned Zündel's conviction, ruling that the statute against speading "false news" was unconstitutional.[102] Zündel held a press conference, during which he reiterated his Holocaust-denying views. The Canadian Jewish Congress videotaped Zündel, and, along with other Jewish groups, has been pressing for a renewed prosecution under the "promoting hatred" statute that Keegstra was convicted of violating.[103]

These two trials[104] raised difficult questions for prosecutors and Jewish community professionals. As in many European countries, Canada has no "First Amendment," although free speech is protected within certain limits. The laws allowing the prosecution of Keegstra and Zündel had problems. Laws prohibiting promotion of hatred against groups and printing "false news" can never be fully precise. They allow a defendant great latitude to put on a defense, allowing him to use the courtroom stage to spread his hate.

An analysis of the first Zündel prosecution, *Hate on Trial,* by Gabriel Weimann and Conrad Winn, suggests that the publicity generated by the court proceedings did not materially alter people's views about the events of World War II—although some of the reporting was unnerving, treating the deniers' claims with respect. The Jewish community generally applauded these prosecutions, although the disproportion between the large cost of repeated trials and appeals, and the small sentences that were imposed, made some pause. On the other hand, the publicity generated by the trials also exposed other disturbing evidence of Holocaust denial which might otherwise have remained hidden—including comments of public officials who agreed with the deniers.[105] Another outcome, of course, was that Keegstra was exposed and removed from his job.

While those working against anti-Semitism weigh the gains and losses from prosecuting Holocaust deniers, the deniers themselves will inevitably call their failures successes, and extract every ounce of legitimacy they can from the trials. Having extensive practice in rewriting the most cataclysmic event of the twentieth century, it is an easy task for them to recast a few weeks in a courtroom. The Institute for Historical Review, for example, promotes *The Holocaust on Trial: The Case of Ernst Zündel,* by Robert Lenski, a 544-page book allegedly documenting the "breakthrough testimony by Fred Leuchter, Robert Faurisson, David Irving, Mark Weber, Udo Walendy, Ditleib Felderer, J.G. Burg, and many more," as well as the "relentless . . . cross-examining [of] Exterminationist cover-up artists."

Canada remains a favored location for the well-traveled group that purveys Holocaust denial. David Irving, after appearances at the IHR's annual International Revisionist Conferences, routinely traveled around Canada, where his speeches were noted in the press. In 1991 in Regina he called the Holocaust "a major fraud. . . . There were no gas chambers. They were fakes and frauds." Although now barred from Canada because of his May 1992 conviction in Germany for Holocaust denial, Irving sneaked into the country later that year and spoke. His message was protested by many Canadians, including Monna Zentner, a 55-year-old professor of sociology. Immediately after the protest, Zentner's house burned in a suspicious fire.[106]

Japan

Japan is a homogeneous society with almost no Jews, but books on Jews, including anti-Semitic books, sell well. *The Protocols of the Elders of Zion* is more easily obtained in Japan than in any other major industrialized nation.[107]

One of the best known anti-Semitic writers is Masami Uno, who praises Hitler, sees a "Jewish peril," blames Jews for the economic problems of the entire world, and offers lectures on the "lies"[108] in Anne Frank's diary. He also claims that the Holocaust is Jewish propaganda.[109]

Uno, however, is not alone. On February 7, 1992, Keiichiro Kobori, a professor at the University of Tokyo, published an article praising the work of the Institute for Historical Review in *Sankei,* a daily paper with a circulation of two million.

The IHR is targeting Japan for its "revisionist" material, which not only denies the Holocaust, but also rewrites World War II to make Britain and the Allies the evildoers and the Axis powers the victims. In 1991, "President" publishers of Tokyo issued a Japanese translation of an IHR book: *F.D.R.: My Exploited Father-In-Law,* by Curtis B. Dall.

Deniers also diminish the Holocaust by comparisons to the racist internment of Japanese-Americans during World War II. As David McCalden told the *Los Angeles Times* in 1981, " 'There is a grain of truth in many Holocaust accusations. . . . Tens of thousands of Jews did die' from famine, typhoid fever, riots and exposure to freezing temperatures . . . Persons of Japanese ancestry who were confined in California camps during World War II might have suffered the same fate if the United States had 'been bombed, invaded and blockaded from Canada to Mexico.' "

Not surprisingly, the IHR's yearly conference has had speakers from Japan. Albert Kawachi, a Japanese professor who wrote *Why I Survived the A-Bomb,* spoke to the 1990 IHR meeting, paying "tribute to IHR and Revisionism for offering his nation a potential for escape from one-sided materialism and return to authentic Japanese values [since] he placed the roots of Japan's current crisis of soul on the American imposition of unilateral Japanese guilt for the East Asian and Pacific War."[110]

Arab Nations and Groups

Holocaust denial has long fascinated certain folk in the Arab world. Saudi Arabian money helped publish two of the earliest Holocaust-denying works.[111] Well before the United Nations equated Zionism with racism, Gamal Baroodi, the Saudi Arabian representative to the United Nations, claimed that the Holocaust never occurred.[112] Yehuda Bauer reports that "As early as 1974, a book entitled *Adolf Hitler, Bergründer Israel,* written by Karl Hunecke, appeared in Switzerland. Apparently written by an Arab, the publication was certainly supported by Arab funds. In 1975, a book by Ahmad Hussein, *Palestine My Homeland,* was published, which also included the claim that the Holocaust never occurred."[113] And in 1977, when New York City decided to introduce study of the Holocaust into its curriculum, Dr. M. T. Mehdi, president of the American-Arab Relations Committee, denounced the decision as "an attempt by the Zionists to use the city educational system for their evil propaganda purposes."[114]

In recent years the PLO has taken up the call of Holocaust denial with vigor.[115] In an April 20, 1990 story in the *Jewish Week,* Daniel Santacruz wrote:

> According to a series of magazine articles published by the Palestine Liberation Organization, the Nazi concentration camps were more humane than Israeli prisons are today. The publication also claimed that the camps did not have the technical capacity to burn millions of bodies.
>
> Concentration camps had sanitary conditions "of much higher standards" than Israeli prisons, wrote Dr. Khaled el-Shamali about his recent visit to the Dresden and Sachsenhausen concentration camps, in the Palestinian weekly *El Istiglal* (Independence). He added that the Israel prisons are "worse than those fit for animals."
>
> The scientist, said to be an expert in intense heat stoves and a member of several scientific associations in Arab countries, wrote: "Jews are complaining of their treatment by the Gestapo whereas the truth is they were served healthy food as proven by the dining rooms observed there."
>
> The articles, "How Did Zionist Propaganda Cloud Science and Mind? A First Quiet Travel Through the Climate of Fear," and "Burning of the Jews in the Nazi Chambers is the Lie of the 20th Century in Order to Legitimize the New Nazism," appeared in the December 13 and Dec. 20 1989 issues of the publication. . . . The weekly was founded . . . by PLO Chairman Yasir Arafat and is regarded as the main news organ for Palestinians inside and outside the territories. Its editor is Luai Abdo, reportedly a top PLO figure in the West Bank. . . . Abdo wrote in the preface to Shamali's Dec. 13 article that the study is "worthy of reading, eloquently described and supported by scientific arguments of the folly of Zionist propaganda concerning the alleged Holocaust."
>
> Because the stoves where Nazis burned the corpses were "very primitive" and belonged to the "Middle Ages," by no means could millions be incinerated, Shamali said in his second piece. In the same article he said that Israeli soldiers

"undergo fascist education more extreme than the Nazis," and that the world must "combat Zionism because it is more dangerous to human civilization than the Nazis."

Later in 1990, the *Los Angeles Times* reported: "PLO ARTICLE ENDORSES HOLOCAUST AS HOAX . . . [T]he Palestinian Red Crescent Society, published, last July, an article which cites Revisionist scholarship in challenging what author Ream Arnouf calls 'the lie of the existence of the gas chambers.' . . . Arnouf writes: 'Faurisson described the lie about the gas chambers as a historical deception, which allowed large scale extortion, which benefited Israel and international Zionism at the expense of the German people but not its leaders and the whole of the Palestinian people.' "[116]

Holocaust denial by Arab groups is a fascinating phenomenon. The Nazis' anti-Jewish policy attracted Arab leaders to the Third Reich during World War II. Arab propagandists have for many years promoted the lie that the Israelis are doing to the Palestinians what the Nazis did to the Jews. Additionally, pro-PLO publications try to delegitimize the state of Israel by ignoring the Jewish historical presence and cultural and religious ties to the land of Israel. Intrinsically linked with this historical rewriting is the claim that Israel only exists because the world felt sorry for Jews after the Nazi Holocaust—a crime that Arabs did not commit, and thus should not have to "pay" for.[117]

Holocaust denial should be a growth industry in Arab countries, with the help of the Institute for Historical Review and the Arab deniers they have promoted. As *Newsletter* #76 of the IHR (November 1990) noted, "As to the future [there is] a major initiative by Ahmed Rami. . . . [T]he former Moroccan tank officer, who has extensive ties throughout the Arab world, is working with Arab intellectuals and leaders to begin serious study of Holocaust Revisionism in the Arab countries."[118] Rami, as well as Abdel-Majid Trab Zemzemi of Tunisia, has ties to the Institute for Historical Review.[119] Apparently, for the PLO and other Arab leaders, the propaganda potential of Holocaust denial has become manifest, despite the need to reframe the claim that it was only because of the Nazi Holocaust that Israel was created. Now, Jews are to be further vilified for making up the existence of the Holocaust itself. As

Robert Faurrison told attendees of the IHR's Tenth Conference, "Arab and Islamic intellectuals . . . have begun a serious study of the case of Holocaust Revisionism and its implications for the Muslim world."

According to the 1992 *Anti-Semitism World Report* of the Institute of Jewish Affairs, Holocaust-denying articles have also appeared in Algeria and Egypt.[120]

Target: Israel

Even in the non-Arab literature of Holocaust denial, hatred for Israel appears prominently. That fact should convince the naive that mere "historical inquiry" is not the goal. Israel was not created until 1948, three years after the end of World War II. If somehow World War II was greatly misinterpreted, as the deniers claim, that would have little to do with a subsequent event—the founding of a Jewish state.

Deniers, however, integrally link Holocaust denial with anti-Israel propaganda, for if the Holocaust is a "hoax," as they suggest, then one of the justifications for a Jewish state is undermined.[121] Holocaust denial not only attacks Jewish history, its inherent anti-Zionism also targets the Jewish present and the Jewish future. Historian Deborah Lipstadt believes "The anti-Israel component is the key. This is where they really come around to their contemporary claims. This is absolutely central to their argument. In some respects, all Holocaust denial is a means of trying to deny the legitimacy of the state of Israel. The troubling thing is that it is going to prove very appealing to people who are inclined toward anti-Semitism. And those people are going to be exactly the ones who are going to fall prey to this kind of stuff."

When Israel is mentioned, many deniers can barely hide their crass anti-Semitism. Their literature asks questions such as "Is the Old Testament the basic plan for the foreign policy of a modern nation?"[122] IHR conferences—especially the earlier ones—have been orgies of classical anti-Semitism. For example, at the 1982 conference Palestinian Sami Hadawi said, "Begin says that a Jew will not bow down to anyone other than God—but does he know who God is?" The keynote speaker that year was Dr. Martin Larson, who said, "The Bible clearly depicts two Gods. On the one hand there is Jehovah—the God of the Old Testament—a God of hate, cruelty and caprice. On the other there is the New Testament God of love. These two Gods cannot be reconciled. Jehovah is not the God of Jesus Christ." If his point was not clear enough, Larson also quoted Harry Barnes: "Israel is Murder, Incorporated, raised to the level of a state."[123]

An IHR *Newsletter* in 1982 said: "Because of the myth of the 'holocaust'—this *idea*—you, dear American, have been maneuvered into footing the entire bill for naked Israeli aggression and pre-meditated genocide. . . . ISRAEL GETS AWAY WITH MURDER AND YOU ALLOW YOUR GOVERNMENT TO FINANCE AND SUPPORT THIS MURDER BECAUSE OF SOME LEGENDARY 'HOLOCAUST' TALE."

Arthur Butz, in an IHR *Journal* article entitled "The International 'Holocaust' Controversy," wrote that "Israel is always in trouble, and will be in trouble as long as it exists as a Jewish state."

Israel plays such a prominent role in Holocaust denial because it is inextricably linked with the deniers' anti-Semitism. The Holocaust-as-hoax belief is rooted in the idea of a world Jewish conspiracy. Israel, of course, would have to be a key part of any such conspiracy. That Israel is being paid reparations by Germany for the Holocaust is seen not as proof of the Holocaust but as a motive for creation of a Holocaust "myth."

The IHR is actively promoting Holocaust denial to Israel's enemies.[124] Even where deniers cannot agree among themselves, they can agree on hatred of Jews and Israel. When David McCalden separated from Willis Carto and started his Truth Missions, one of his earliest fliers spoke not about World War II, but Israel, highlighting the "truth" of the United Nations' equation of Zionism with racism.

Left Wing

The principal ideological connection between right-wing neo-Nazis promoting Holocaust denial and those who do the same on the left is hatred of Israel.

Noam Chomsky, one of the great intellectual heroes of the far left, wrote in support of French Holocaust denier Robert Faurisson.[125] Chomsky's piece was published as an introduction to Faurisson's *Treatise in Defense Against Those Who Accuse Me of Falsifying History.*[126]

Across the globe, the far left can be counted on to criticize the KKK or neo-Nazis at any opportunity. But if the PLO, rather than the Aryan Nations, spouts Holocaust denial, the far left is conspicuously silent.

Perhaps the greatest contribution of the far left to the denial of the Holocaust has been its relativizing and diminishing the horrors of the Nazis as a strategic tool to better attack Israel.

Israel-bashing was part of the "politically correct" dogma of the far left long before the first Israeli settlements in the West Bank, or its incursion into Lebanon, or the right-wing governments of Menachim Begin and Yitzhak Shamir. The anti-imperialist far left that was born in opposition to the Vietnam War viewed Israel as a tool of "American imperialism," to be opposed. Coupled with the embrace of the PLO, which touted itself as a "revolutionary" movement aligned with "people of color," Marxist parties such as the Socialist Workers Party and the Revolutionary Communist Party, as well as independent Marxist groups like the collective that published the far left's premier paper in America, *The Guardian,* became vehemently anti-Israel.

Theoretically, unfair attacks on Israel need not diminish the Holocaust. But the diminution of the Holocaust becomes inevitable when, for the last twenty years, the far-left press has gleefully compared Israelis to Nazis, and the treatment of Palestinians to the treatment of Jews in the death camps. Rather than target specific Israeli policies, practices, or programs as they might with a government that was otherwise "politically correct" (e.g., Nicaragua's Sandinistas) or simply disliked as capitalist (the United States, Britain), polemicists on the far left continually diminish the horrors of Nazism by claiming that the Israelis are doing what the Nazis did.

The far left also trivializes the Holocaust in another way. Starting with a commendable proposition—that many genocides throughout history have been ignored based on who the victims were—it has become "politically correct" to see all genocides[127] as "holocausts" and all "holocausts" as indistinguishable. Certainly, the mass killings and deportations of Armenians, American Indians, Cambodians, and black slaves were deplorable events that need to be studied, remembered, mourned, and learned from. So too are the other killings also referred to as "holocausts" in the far-left press (e.g., East Timorese, Vietnamese, etc., mentioned in Edward Herman's "Politically Correct Holocausts," *Z Magazine,* April 1992). All of these testimonies to human horror share much in common—a state killed or dehumanized people of another race or religion. But the Holocaust was unique in that a modern state—not to aid its war effort, but despite the hampering of that effort—committed genocide. The killing of American Indians, or the horrors of the slave trade, or the targeting of Armenian Christians by Turkish Muslims during World War I, were all done to benefit the majority population, usually economically. But in Germany the Nazis' "Final Solution" was a hindrance to their war effort—and may have cost them victory. And whereas millions of black slaves, and Indians, and Armenians, and Cambodians, died horribly, it was never the policy of the criminal state to target *every* member of the group that could be rounded up. Only those who were "in the way," or otherwise deemed "worthwhile" killing, were murdered. And although those otherwise "worthwhile" killing throughout history often included women and children, it was the Nazis alone who aspired to obliterate the presence of a people—Jews and Jewish culture and Jewish history—from the planet. Americans did not kill anyone they could find who had one Indian grandparent, the Turks did not kill anyone they could find who had one Armenian grandparent, and the world did not kill anyone who had one African grandparent. The Nazis, however, felt a holy mission to target anyone who had a trace of what they called Jewish blood. Nazi Storm Troopers had a song: "Wenn das Judenblut vom Messer spritzt, dan gehts nochmal so gut" ("And when Jew blood spurts from the knife, things will go twice as well").[128]

This is not to diminish for a second the horrors of genocide, or to label one victimized group any more worthy of compassion than another. But those who, like many on the far left, want to reclassify genocides by the skin color of the victim, or call them all identical, create their own brand of Holocaust denial by obliterating any understanding of the unique aspects of the Holocaust in human history. It was what the Nazis did, and not that it was done primarily to Jews, that makes the Holocaust a singular tragedy.

Holocaust denial on the far left also expresses itself in another way. Lenni Brenner, himself a Jew, is anti-Zionist and anti-Semitic. "Just as there were no good Nazis," he said, "there are no good Zionists."[129] Despite Brenner's left credentials, his writings have been promoted and sold by the IHR. This is not incidental. There is an intellectual strain on the far left magnetically akin to basic tenets of the far right. Speakers from both extremes spoke to their opposite numbers during the Persian Gulf War in similar tones, agreeing that the war was only being waged to help Israel.

For both Marxist and right-wing isolationist,[130] the general societal baseline of anti-Semitism, coupled with a shared dislike of Israel, make Holocaust denial, or at least Holocaust relativism, an easily digestible philosophy.

Should Denial of the Holocaust Be a Criminal Offense?

Different societies have different histories, cultures, and means of addressing hateful speech. There is no one "correct" way to apply law to Holocaust denial. What may be logical in one society may be ridiculous in another.

The United States is unique in its First Amendment constitutional guarantees. Non-Americans may be astounded to learn that Americans can print or say anything they want, as long as their utterances are not "fighting words," threats against the life of the president, or a few other carefully guarded expressions.

Other countries, with other traditions and without constitutionally enshrined guarantees of free speech, criminalize certain expressions. After World War II, displays of the swastika and similar exhibitions were outlawed in Germany. Germany today also outlaws Holocaust denial. Other countries, such as France and the Netherlands, have used court cases to curtail the dissemination of Holocaust-denying literature.[131] Laws, however, are never an entire answer to any social problem, including anti-Semitism and Holocaust denial. Laws to combat expressions of hate are also particularly difficult to enforce, as the Canadian experience in the Zündel and Keesgtra trials attests. Laws also create paradoxes. If a prosecution is not brought because a conviction may be hard to secure, people may believe that the authorities are condoning illegal expression. And because people see prosecution as what the authorities are "supposed" to do about hatred, other necessary governmental responses, such as education and community-relations work, may be ignored.

Stephen Roth, writing in "Denial of the Holocaust: A Criminal Offense?"[132] describes how a denier "boasted" that it was now legal to deny the gas chambers after he was acquitted for making such statements in Austria. The Austrian Constitutional Law of May 8, 1945, prohibits "activities . . . in a National Socialist spirit," and prescribes a minimum punishment of five years imprisonment. Roth notes that the provision has "two shortcomings." First, the language is imprecise as to what it outlaws. Second, the punishment is so severe that judges—especially the lay judges who sit on such cases—would rather acquit than impose the mandatory minimum sentence.

The Jewish community has requested that the law be changed to increase the possibility of conviction. "Considering that this involves an amendment to a Constitutional Law, and having regard also to the mood of the Austrian populace, the chances of success are not very great," Roth concludes.

Laws, then, are insufficient to combat Holocaust denial, which is no more exclusively a legal question than it is exclusively a cultural, political, or historical question. An effective strategy requires a multifaceted approach.

Chapter 3

REFUTING HOLOCAUST DENIERS

Exposing Holocaust Deniers

Holocaust deniers crave legitimacy above all else. As long as they are seen as neo-Nazi hacks, and not scholars, their task is harder.

Part of their strategy is to repaint the entire portrait of World War II, rather than focus exclusively on the extermination of Jews. By doing so, the IHR crowd has attracted others whose names they exploit. Pulitzer prize-winning author John Toland spoke at the Tenth International Revisionist Conference in 1990. Thereafter the IHR has been promoting his works on Japan.

The Institute for Historical Review also tries to portray itself as legitimate by quoting denunciations from real scholars as praise. For example, IHR promotes a book entitled *The Dissolution of Eastern European Jewry* by Walter N. Sanding which purports to prove that "there were never 'six million' Jews under the control of the Germans at any time, and that only the *presumption* of a higher Jewish population-growth rate than actually existed in Europe during the twentieth century, combined with the overcounting of Jews in countries from which they emigrated and their undercounting in countries to which they immigrated, has allowed the 'six million exterminated' story to claim a demographic justification." A leaflet promoting the book quoted professors and Jewish sources:

"The danger of this book (and those that will doubtlessly follow) is its clever veneer of scholarship. The bibliography is international in scope and the text has the panache of objectivity. Not one in a thousand undergraduates could find fault with it."—Professor Henry Huttenbach of the City College of New York.

"This book makes a great parade of statistics to show that whatever diminution in the population of the European Jews took place during World War II was only part of a long-term demographic 'dissolution,' exacerbated by the rough treatment accorded Jews by the Soviet Union."—Gordon Mork, in *Shofar*

By quoting their (Jewish) critics, IHR tries to create the illusion of legitimate debate.

But there should be no debate between fact and fiction. The deniers' claims can and must be debunked—not with debate, but with exposé.

First, Jews, historians, and others of goodwill have to make clear why we will not debate deniers. Second, we have to expose the disingenuousness of the deniers' insistence on debate. Professional deniers are not Holocaust scholars, but anti-Semitic impostors with a neo-Nazi political agenda burdened by what Gerry Gable terms a "moral albatross around their neck of enormous proportions. And that's the Holocaust. All the other things, they can argue Hitler's a good anti-Communist, they can argue he made the trains run on time, but when it comes to a state writing into its statute book, into its law, the Nuremberg laws, the laws based on race and eugenics and so on, and the creation of an extermination program that killed millions of people in the camps, you've got something they're stuck with." It is important that people know that deniers want to rehabilitate Nazism and create a new world order based on the Third Reich. In order for there to be an honest debate, both sides have to be committed to honest historical inquiry. The deniers' agenda is easily exposed: their literature is produced by Nazis who sell glowing biographies of Hitler, tapes of Nazi marches, the enthusiasts' edition of *Mein Kampf,* and *The Protocols of the Elders of Zion.*[1] Just as a parent would not take a child to a doctor whose hero was Dr. Mengele—the Nazi who experimented on twins—one should not get one's history from people who think the Third Reich had it right.

There is much validity to Deborah Lipstadt's comment that "We need not waste time or effort answering the deniers' contentions. It would be never-ending to respond to arguments posed by those who freely falsify findings, quote out of context, and simply dismiss reams of testimony. Unlike true scholars, they have little if any respect for data or evidence. Their commitment is to an ideology and their 'findings' are shaped to support it."[2]

Deniers also insist upon "debate" on unfair terms. As Deborah Lipstadt says, they cite, or miscite, specific factoids about events fifty years ago that require knowledge to refute. One need not be an expert historian on any issue to believe, with confidence, that certain events occurred, the Holocaust among them. Yet, if one relies on belief, the deniers will claim that the conviction is false, based on faith rather than knowledge. Once one admits that he or she cannot debunk the deniers' "facts," the deniers move in for the kill. Belief in the Holocaust is then no different from belief in Santa Claus or the Easter Bunny. In fact, belief in the Holocaust is more suspect—it is a religiously grounded, politically correct "official truth." "Official truths," such as the "official" story of the attack in the Gulf of Tonkin, or for some the "official" story of the John F. Kennedy assassination, are always to be viewed skeptically.

Eric Zorn of the *Chicago Tribune* describes the dilemma well. "Ignore the revisionists," he argues, "and their pronouncements float in the air unchallenged. Answer them in general but refuse to debate head-to-head, as mainstream historians and Jewish groups have, and you risk seeming afraid of confrontation. Respond to their allegations one by one and you appear to dignify the arguments, perhaps making it seem to the uninformed as though the existence of the Holocaust is a question serious people consider seriously, when, in fact, the revisionists have failed to make their case with virtually every active scholar in the field."[3]

As the long list of publications at the end of this study (see Appendix D) suggests, Holocaust denial is a growth industry. Yet most people around the world will not learn of Holocaust denial through the denying literature; they will learn of it through the media. (For example, Canadian newspapers, during the Zündel trial, had headlines: "No gas chambers in Nazi Germany, expert witness testifies"; "Women Happy at Auschwitz, Trial Told [subheading: "Guards respectful, ex-soldier says"]; "Auschwitz Called Fake" [subheading "Nazi Camp Had 'Pool, Ballroom' "]; "Lawyer Challenges Crematoria Theory."[4]) Those who have written well and extensively about denial, such as religion writer Jim Davis of the Fort Lauderdale *Sun Sentinel,* suggest that the lies should be directly rebutted. "We journalists are only as good as our sources," he said.[5] "If the American Jewish Committee and others had not done hard and fast research on this, I would have been only left with how they portray themselves."

When the first director of the IHR, David McCalden, was lying about his identity, calling himself Lewis Brandon, he was interviewed by the San Francisco *Examiner.* "He was asked if the thousands of books written on the Holocaust could all be mistaken," the article reported. " 'I'm afraid,' Brandon said, 'I have to say most of this literature is fake.' "

To believe deniers, one has also to believe—as McCalden did—that historians worldwide have faked history. That is a hard nut for even the most cynical to swallow. Obviously, historians have not conspired to fake history—but because the deniers have, their methods can and must be exposed.

What the Klarsfeld Foundation did in its exposé of Fred Leuchter,[6] and what Deborah Lipstadt has done in her book *Denying the Holocaust: The Growing Assault on Truth and Memory* (New York: Free Press, 1993) are important contributions to a type of scholarship that is frequently overlooked: setting the historical record straight by debunking both the deniers' claims to be serious historians and their historical claims. As Leonard Zeskind notes, there is a need to "take on directly some of the mythomania of the Holocaust deniers. That is critical for the period 20 years hence. There must be, on the record, a rebuttal of essentially these historical slanders. The funding of that kind of work, and the actual production of that type of work is critical. That's not getting done, for the most part."

The deniers' claims are not difficult to expose. In fact, by exposing their methods, we can further illustrate their neo-Nazi agenda:

Claim: Hitler Did Not Order, and Did Not Know about the Extermination of Jews

ANSWER: Deniers note that there is no single signed document by which Hitler ordered the Holocaust. From this they contend that if any extermination took place, Hitler did not know about it, rather than the more logical explanations: that he was not foolish enough to sign such a damning document, or if he was so foolish, one has not been found. Deniers also do not acknowledge that a job so massive as the destruction of the Jews would by necessity require the knowledge and approval of the Nazi head of state—what historian would claim that President Johnson's failure to sign a formal declaration of war against Vietnam meant he was unaware of that war?

Professor Robert G. L. Waite of Williams College, in calling David Irving's work (which advances the "the führer didn't know" thesis) "a calumny both on the victims of Hitler's terror and on historical scholarship," noted that "no one but Hitler had the authority to give the orders to murder more than six million people in the midst of war."

Aside from Hitler's warrant for genocide neatly laid out for all to see in *Mein Kampf,* deniers conveniently "forget" that he spoke about the need to exterminate the Jews.[7]

On January 30, 1939, for example, Hitler gave his famous Reichstag speech.

> During the time of my struggle for power it was in the first instance the Jewish race which received my prophecies with laughter when I said that I would one day take over the leadership of the States, and with it that of the whole nation, and that I would then among other things settle the Jewish problem. Their laughter was uproarious, but I think that for some time now they have been laughing on the other side of their face. Today I will once more be a prophet: If the international Jewish financiers in and outside Europe should succeed in plunging the nations once more into a world war, then the result will not be the bolshevisation of the earth, and thus the victory of Jewry, but the annihilation of the Jewish race in Europe![8]

In a two-hour meeting with his confidant Alfred Rosenberg in April 1941, Hitler outlined the plans for that prophecy, something that Rosenberg did not "want to write down, but will never forget."[9]

In a public speech on February 24, 1943, Hitler spoke about the extermination of European Jewry. He compared the need to exterminate the Jews with having "exterminated a bacterium because we do not want in the end to be infected by the bacterium and die of it."[10] On June 19, 1943, Hitler ordered Himmler to press forward radically with the "evacuation" of the Jews—a term used, and understood, as a euphemism for extermination. Referring to this order, Himmler spoke to a group of generals in May 1944, telling them that he had "uncompromisingly" solved the Jewish "problem." He added: "You can imagine how I felt, executing this soldierly order issued to me, but I immediately complied and carried it out to the best of my convictions." In another speech, to SS generals in Posen, Poland, on October 4, 1943, Himmler was equally clear. "The Jewish race is being exterminated," he said. "It's our programme, and we're doing it. . . . We had the moral right, we had the duty towards our people, to destroy this people that wanted to destroy us."[11] Himmler also told his SS audience that while "we can talk about it quite openly here . . . we must never talk about it publicly. . . . I mean the evacuation of the Jews, the extermination of the Jewish people . . . You know what it means to see 100 corpses piled up, or 500 or 1,000. . . . This is an unwritten, never to be written, glorious page of our history."[12]

That "evacuation" meant "extermination" is unquestionable from German documents. "The result to date of this 'resettlement action,'" wrote SS Major Francke-Griksch in a 1943 report on Auschwitz, "[is] 500,000 Jews. The present capacity of the 'resettlement action' furnaces: 10,000 in 24 hours."[13]

Deniers like David Irving perpetually harp on the fact that there was no single extermination order signed by Hitler, as if that proves something.[14] Sybil Milton, a historian at the U.S. Holocaust Memorial Museum in Washington, D.C., notes that "Hitler did initial the Euthanasia Order of 1939, which ordered the deaths of deformed and mentally ill patients. The resulting questions from medical and law officials . . . convinced him to sign no more orders that explicitly mentioned killing—a decision reflected in the fifteen-page blueprint for the Final Solution produced at the Wannsee conference which contained carefully sanitized language. Instead, from 1941 on, Himmler and his assistant Adolf Eichmann filed frequent reports with Hitler on the progress of the Holocaust. And the remark 'it is the Führer's wish' came to have the force of law."[15]

Detailed reports were made about the numbers killed by murder squads that hunted Jews and others.[16] The efficiency of these operations was described by the Nazis. For instance, Herman Graebe, a German engineer, detailed the killing of Jews in the Ukraine town of Dubno:

> The people who had got off the trucks—men, women, and children of all ages—had to undress upon the order of an SS man, who carried a riding or dog whip. An old woman with snow-white hair was holding a one-year-old child in her arms and singing to it and tickling it. The child was cooing with delight. The parents were looking on with tears in their eyes. The father was holding the hand of a boy about ten years old and speaking to him softly: the boy was fighting his tears. The father pointed to the sky, stroked his head and seemed to explain something to him.
>
> At that moment the SS man at the pit shouted something to his comrade. The latter counted off about twenty persons and instructed them to go behind the earth mound. . . .
>
> I walked around the mound and found myself confronted by a tremendous grave. People were closely wedged together and lying on top of each other so that only their heads were visible. Nearly all had blood running over their shoulders from their heads. Some of the people were still moving. Some were lifting their arms and turning their heads to show that they were still alive. The pit was already two-thirds full. I estimated that it contained about a thousand people. I looked for the man who did the shooting. He was an SS man, who sat at the edge of the narrow end of the pit, his feet dangling into the pit. He had a tommy gun on his knees and was smoking a cigarette.
>
> The people, completely naked, went down some steps and clambered over the heads of the people lying there to the place

to which the SS man directed them. They lay down in front of the dead or wounded people; some caressed those who were still alive and spoke to them in a low voice. Then I heard a series of shots. I looked into that pit and saw that the bodies were twitching or the heads lying motionless on top of the bodies that lay beneath them. . . . The next batch was approaching already. . . . I swear before God that this is the absolute truth.[17]

Claim: That the Crematoria Could Not Have Accommodated the Number of Corpses Necessary

ANSWER: The deniers, as they have with the gas chambers, advance reasonable sounding theories that are scientifically unsound. As Holocaust scholar Yehuda Bauer noted: "An article by Prof. Reinhard K. Buchner of California State University in San Diego . . . argues that since an incinerator in any American crematorium can cremate one body in five hours, and in Auschwitz there were fifty-two incinerators, it was impossible to have cremated six million Jews. Buchner estimates that there were 100,000 victims in Auschwitz and that the total number of victims could have reached 219,000. In fact, the incinerators in Auschwitz were built to cremate nine corpses per hour. There were forty-six ovens, and, at peak times, fifty-two, which were in operation ten to twelve hours per day. Thus there was a *potential* possibility of cremating 4,043,520 corpses during the two years the incinerators were operational . . . In addition to Auschwitz, there were other extermination camps, such as Belzec, Treblinka, Sobibór, Chelmno, Majdanek and Mauthausen (where the inmates were worked to death), and approximately one and a half million Jews were shot to death by the Einsatzgruppen."

In 1944, when Hungarian Jews were being shipped to Birkenau faster than the crematoria could accommodate the corpses, "the dead bodies were burned in open pits."[18]

Claim: That Only a Few Hundred Thousand Jews Died During World War II, These the Victims of Hunger, Thyphus, Etc.; That the Figure of 6 Million Exterminated is Fiction

ANSWER: The deniers who tout demographic studies do so deceptively. In "Auschwitz: Truth or Lie," by Thies Christophersen, the number of Jews in 1938 is given as 15,688,259—source, the American Jewish Committee; and 18,700,000 in 1948—source, a *New York Times* article. The contention is that if there were three million more Jews after the war than before, how could six million have been killed?

The 1938 *American Jewish Year Book*—where the American Jewish Committee publishes these data when available—had no precise data for 1938. However, the 1939 *Year Book* gave the world Jewish population as 16,633,675. The 1948 *Year Book* listed world Jewry at 11,373,350. That, of course, was not mentioned by Christophersen.

The Nuremberg trials, based on evidence presented by Justice Jackson (on leave from the U.S. Supreme Court), put the figure of Jews who died during World War II as 5,700,000. According to scholar Lucy Dawidowicz in a 1977 memo for the American Jewish Committee, "the round number of 6,000,000 has subsequently been the generally accepted assumption, arrived at by various estimates of Jewish pre-war and post-war populations in the different countries and confirmed by various German documents and witnesses before the International Military Tribunal."

One of these documents (Nuremberg Document PS 2738) is an affidavit from SS Major Dr. Wilhelm Hoettl, quoting Adolf Eichmann as having told him, at the end of August 1944, that "approximately four million Jews had been killed in the various extermination camps, while an additional two million met death in other ways, the majority of which were shot by operation squads of the Security Police during the Russian campaign."[19]

The Anglo American Committee of Inquiry, in an April 20, 1946, report, put the number of European Jews missing as 5,721,-600.

Some reputable estimates put the figure between four and five million (English historian Gerald Reitlinger, in his *The Final Solution,* published in 1953 and revised in 1968); some between five and six million (Martin Gilbert, a fellow of Merton College, Oxford, in his *Recent History Atlas—1870 to the Present Day,* printed in 1969); some between six and seven million (Dr. Helmut Krausnick, former director of the Munich Institute, in his 1956 publication *Zur Zahl de Judischen Opfer des Nationalsozialismus*).

As Reitlinger wrote: "Constant repetition of [the six million figure] has already given anti-Semitic circles . . . the opportunity to discredit the whole ghastly story and its lessons. I believe that it does not make the guilt . . . any less if the figure of six million turns out to be an overestimate . . . it was still the most systematic extermination of race in human history. . . . As a German, Walter Dirks, has written: 'It is shameful that there should be Germans who see a mitigating circumstance in reducing the sum from six million to two million.' "

For scholars, the chore of trying to pin down the actual number of Jews and other killed by the Nazis continues. New sources of information, such as documents that are bound to be found in the former Soviet Union, will shed light. Most reputable scholars still hold to the six million figure as probably the best estimate—the numbers killed in some camps is lowered, in others increased. Deniers seize on every reduction to prove their thesis, and ignore all the increases.

Another tactic used by the deniers, but with decreasing frequency since the death of David McCalden (this was his piece of denial "expertise"), pointed to survivors finding each other after many years. Clipped from the mainstream presses, the stories were usually about close relatives who had been separated at a camp, both presuming the other had died, until some freak event brought them together. For others, these stories of separation and discovery were heartwarming. For McCalden, these were evidence that millions of Jews presumed dead were merely misplaced.

Jim Davis, religion reporter for the *Sun Sentinel,* noted that if, as the deniers suggest, the six million figure is "irresponsible exaggeration," then "a wide range of researchers have agreed to exaggerate together [including] historians, a 1946 commission of the United Nations, and even German schoolbooks."[20] Peter Hayes, associate professor of history and German at Northwestern, asks: "Is it plausible that so great and longstanding a conspiracy of repression could really have functioned? That no genuine scholar would have long since emerged to blow the whistle on it, if it had? That everybody with a Ph.D. active in the field—German, American, Canadian, British, Israeli, etc.—is in on it together?" Not only historians, but six million people who were supposed to have been killed, but who in fact survived, would have to be part of the plot.

Michael Allen, the director of the Holocaust Awareness Institute at the University of Denver, notes that "the figure 6 million came from the Germans' own documents. The Germans kept meticulous records of who was sent where . . . and who was sent to the gas chambers. A lot of people starved, but it was only the Jews and a few others who were singled out for mass execution."

The Nazis, of course, did not document every death. Those who arrived dead in the railcars, or who were directed in the "wrong" line were frequently unregistered. As Shelly Shapiro, director of Holocaust Survivors and Friends in Pursuit of Justice, notes, some historians "counted trains, and by knowing who got on, who registered for transport, where the trains arrived, and what percentage were unregistered at the camps, they could compute deaths. The Nazis also usually did not count dead babies."[21]

Among the Nazi documents that support the six million figure is a report from Himmler to Hitler showing 363,211 Jews killed in the last quarter of 1942 alone, and a report from SS statistician Richard Korherr[22] documenting the murder of 2.5 million Jews as of March 31, 1943. The documents even detail how seriously the Nazis took the minutiae of their genocide. A 1942 report from SS Dr. Becker described how the gas van drivers should press on the accelerator, so that "death comes faster and the prisoners fall asleep easier."

Claim: That the Nuremberg Trails Were a Fraud

Answer: The Nuremberg trials, conducted after World War II, were indeed a "victors' " court. Reams of testimony and memoranda documented the war crimes of the Nazis, including their genocide against Jews and others. As Hans Frank, governor general of occupied Poland for Hitler, said during the proceedings, "A thousand years will pass, but the German guilt will not be repealed."[23] The trials documented the Nazi genocide machine. For example, Rudolf Höess described to British investigators on March 16, 1946, how he "personally arranged on orders received from Himmler in May 1941, the gassing of two million persons between June-July 1941 and the end of 1943, during which time I was Commandant of Auschwitz."[24]

It is precisely because the Nuremberg trials were so exhaustive in their documenting of the crimes of the Nazis that the deniers have to discredit them in order to pursue their claim. Their strategy rests on the assumption—a correct one—that few people beyond the participants and a handful of scholars know the exact details of the trials.

First, the deniers claim that the trials should be discredited because they were conducted by the victors, who were not interested in justice but in propaganda. Never mentioned, of course, is that the Nazis committed unspeakable crimes, and the world did indeed need to punish those responsible for mass murder. Also not mentioned is that the trials were conducted with safeguards for due process—defendants were allowed a defense, with the aid of counsel.

Second, deniers point to inconsistencies inevitable in any court proceeding, let alone one documenting crimes against millions of people during a multiyear war, and use them to paint a picture of a fraud.

Third, the deniers suggest that the confessions of the Nazis were tainted or the result of torture.

For those disinclined to immerse themselves in the voluminous record of the trials to refute the deniers, there is one simple observation that will suffice: the Nazis were allowed a defense, with defense counsel. If the Nazi "plan and design . . . to annihilate the Jewish people," as Robert Jackson, the chief U.S. prosecutor termed it, did not exist, *none* of the defendants would have admitted to it. The defense of choice was "I was only following orders." A defense of "it didn't happen" would have been untenable because the proof of the Holocaust was overwhelming. But even if one indulges the deniers' assertions, why wouldn't every Nazi accused of a crime against humanity not have defended himself with a complete defense that "It may have happened, but I did not know about it, and took no part in it," rather than a partial defense that admits personal action in the extermination of Jews, but seeks mitigation for "following orders"? No petty criminal would admit guilt unless caught red-handed; certainly, no one accused of crimes against humanity would admit their actions unless overwhelming proof left them no choice.[25]

Like all people who fabricate, Holocaust deniers end up contradicting themselves. On one hand, they paint the trials as so eager to blame Nazis for crimes they did not commit, any evidence was used. Yet Paul Rassinier, in his *The Drama of the European Jews,* noted in refutation of a Polish Jewish refugee named Rafael Lemkin[26] that "The Tribunal at Nuremberg even refused to admit [Lemkin's] impossible forgery into evidence."

Claim: That the Survivors' Recollections Are Unreliable

Answer: There are literally thousands upon thousands of testimonies about the Holocaust collected in Holocaust museums and oral history libraries all over the world. Only a hard-core anti-Semite who believes in magical conspiratorial witchlike powers of Jews would believe that all these eyewitnesses would be in on a conspiracy. No person of goodwill could believe that thousands of people would be merely "mistaken" about such important months and years of their lives. And it is not only the Jewish survivors who would have to be mistaken: it is the liberators as well.

The survivors not only are living proof of the scope and details of the Holocaust, they are doubly dangerous to the deniers because they can discredit many of the deniers directly. For example, Thies Christophersen, a Wehrmacht officer who was stationed at one of the camps in the Auschwitz complex, wrote a booklet entitled *Die Auschwitz Lüge,* in which he claimed that Auschwitz was not a death factory. (The stench of burning bodies, he claimed, were not from crematoria, but "a horse-shoeing shop and the stench of the burned horse hooves was not pleasant."[27]) Four Auschwitz survivors who worked under Christophersen have signed affidavits. "If you are not going to work more," Christophersen told them, "I shall dispatch you through the chimney."[28] Of course, deniers around the world still use Christophersen's work.

Another example is that of Arthur Butz's *The Hoax of the Twentieth Century.*[29] A large part of Butz's argument is that the survivors' testimonies presented at Nuremberg were unbelievable. He "exposed" a book by Rudolf Vrba[30]—an escapee from Auschwitz—claiming that Vrba was never a prisoner there, as proved by the absence of his name in the official camp record. "The story of this person is not credible," Butz deduced, "[in] this way, lies about Auschwitz are born."

Vrba's real name was Walter Rosenberg. After his escape, he secured documents in the name of Rudolf Vrba, which he continued to use, not mentioning this fact in his book *Ich Kann Nicht Vergeben*. Vrba wrote to Butz, explaining his name, proving it with documents. Butz did not alter his assertion.[31] His book has appeared in at least forty countries, and has sold over a million copies.[32]

Claim: That Neither Churchill Nor Eisenhower, in Their Memoirs, Mention Either Gas Chambers or a Genocide Program

ANSWER: As the deniers well know, the death camps were not on German soil, but in eastern Poland. The American and British forces did not capture eastern Poland—the Russians did. Eisenhower, however, visited a concentration camp near Gotha, and wrote about the atrocities he witnessed in a April 15, 1945, letter to General George Marshal.[33]

Claim: That Auschwitz[34] Was Not a Death Camp

ANSWER: The deniers quote Fred Leuchter, who supposedly went to Auschwitz, examined the camp,[35] and concluded that it had never had gas chambers. Leuchter, they will claim, was even certified as an expert witness at the trial of Ernst Zündel in Canada in 1988.

What they don't say is that Leuchter's report was not accepted in that trial, the court ruling that he lacked sufficient credentials to admit his findings into evidence. "[Leuchter] is not a graduate engineer," the court said, "he's got a B.A. [in history]."[36] (In June 1991, Leuchter admitted in court that he had misrepresented himself as "an engineer able to consult in areas of engineering concerning execution technology," in violation of Massachusetts criminal law.[37])

French pharmacist Jean-Claude Pressac made thirteen visits to Auschwitz, and having analyzed the camp plans, work crew slips, poison gas specifications, and photographs, concluded that the camp was built for mass murder. After Leuchter wrote his "report," Pressac wrote a rebuttal, concluding that Leuchter both ignored sound scientific practice and plain evidence that showed that gassings took place.[38]

Leuchter's claims were so extensive and absurd and touted as credible by deniers,[39] a book was written to refute him. *Truth Prevails: Demolishing Holocaust Denial—The End of "The Leuchter Report,"* was published in 1990 by the Beate Klarsfeld Foundation and Holocaust Survivors and Friends in Pursuit of Justice. It takes Leuchter's "science" step by step, and exposes it and him as fraud.[40]

The refutation notes that Leuchter took brick and cement samples (illegally) from ruins that had been exposed to the elements since 1945, hardly scientific practice since cyanide is soluble in water, and the rubble he collected may or may not have been residue from the gas chambers (the SS blew up Crematorium II in January, 1945).[41]

Leuchter claims that he found concentrations of cyanide residue 150 to 1000 times greater from material he identifies as from delousing chambers than that from the gas chambers—and since the same gas, Zyklon-B, was used for both, the latter (supposedly used to kill thousands of people daily), rather than the former, should have the greater residue—in fact, should have been tainted blue given the staining properties of the gas. Pressac patiently explains that, even ignoring Leuchter's illegal removal of samples and poor scientific procedures, the discrepancy and lack of blue stain proves, rather than refutes, the existence of gas chambers.

Pressac wrote:

> A hydrocyanic gas concentration of 0.3 g/m³ [grams per cubic meter]—a lethal dose—is immediately fatal to a man, while killing lice requires a concentration of 5 g/m³ for a period of at least two hours. Maintaining that concentration (5 g/m³) for six hours will kill all insects. . . . The dose used at Birkenau was lethal 40–70 times over (12–20 g/m³), which infallibly killed a thousand persons in less than 5 *minutes.*
>
> Afterwards, the place was aired out . . . The HCN was in physical contact with the gas chamber walls for no more than ten minutes a day at a temperature of about 30 degrees Cel-

sius. In the delousing chambers, a minimum concentration of 5 g/m^3 was used over the course of several daily cycles, the length of which varied according to the amount of time chosen for the period of contact. This cyanide saturation for 12 to 18 hours a day was strengthened by the heat the stoves in the room emitted, providing a temperature of 30 degrees Celsius. The walls were impregnated with hot HCN for at least 12 hours a day, which would induce the formation of a stain: Prussian Blue, or potassioferric ferrocyanide of varying composition depending on the conditions in which it was obtained. . . . The appearance of blue walls in the delousing gas chambers now allows us to distinguish them visually from the homicidal chambers, where this phenomenon did not occur, in an empirical but absolutely certain manner. Without heat induction of long continuance, the cyanide doses, as high as they were, were not in contact with the walls of the homicidal installations long enough to provoke the reaction to an appreciable—that is to say visible—degree.

Faurisson and Leuchter concurrently propound incoherences concerning the Zyclon-B delousing chambers. The first one is that Faurisson alleges that the homicidal gas chambers were too primitive to be used by the SS without endangering themselves, in light of the highly secure American execution gas chambers. But since delousing buildings and homicidal chambers were built on the same design, differing only in operating process, one wonders how he manages to accept the delousing chambers whereas he ferociously denies all reality of the homicidal ones.

As for the second incoherency, Leuchter is the guilty party. Faurisson confirms, according to Leuchter's "judgment," that the gas chambers at Maidenak could not have been homicidal either. I, having visited Maidenak, knew that three areas using Zyclon-B had walls of a particularly intense blue. I naively thought that if Leuchter admitted Birkenaus' BW 5a was a delousing gas chamber, Leuchter at least had to admit by his own erroneous blue wall theory that three premises suspected at Maidenak could be homicidal, since there were blue areas all over the wall. Against all evidence, Leuchter denied their function.

Faurisson was annoyed by the "infintessimal" cyanide traces found in the former gas chambers of the Auschwitz-Birkenau crematoriums, since he was expecting a completely negative result, conforming to his "vision." He draws upon one of the most often-used lies in explanation: The minute traces come from the fact that the "morgues" were sometimes disinfected with Zyclon-B. (The term "morgues" in the crematorium blueprints denotes ground level rooms to be used ostensibly for this purpose, but which were transformed into homicidal gas chambers. Faurisson only accepts their former state.) Hydrocyanic acid is used first and foremost to exterminate such vermin as insect pests and rodents. Classified as an insecticide and vermin killer, it has no bactericide or germicide properties for use as an antiseptic. Places and things are disinfected with various kinds of antiseptics: solid (lime, lime chloride), liquid (bleach, cresol), gas (formaldehyde, sulfur anhydride). To remove lice from clothing required either an insecticide, or dry steam disinfecting in an autoclave. But a morgue is not disinfected with an insecticide or vermin killer like hydrocyanic acid, as Faurisson foolishly claims, which would be as much use as a poultice on a wooden leg. Leuchter, who claims to be scientifically trained, whereas Faurisson is not, similarly used this stupidity in his report.

The discrepancy between the recorded cyanide ration in the delousing chambers and the ration in the gas chambers, the latter being lower, allowed the deniers to impose their "terrible" line of questioning. But these results actually conform to our current knowledge of history. If Faurisson and Leuchter had been willing to compile their information more carefully, they would have understood, rather than raving that they had "unmasked the great hoax." . . .

Leuchter, like Faurisson and others, also claimed that Zyklon-B could not have been used, because the gas is combustible. Once the chamber doors were opened, there would have been explosions.

Pressac—who flirted with Holocaust denial until he researched the question himself—ridicules the "explosion" theory. He writes that the gas's "flammability limits in air are from 5.6% (minimum) to 40% (maximum) in volume (6%–41% according to Du Pont).

This signifies that upon contact with a flame there is an explosion if the concentration of hydrocyanic acid in air comprises between 67.2 g/m^3 and 480 g/m.^{3} Below 67.2 g/m^3 there is no risk. . . . The SS used doses of 5 g/m^3 in delousing and 12–20 g/m^3 in killing,[42] well under the 67.2 g/m^3 threshold."[43]

Another favorite claim of those who cite Leuchter is that the people who dropped the Zyklon-B into the chambers would have died if the gas chambers existed. The deniers fail to note that the Nazis took procautions, that they used gas masks, and that so many people were crowded into the chambers, that a tremendous volume of air was displaced.

At the trial of Ernst Zündel in Canada, Leuchter was asked the following questions by the prosecutor, Mr. Pearson, and gave the following answers:

> **Q:** So this stuff you told us about people on the roof who dropped the gas down and how they would be committing suicide, it would take a matter of minutes before the gas got to them, wouldn't it?
>
> **A:** Unquestionably.
>
> **Q:** So, if they closed the vent and got off the roof, there would be nothing to concern them, would there?
>
> **A:** If they got off the roof. But at some point they have to do an inspection to determine whether the parties are deceased.
>
> **Q:** They send in the Sonderkommandos to do that, sir, and they don't care what happens to them.
>
> **A:** Right, all right.
>
> **Q:** So, if someone's on the roof with a gas mask, you agree that they've got all kinds of time to get off the roof after they've closed the vent?
>
> **A:** Perhaps.
>
> **Q:** Right. And in a room that has 2,000 people squeezed into 2,500 square feet, would you agree that the amount of air in that room is going to be displaced by the people?
>
> **A:** Unquestionably.[44]

Perry Broad, a *Rottenführer* in the *Kommandatur* at Auschwitz, described the process as follows:

Q: Will you tell us what you learned on the subject of exterminations while you were employed at Auschwitz?

A: In May 1942, I heard at that time only as a rumour that gassing on a bigger scale had been done in the concentration camp at Auschwitz. At that time I had not seen it myself. In July 1942, I was in the neighbourhood of the Truppentivier about 40 to 45 kilometres from the crematorium of Auschwitz, and there I saw for the first time a gassing action.

Q: What gas was used?

A: At that time I did not know, but I saw that several people with gasmasks were working on the roof of the crematorium and that they opened with hammers tins.

Q: Where did you see this, in Auschwitz or Birkenau?

A: At that time, 1942, it was in Auschwitz.

Q: Was this crematorium what was known as the old crematorium?

A: Yes, it was.

Q: Will you tell us what you saw in connection with exterminations at the old crematorium?

A: The installation at the crematorium was the following. The roof was plain, and there were six holes of the diameter of ten centimetres. Through these holes, after the tins had been opened, the gas was poured in.

Q: How many people were they putting in at a time in the old crematorium?

A: At the time when I observed it, there were about 300 or 400 or there might have been even 500.

Q: How long did the gassing take to finish the 500 off?

A: One could hear the screaming of the people who were killed in the crematorium for about two or three minutes.

Q: Did you later get to know more about the gassing operations?

A: Yes, later on I got to know the name of that particular gas, it was Zyklon.

Q: Did you ever see any gassings at the new crematoriums at Birkenau?

A: Yes.

Q: How many gas crematoriums were there at Birkenau?

A: There were four crematoriums at Birkenau.

Q: How many people a day were they gassing at Birkenau?

A: In the months of March and April 1944 about 10,000.

Q: Per day?

A: Yes, per day.

Q: Who were the men who actually did the gassing? What type of man was that in the camp?

A: They were called disinfectors.

Q: Will you tell us about these disinfectors shortly?

A: They were under the orders of the doctor and their duties comprised, apart from killing human beings, also the disinfection and the delousing of the internees' clothes.

Q: How was that delousing and disinfection of the clothes carried out?

A: In airtight rooms. The clothing was dealt with in the same way as the human beings.

Q: Will you look at this extract from this report and tell me if you know anything about it? Who wrote that report, which is set out there in inverted commas?

A: I myself.

Q: The disinfectors are at work . . . with an iron rod and hammer they open a couple of harmless looking tin boxes, the directions read Cyclon [sic] vermin destroyer, Warning, Poisonous. The boxes are filled with small pellets which look like blue peas. As soon as the box is opened the contents are shaken out through an aperture in the roof. Then another box is emptied in the next aperture, and so on. And in each case the cover is carefully replaced on the aperture . . . Cyclon works quickly, it consists of a cyanic acid compound in a modified form. When the pellets are shaken out of the box they give off prussic acid gas (Blausauregas). . . . After about two minutes the shrieks die down and change to a low moaning. Most of the men have already lost consciousness. After a further two minutes . . . it is all over. Deadly quiet reigns. . . . The corpses are piled together, their mouths stretched open. . . . It is difficult to heave the interlaced corpses out of the chamber as the gas is stiffening all their limbs. Is that based on your experience?[45]

A: Yes.

Höess, the commandant of Auschwitz, said:

The "final solution" of the Jewish question meant the complete extermination of all Jews in Europe. . . . It took from three to fifteen minutes to kill people in the death chamber. . . .[46]

The deniers perpetrate fraud regarding Auschwitz by ignoring historical documents, using fallacious scientific assumptions,[47] and distorting what the documents do and do not say. Robert Faurisson's claim that Auschwitz had no gas chambers, for example, relies in part on the diary of Johann-Paul Kremer, an SS doctor. Kremer's diary for October 18, 1942 read: "This Sunday morning in a cold and humid weather I was present at the 11th special action (Dutch). Atrocious scenes with three women who begged us to let them live."

Faurisson claims that a "special action" was not the selection of who would go to the gas chamber and who would not. Rather, he claims it was a division of the healthy from the sick who, suffering during a typhus epidemic, were executed. Faurisson wrote that the three women were shot. He attached a footnote, citing prison records.

What Faurisson did not mention was that there were 1,710 people in the convoy Kremer noted in his diary. Only 116 were brought into camp. The rest were the subject of the "special action," the eleventh of fourteen that Dr. Kremer would participate in.

What about Faurisson's claim that the three women mentioned in Kremer's diary were shot? The diary said nothing about their fate. Rather, Faurisson referred to Kremer's testimony during a war crimes trial in Poland. The good doctor testified: "Three Dutch women did not want to go into the gas chamber and begged to have their lives spared. They were young women, in good health, but in spite of that their prayer was not granted and the SS who were participating in the action shot them on the spot."

Faurisson used the doctor's testimony to supply the fate of the three women, but ignored the doctor's testimony about the existence of the gas chambers.[48]

Claim: That Anne Frank's Diary Was a Fraud

ANSWER: Anne Frank's diary detailed a young girl's feelings and family travails while hiding from the Gestapo in an Amsterdam attic (the deniers admit that the Nazis discriminated against Jews). Anne Frank in hiding was hardly a witness to the events at Auschwitz and Treblinka. Why, then, do the deniers put so much energy into the claim that the diary was a fraud?

There are two reasons. One is the power of this young girl's prose. Her words have touched generations of schoolchildren around the world, proving the moral horror of Nazism, something the deniers would prefer the world forget.

More importantly, the deniers question Anne Frank's diary because their anti-Semitic attitudes compel them to. Intellectually, one could believe that the world was mistaken about what happened to the Jews of Europe without believing that there was a purposeful conspiracy to hoodwink everyone. For the deniers, however, the claim of Jewish conspiracy is an integral part of their anti-Semitic delusions. If Jews somehow magically conspired to create what the deniers call a "Holohoax," then wouldn't the seminal piece of Holocaust-era literature have to be fake? The claim that the diary is a fraud is both a natural outgrowth of the denier's own anti-Semitism, and a part of the effort to promote the old anti-Semitic canard of "Jewish conspiracy," Jews having demon-like power to make the world believe a lie.

The seminal "work" attempting to prove the falsity of the diary was the Swedish Ditlieb Felderer's *Anne Frank's Diary: A Hoax*. It is referred to extensively by the deniers around the world today. Felderer's gross anti-Semitism is not. For example:

All the way back in antiquity the Zionists have peddled their ware, a disease far worse than the leprous plague.[49] In this way they have brought havoc, confusion, butcheries, cruelties and death to millions of innocent people. Wherever they have tread—crime, corruption, perversion and pornography has come. Whoever has aligned himself with them has finally become the victim of their crime and succumbed to their satanism. The Zion-racists continue on to our present day to whore their race merchandise, often under the guise of equality, brotherhood and democracy. In truth, their form of 'democracy' is no other thing but a chronic state of democracy—a rule by incarnated demons.[50]

From such an "objective" historian comes the following "proof" that the diary was a fraud:

(1) That it made no sense for Anne Frank, after her capture, to be sent to Bergen-Belsen through Auschwitz-Birkenau and Westerbork. "How anyone," Felderer wrote, "in a time of full-scale war, where transportation and food supplies are severely hampered, can proceed in this manner to 'exterminate' people is beyond our comprehension."

(2) That two pieces of Anne Frank's handwriting are dissimilar, one more adult, the other more childlike.

(3) That a child of her age could not have had the sexual feelings she describes, and thus the diary must have been written by a pedophile.

These claims are easily refutable. First, Dutch Jews were routinely sent to Westerbork for "sorting." And what Felderer finds so mysterious—that the Nazis sacrificed the efficiency of their war effort to kill Jews—is what made Nazism so uniquely horrible. Killing Jews was a mission beyond all others.

Second, one handwriting sample was script, the other print. And if, as Felderer claims, a sample of her more child-like writing with her signature had a later date affixed to it, the obvious explanation is that she signed an earlier piece of writing. Her affixation of a signature to an earlier document was entirely consistent with her personality and her predicament: she was, after all, trying to preserve a part of herself on paper, knowing that at any time the Nazis might discover her.

The third claim is the most bizarre. Child development experts, as well as anyone who has ever known children of Anne Frank's age, know that the thoughts she expressed were honest and natural—in fact, that is part of the reason why her diary is such compelling reading for young adolescents.

Added to Felderer's claim[51] is another, which was mentioned during the trial of Ernst Zündel in Canada. As Gabriel Weimann and Conrad Winn wrote in *Hate on Trial*,[52] "When a student pointed to *The Diary of Anne Frank* as evidence [of the Holocaust], Zündel insisted that it was a fraud. Zündel claimed that West

German forensic experts had proved that it was written in 1951 and in ballpoint pen, a postwar invention. Hence, Anne had to have survived the war. Zündel did not explain how the diary could have been written in 1951 in view of the fact that it was first published in 1947. Nor did he attempt to explain away the considerable documentary evidence that the fifteen year old girl was shipped to her death in 1944."

Recently, the Netherlands Institute for War Documentation produced a 714-page book, proving that the diary was not a forgery. The deniers, however, will continue their false claims. These lies do not die, and will have to be exposed repeatedly. Anne Frank's diary was first proved authentic in court in 1961, when Anne' father Otto sued a teacher who claimed the diary was a "fake."[53]

Chapter 4

LONG-TERM BATTLE AGAINST HOLOCAUST DENIAL

Holocaust denial is a problem with many dimensions. It is part anti-Semitism, part antihistory, part antiauthority, part antidemocracy. Like all forms of hatred, and all ideologies that promote or apologize for fascism, it must not be dismissed as either something "silly" or as something to be combated with platitudes or incantations of "the truth." It must be fought as hatred, as ignorance, and as ideology. Those who dismiss Holocaust denial as the stuff of flat-earth types forget a simple historical fact: all bigotry and anti-Semitism is palpably absurd. People throughout history have accepted these absurdities as empowering truth. The painstaking effort to debunk the deniers' agenda and their claims, as outlined in Chapter 3, is only a small part of what we must do.

Holocaust Studies

Some, but not all, American school systems mandate study of the Holocaust. They all must.

Sometimes, when Holocaust study has been proposed, some groups have objected, claiming that Holocaust curriculum will promote anti-German attitudes, or that the travails of one group should not be showcased above others.[1] But Holocaust study need not promote anti-German prejudice, and its importance is not that one group was the primary victim, but that it is the most powerful

82

example of a state pursuing genocide as a glorious mission.

In teaching the Holocaust, students must learn the lessons not as dry history but as something relevant today. Elizabeth Rickey says, "Eighty percent of my students had never heard of the Holocaust.[2] The reaction I get is 'how long are we going to have to hear about it?' It's the same as those who say, 'we gave blacks the right to vote in '65, what more do they want?' Education, to be meaningful, has to start bridging the gap between history and a person's own experience." Almost every heritage has experienced mass murder. The Holocaust, if taught properly, should make every student connect not only with a larger human lesson, but also his or her background. If the Holocaust is presented only as a horrible thing that happened to Jews in the mid-twentieth century, non-Jewish students will not be able to see themselves in the lessons. Without such personal identification, the unique horror Jews suffered during the Holocaust cannot be grasped.

Some believe that by simply learning about events, those events will not be repeated. That belief is well-intentioned fantasy. History teaches that genocide, bigotry, racism and intolerance are an inescapable part of the human story; that there are baser instincts and societal patterns at work that cannot be transformed with simple knowledge of important facts alone. Hate, at its most frightening, is not perceived as hate of other but love of self. Nazis needed Jews to make themselves feel good about being "Aryans." White racists need blacks to make themselves feel superior. If all we demand is accurate memory of past genocide as a complete prophylaxis against future genocide, we create our own historical denial by ignoring a self-evident truth: it is not memory alone, but also social, cultural, political and economic forces that have to be changed in order to effect the human indulgence in hate, genocide and anti-Semitism. Teaching about these forces should be part of Holocaust education.

Because Holocaust education (in this broader context) is essential, it cannot be simply an add-on to the social studies curriculum, or a lesson learned during visits to museums, no matter how well presented. It must be part of a larger commitment of schools to teach youngsters "communal literacy," how to live in a society where everyone does not look the same or share the same religion or background.

Teaching about hatred must be designed to touch students indelibly. Years ago an elementary school teacher taught a simple lesson on prejudice. She divided the class into blue-eyed and brown-eyed children. One day the blue-eyed children were told they were— and were treated as—superior. The next day, it was the brown-eyed children's turn to be better than their neighbors. That powerful lesson of bigotry was easily learned, because the students experienced how easy it was to feel superior, how tormenting it was to feel inferior, and how easily discrimination and prejudice work. Teaching of the Holocaust must take place in a system that is committed to inoculating children against the all forms of the disease of human hate. Otherwise, the lesson is simply one of increasingly stale events that caused one group suffering.

To make Holocaust studies more relevant and to combat today's anti-Semites, the curriculum must mention that there are people who deny the Holocaust, and expose them for the haters, bigots, and Nazi-lovers that they are. And while Holocaust education has to be designed to be compelling to future generations, today we can still utilize survivors and liberators to give a human dimension to genocide, people who can say "this is what happened to me and my family" and "this is what I saw." There are programs of survivors and/or of liberators who speak to young people today and tell their stories in American classrooms. And there are organizations, such as the Oral History Library of the American Jewish Committee and Facing History and Ourselves in Boston, that are collecting these histories. They should be fully used.

Planning Ahead for a World Without Witnesses: Holocaust Denial in the Next Century

Holocaust denial is already the glue that holds various anti-Semitic factions together, and is a dogma that provides ideological incentives to feel good about Jew-hatred.[3] In the next century, the Holocaust-denying industry will continue to market its hateful lies in the United States, Europe, Canada and elsewhere.

The venues for Holocaust denial will also expand with changes in technology. In addition to rallies, conferences, ads on campuses, and radio programs, the deniers have already begun to target cable television stations and interactive computer bulletin boards, such as

Compuserve, Prodigy, Internet and USENET. Tom Marcellus, the director of the Institute for Historical Review, has promoted the use of computer bulletin boards as an easy way to reach millions of "readers" worldwide. According to Marcellus, by early 1992 over 500 Holocaust-denying messages had been posted on the General Electric bulletin board named GEnie.[4]

Regardless of what avenues new technologies will offer for anti-Semitism, our human immune system against bigotry is still deficient. Assuming that there is no quantum change in the human capacity to organize ideologies around hate, Holocaust denial may be to the beginning of the twenty-first century what the *Protocols of the Elders of Zion* was to the beginning of the 20th century—an intellectual warrant for anti-Semitism. But it has the potential to become even more dangerous for three reasons.

First, to accept the *Protocols* as true, one had to posit an evil little Jewish group that met secretly, and somehow had the power to control the destiny of the world. The Holocaust as hoax is, inherently, a more believable delusion, especially once all the witnesses to it are gone. Historical events are always viewed from differing perspectives. The claims of picture forgeries, of diary hoaxes, of chemical disproof of the gas chambers, of kangaroo courts and forced confessions, are all small, digestible lies that, added together, make the big lie palatable. One need not believe in a Jewish "Holohoax" conspiracy to end up at that point. But if the occurrence of the Holocaust is an open question, then the idea of a Jewish conspiracy becomes inevitable.

Holocaust denial both feeds into and benefits from the traditional modern stereotype that the "Jews control the media." As Charles A. Weber wrote in his book, *The "Holocaust"—120 Questions and Answers,* "the extermination thesis . . . derived from Zionist sources." And as he wrote for the 1982 issue of IHR's *Journal,* "As a result of heavy Jewish influence in the American news media . . . few typical American political figures would dare to question the 'Holocaust.' " The inevitable anti-Semitic conclusion of Holocaust denial unfolds like a prosecutor's dream: the "crime" is the conspiracy, the "motive" is money for Israel, the "opportunity" is control of the media.

Second, the transference of classical anti-Semitism into political anti-Zionism ("Israel" is substituted for "Jew" as the object of

85

hate) allows further fuel for those who would not otherwise be enamored with Holocaust denial. Like the "Zionism is racism" canard, Holocaust denial provides a reason for disliking the mere existence of Israel.

Third, and most important, histories of genocide have always been purposefully misremembered, especially when those genocides have occurred during wartime. Even other victims of genocide have contributed to this phenomenon.

Take Armenians, for example.[5] With less sophistication than the Germans, but with the similar intent of organizing state machinery for the killing of a people, the Turkish government victimized Armenians. Beginning on the night of April 24, 1915, first the Turks came for the community leaders, and then the males, who were told they would be deported. Many were marched a distance, then summarily shot. Others had their feet beaten until they burst. Or had horseshoes nailed to their feet. Or had their eyebrows and beards extracted one hair at a time. Or had their finger and toe nails ripped off. Or had their flesh pulled off with pincers. Or had their skin burned with red-hot rods. Or had boiling liquid poured into their wounds. Or were crucified or hung in public squares.

Then came the Armenian women and children and old men. They were marched into the desert and massacred along the way, for example: 70,000 at Res-ul-Ain; 50,000 at Intilli; 200,000 at Deir-ex-Zor. According to Henry Morgenthau, the U.S. ambassador to Turkey at the time, many Armenians were killed with "clubs, hammers, axes, scythes, spades and saws." The Turkish officials "boasted" that these methods were "more economical, since they did not involve the waste of powder and shell."

Turkish interior minister Taalat Pasha proclaimed that "all the Armenians—women, children, invalids—must be eliminated." Deportation was the most effective method. 18,000 Armenians were marched out of Kharput and Sivas. Only 350 survived. 1,900 Armenians were marched out of Erzerum. Only 11 reached their destination.

The government of Turkey, only decades before the government of Germany, had plotted to kill a people. The effort was documented by many, including U.S. Ambassador Morgenthau. The Turkish government did not hide its intent. Its excuse was that Armenians could not be trusted in Turkey's World War I effort.

Armenians were to be exterminated, and not only the disloyal ones because, as Taalat Pasha explained, "those who were innocent today might be guilty tomorrow."

Even though population figures are not entirely precise, it is possible that half the Armenian population was murdered. Perhaps as many as 1.5 million Armenians were killed.[6]

Nearly eighty years ago, the Turkish officials then in power took credit for this genocide. The current Turkish government denies history. It says it never happened, or seeks to excuse the massacres as a consequence of war. The rest of the world, for its own reasons, allows this denial to go unchallenged.

In 1982 an International Conference on the Holocaust and Genocide was held in Tel Aviv. The Armenian genocide was on the agenda. The Turkish government warned that the topic should not be included, and mentioned, threateningly, the well-being of Turkish Jews. Turkey has been historically the most hospitable Muslim country to Jews. The threats were taken seriously. The Israeli government tried to abort the conference, and encouraged scholars to stay away. The conference was held nevertheless, and the Armenian genocide was discussed.[7] The Turkish government also raised the specter of harm to Turkish Jews in 1990, when many American Jewish groups were considering whether to support a congressional commemoration of the Armenian genocide. Academics have also been used to give a veneer of legitimacy to the denial of the Armenian genocide. Sixty-nine academics signed a *New York Times* ad in 1985, protesting a proposed day of remembrance for the victims of the Armenian genocide. According to Professor Peter Sourian, most of these academics "apparently benefit[ed] directly or indirectly from Turkish largess."[8]

Jews, like Armenians, were seen as a hostile minority during wartime. Because the genocide occurred during a war, the exact number of victims is not precisely ascertainable. Differences between scholarly estimates are used to suggest that "estimates" of the deniers are no less believable. Jews, like Armenians, were painted as having a reason for exaggerating claims (and thus the scholarship of those most likely to care was dismissed).

Adolf Hitler, in a speech to his military commanders on August 22, 1939, reportedly asked, "Who still talks nowadays of the extermination of the Armenians?" That the Armenian genocide is now considered a topic for debate, or as something to be discounted as old history, does not bode well for the those who would oppose Holocaust denial.

Or take another example: American Indians—the clearest answer to those who say what happened in Germany was peculiarly German, that "it" could never happen here. "It" did.

America, for all its celebration of diversity, has one great division beyond all others: those who came to the United States from other parts of the world and the indigenous population. For the needs of expansion, the government organized to push Indians out of the way and, whenever that became inconvenient, to kill them.

Indians, like the Armenians, were marched until they died. Cherokees were forced to leave their ancestral home in the Southeast, and were marched to Oklahoma in the dead of winter. One out of four died. It was called the "Trail of Tears."

Americans built an ideology around dehumanizing Indians in order to gain support for policies designed to kill them. "Savages," Americans called them. Colonel John M. Chivington, asked why Indian babies had to be targeted for death as well, explained, matter-of-factly, "nits make lice." Killing Indians was an effective political strategy. Cherokees, Seminoles, Chickasaws, Choctaws and Creeks referred to one soldier as "Sharp Knife." Sharp Knife was responsible for the murder of thousands of Indian people, including women and children. The American people elected Sharp Knife—Andrew Jackson—president of the United States. A sentiment so old as to be irrelevant? William Janklow won the governorship of South Dakota in the 1970s after advocating dealing with certain Indians in that state by "put[ting] a bullet in their heads."[9]

Unlike the Holocaust or the Armenian genocide, there is no political movement afoot to deny the killing of Indians. That is why, a century after the killing ended, the Indian genocide is so instructive. Even though there is general acknowledgment that Indians were targeted and killed, the memory of that killing has always been recast for then-current social and political needs. On some basic level, it is impossible for any society that indulged in genocide to fully comprehend what a horrid act it committed. It is as if an otherwise good-hearted person had to look in a mirror, see him or herself as a murderer, then go on about his or her affairs. It is easier to let the mind refract what one sees than fundamentally to reexamine who one is. Perhaps that is why, the killing acknowledged, nineteenth century Indians still tend to be pictured as lesser human beings—either as evil savages or as noble savages. That ideological dehumanization of Indian people, so necessary to commit genocide a century ago, has its effects on America today. Racism against Indian people is so entrenched that people discount it and the pain it causes its victims. For example, America still employs Indian caricatures as mascots for sports teams (who would accept the "Washington Blackskins" or the "Kansas City Rabbis"?), coupled with trivializations of Indian religious symbols (chicken feathers as mock eagle feathers—what would the Jewish reaction be to a foam toy used as part of a crowd-pleasing chant, the "torah scroll"? What would the Catholic reaction be to a mascot prancing along with 50-yard line with a foam cross, the symbol of the "St. Louis Pontiffs"?) Think what it feels like to be an Indian child, learning that his ancestors were "discovered" by Columbus, whereas Chinese people were "visited" by Marco Polo.

Certainly, there are fundamental distinctions between what happened to Indians in America, Armenians in Turkey, and Jews in Europe. Neither of the prior two genocides reflected a state policy of hunting down every victim it could find that was as aggressive and efficient as the Nazi's. For example, there was no attempt to eradicate even those who had one grandparent with either Indian or Armenian blood. And despite Pasha's remarks about the need to eliminate all Armenians, not all Armenian women were targeted for death—some were forced into marriages with Turks—illustrating a different "blood" concept than the Nazis had of Jews. But the special efficiency and scope and quintessential evil of the Nazi Holocaust should not be used to lose sight of the fact that it fit into a pattern of genocides—something most peoples, in one form or another, have experienced. And if you think that Americans' treatment of Indians was somehow an exception to that human pattern, remember how black people came to America, how many millions died in the slave trade, especially in the Middle Passage.

Do we know better today? Consider the murder of millions of Cambodians during the late 1970s to early 1980s. The world knew. It recognized the images. Just as Indians and Armenians were marched until they died, and as Jews were herded onto cattle cars, whole cities were marched to rendezvous with death—their crime not race but the preception that they could not become true enough believers in the Khmer Rouge's political religion because they had been exposed to a measure of knowledge.

We've progressed since then? Look at Bosnia in 1993. The images are the same. "Ethnic cleansing." Organized mass slaughter. Organized mass rape. Baby killing. The world knows. This, too, is a world that remembers the lessons of the Holocaust, but is too self-interested, or too slow, to act as if it does. Memory alone is not a defense against genocide, for either participants or observers.

Huey Long once said that if fascism came to America, it would be called Americanism. That, essentially, is how the ideology of genocide works. There is some recognition that something that gets the blood boiling is going on, but the mistreatment of other human beings is easily justified. Armenians have to be killed as state policy because they (who are also nonbelievers) hurt the war effort. Indians have to be killed as state policy because they (who are also nonbelievers) are savages, and are in the way of our plans. Jews have to be killed as state policy because they (who are also nonbelievers) are degenerate and evil and leechlike.

Once the genocide is over, what happens? The realization that the state has organized, with the population's support, to kill other people based on bigotry has to be made acceptable somehow. The Turkish government ultimately decided to deny the truth, knowing that the Armenians have no state of their own, no apparatus to fight the historical denial. Americans continued holding onto the 19th century images of Indians, or repainting those images into the "noble savage" concept. They have never fully comprehended how their predecessors organized a government to kill a people simply because they were in the way of economic expansion.[10]

The West Germans after World War II did something absolutely unique, remarkable and commendable. They went out of their way to incorporate teaching about the Holocaust in their society. With the help of groups such as the American Jewish Committee and the Adenauer Foundation, many West Germans learned about the genocidal policies of Nazism, and the extermination of Jews, Gypsies, homosexuals, and political dissidents.

In East Germany, there was no Holocaust education. The official Communist party line was all that mattered—that the Soviet people and other Marxists were the victims of Nazism. Shortly after reunification, the American Jewish Committee conducted a public opinion poll in Germany. Forty-five percent of West Germans and 20 percent of East Germans agreed with the statement "Jews are exploiting the Holocaust for their own purposes." Sixty-five percent of West Germans and 44 percent of East Germans agreed that "it is time to put the memory of the Holocaust behind us." Fifty-seven percent of West Germans and 40 percent of East Germans agreed that Israel had no special claim on Germany, that "Israel is a state like any other."

While some of the difference in reaction between former East and West Germans might be explained by the easterners' desire to reject the official Communist "truth," the results are inherently disturbing. Most Germans have troubling attitudes on the Holocaust, with the more disquieting attitudes coming from the West, which had programs and curricula and leaders' speeches on the subject. In Germany, at least, people who learned about the true horror of Nazism were more likely to think that the Holocaust was not so important; those who grew up without a Holocaust curriculum had less troublesome attitudes.

To be fair, more polling is necessary. The West German program for teaching about the Holocaust could also have been better.[11] And since the German government commendably created a taboo against public expressions of anti-Semitism, one has to wonder what the effect of privatizing the expressions has been. Nevertheless, there is an inevitable question: Is there a *negative* correlation between teaching about the Holocaust and an understanding of the importance of the Holocaust? If so, what does this say for Holocaust education as an answer to Holocaust denial? Could it be that the capacity of humans to grasp and internalize the lessons of genocide is inherently limited? That the horrors are too gross to accept as truth? If so, what should we be doing?

The Holocaust is a unique experience in human horror, and the logical endpoint of anti-Semitism. Yet Jews make a mistake when they see anti-Semitism as something *sui generis* in human experience, and combat it as such. Anti-Semitism is a form of human bigotry. It may be the most pernicious. Certainly the longest-lasting. Certainly the most adaptable to different political needs in different cultures over time. Certainly among the most deadly, and the most religiously fueled. But it exists as a strain of a virus called human hate. By focusing on anti-Semitism alone, we ignore all other strains of hate, and allow them to grow. Anti-Semitism flourishes best in a climate of hate. Only by building institutions that confront all forms of hatred can anti-Semitism be combated. Want an example? Just look at college campuses in the United States today. Bias incidents against all groups are increasing. If a university has no antibigotry hotline, no victims services, no response plan; if it does not survey its climate of intergroup relations, or send messages that it cares about bigotry against women, gays, American Indians, blacks, Asians, everyone, the programs and policies and offices and messages needed to fight anti-Semitism on campus will be lacking as well.[12]

But just as anti-Semitism cannot be tackled effectively without recognizing it as a subset of human hatred, the effort to call the Holocaust a hoax should not be seen as *sui generis* either. Even without the catalyst of neo-Nazis and other Jew-haters, Holocaust denial or diminution efforts are inevitable. "Never again" is a noble thought, and an excellent goal, but the importance and emotional punch of historical events always recede with time, even if they are remembered as tragic. World War I is recalled today as the epitome of cruelty in warfare, but it had a larger significance for those who lived through it. The bubonic plagues are still remembered as an extreme human suffering, but their emotional impact today is quite different from that in the 14th century, during which two-thirds of the population succumbed in some areas.

Today some deny the Holocaust as a vehicle for attacking Jews or Jewish interests. A century from now, there will be new vehicles for anti-Semitism. And although it will be of great importance whether our great-grandchildren believe that Auschwitz was a death camp rather than the locus of the "great Jewish Hoax," the events of Auschwitz, so long before their birth, will inevitably be understood differently than it is by the generations that were touched by it. What Jewish child today knows all the details of the Inquisition or the destruction of the Temple?[13] What do non-Jewish children know of these cataclysmic anti-Semitic events?

What will be relevant to our great-grandchildren is that they will live in a world where the machinery of state will still have the ability to organize its power behind an ideology of hate and to implement that policy through genocide. Governments have, throughout history, made the hatred of others a tool of power. They will continue to do so, regardless of what people believe about the Holocaust.

While the memory of the Holocaust is still fresh, while the evil intent of the deniers is most clear, it is time to take action.

Certainly as noted above, Holocaust education, speakers, memorials, museums, movies, article, books, are all essential—but not sufficient. If the study of those who deny the Holocaust (or the Armenian genocide, or who trivialize the killing of Indians) teaches anything, it is that bigotry skews, and is stronger than, accurate memory. The process is psychological as well as an historical and ideological. Dr. Walter Reich, a psychiatrist who taught at Yale, wrote: "The Holocaust was carried out by a nation that was among the most civilized on the planet. The urge to deny it is, in some primitive sense, in all of us: We would all like to forget how frightfully weak are the safeguards, both psychological and cultural, that protect us from our worst impulses."

If "Never again" is to mean anything in a world that sees genocides anew each decade, it is essential that groups who understand and remember their own experiences with genocide push together for more than remembrance—for policies in all our key institutions and government bodies that will reduce the likelihood of intergroup hatred today, and genocides tomorrow.

Peter Sourian, writing about the denial of the Armenian genocide, could not do so without alluding to the Holocaust. "It is true," he wrote, "that each crime is unique and each victim is unique. To the degree that it understands these dynamics, humanity is better able to develop in positive ways."[14]

Yosef Goell, an Israeli journalist, wrote:

> There is an important lesson to be learned here. As victims of the most horrible planned mass slaughter in human history, we the Jewish people, and its state, Israel, have a legitimate claim on the sympathy of the world. But it is essential, in demanding the world's sympathy for our own tragedy, that we openly recognize the tragedy of other peoples, and that we acknowledge that we have not been the sole victims of orga-

nized mass slaughter in this horrible century in human history. The Armenians preceded us, and the Cambodians followed us.[15]

There is an impediment for groups with so much in common to work together to prevent the recurring horror of genocide. Too often the victims of one genocide are reluctant to acknowledge other genocides, as if by doing so they would diminish the significance of their own. In the Jewish community, for example, there has been some hesitation to recall the killing of Gypsies, Poles, Ukrainians, homosexuals and others by the Nazis, on the understandable belief that if the Holocaust is seen only as an example of man's inhumanity to man, then the centrality of Jew-hatred to Nazism—indeed, the existence of anti-Semitism—is diminished, if not forgotten.

But it is essential that groups work together to acknowledge and build upon the legions of examples of state sponsored genocide. By focusing only on one's own tragedies, strategies, lessons, and power are lost. Holocaust denial is not just about historical truth any more than the claim that Jews poison wells, or killed Christ, or commit ritual murder, or secretly run the world are about truth. As Judge Hadassah Ben Itto, president of the International Association of Jewish Lawyers and Jurist, said, "They don't replace each other, these lies; the list becomes longer all the time."[16] Truth is only a partial answer to lies, especially because these are not simple lies, but lies fueled by hate, with an ideological purpose—lies that have the potential to fuel deadly acts.

Holocaust denial is, in reality, not about the Holocaust. It is about politics, ideology and power. It must be combated politically. President Reagan went to Bitburg and blurred the distinction between the victims of the Nazis and the Nazi victimizers. As time goes on symbols associated with the Holocaust may become political footballs—the balance between who is harmed and who is helped by any political gesture will shift as those directly harmed die out. Groups, today, in Europe and elsewhere, are actively encouraging attacks on the symbols of the Holocaust while reclaiming the symbols of Nazism. These groups could care less about historical truth. The neo-Nazis are not marching in Germany because they want another view of history in textbooks; they want influence.

94

Neatly displayed exhibits in museums and twenty pages of curriculum in high school are important—but they do not challenge the politics of what is going on. In order to have a chance at diminishing Holocaust denial, our focus has to be not only on the lies but also on the political agenda of the promoters of the lies.

Leonard Zeskind, research director of the Center for Democratic Renewal, is precise when he comments:

> You oppose the Holocaust deniers with a political movement that contests the hate movement, of which these guys are the glue, contests them on all their issues. There's a tendency to treat this as sort of an isolated and isolatable issue, primarily of Jewish concern, and not related to other issues related to democracy. I think that you have to oppose your political and social movement to their political and social movement. . . . All this will be decided by politics. I don't want to minimize the importance of establishing the historical record. But, ultimately, what will matter in 50 years is the relative political strengths of folk for whom Nazism is anathema, versus folks for whom Nazism represented a period of national sovereignty and national growth. It may be possible that in 20 years the Germans would regard Hitler as the last person to run an unoccupied regime. It may be possible in 20 years, or five years, or next year, for the Slovaks to regard Tiso as the person who ran the last sovereign government of Slovakia. It's possible in Russia for people to come to the conclusion that communism is Jewish, and therefore their trials and travails under the communist regime were due to the power and impact of the Jews. Now, if that's all the case, what that points to is the need for not just sort of this namby pamby lets-all-get-along stuff, I think it points to the need for real political alliances, real political power that can hold up for the long haul. And the caveat on that, I think that the tide is running in the direction away from us.

Zeskind is right. A large part of the effort must be political. Democratic institutions are the only ones that have had *any* success combating hatred. They are also the only ones that hold any promise for adopting a mission that goes beyond the primitive when it comes to tackling bigotry against all groups.

It is no surprise that those who espouse Holocaust denial are also antidemocratic. Deniers do not deny in a political vacuum. On the right they are, like David Duke and Willis Carto, supporters of fascism. On the left, they are opponents of what they call "bourgeois democracy." Even those who dabble with denial—like Patrick Buchanan—have conceptual problems with democracy as a form of government designed to protect minorities from overbearing majorities. Pluralism—a system that sees differences as contributing to the strength, beauty, and cohesiveness of the whole—is a frightening concept to deniers of all political stripes.

It should be a matter of faith—but it is not—that one way to fight Holocaust denial is to combat the larger political agenda of those who use denial as ideology. This is especially true in Europe. In the cataclysmic restructuring following the collapse of communism, hatred, xenophobia, and a nostalgic attraction toward fascism are emerging. Who today would discount the possibility of right-wing anti-Semitic groups gaining significant power in more than one European country before the end of the twentieth century? Anti-Semitism, and of course Holocaust denial, could become an officially endorsed, or at least an officially ignored, ideology. It is imperative that Jews and others who cherish freedom and democracy do all they can to combat a real possibility: multiple European societies in which full-scale bigotry is again released. The European New Right must be combated at the United Nations and at every other appropriate venue. It is not enough for people of goodwill to celebrate the end of communism with nice-sounding words about a new democratic Europe. Not all problematic governments are succeeded by democracies, as the recent history of Yugoslavia and Iran amply demonstrate. Holocaust denial must been seen as a danger to all those who cherish freedom. How well can fledging democracies with massive social and economic challenges survive if the symbols of fascism (which imply government sanctioning of the old hatreds) are restored?

The political nature of this problem must be made clear to the American people and the U.S. government. Fighting the nascent forces of fascism in Europe is not simply a matter of fostering foreign democracy, or of learning lessons missed fifty years earlier. It is about forces that shape our world today. Growing anti-Semitism and fascism abroad—there are now more than 1,000 anti-Semitic organizations in Europe alone[17]—cannot be good for America.

Even if we do not agree with the complete agenda of the current Europe organizations that have a mission to fight fascism—such as some of the mainstream left-wing "antifascist" groups—we should be more active in helping them.[18] We should be supporting particular projects of these groups that work with the thousands of young neo-Nazis across Europe today, telling them, in the words of Gerry Gable, "that the people who are trying to recruit you are no-goodniks, not because they killed 6 million Jews and 4 million others, but because today, in 1996 or the year 2000, they are no bloody good. Because they don't offer you anything." If postcommunist Europe develops a significant minority that has a neofascist flavor, Holocaust denial as ideological glue (rather than as historical illiteracy), and consequently anti-Semitism and anti-Zionism, can only find fertile ground.

We live in a generation where, for the first time, some anti-Semitic lies have been effectively combated. The foundation of religious anti-Semitism on which Nazism flourished was painfully obvious to church leaders after World War II. Liturgy was revised. In 1975 the lie that Zionism was racism was endorsed by the United Nations. Sixteen years later, through political power and political change, the lie was repudiated.

Perhaps future historians will find the years after the Holocaust to have been a relatively "golden age," where anti-Semitic attitudes and expressions were diminished by remembrance of the horrors of the Holocaust. They may also conclude that that relatively good state diminished as the memory of, and lessons drawn from, the Holocaust fade. They may also bemoan the fact that Jews did not take advantage of the "quiet times" to build better structural barriers against future anti-Semitism. While the times were quiet for anti-Semitism, there were still screaming signs that hatred can become state policy, without an adequate world response—Cambodia, Bosnia, Croatia, Serbia, the former Soviet Union.

If this theory is reasonable—that memory of the Holocaust caused a temporary pause on the world's reliance on anti-Semitism—then those alive during the "golden age" must push for societal changes that will both reduce anti-Semitic attitudes in the long run and enhance society's commitment to combat all forms of hate. This means that Jews, and Jewish organizations, should not merely be running around documenting what the most anti-Semitic do (although that is important); we must insist that our institutions see combating bigotry and anti-Semitism as a mission, a mission that requires lasting plans and structures. As long as we are satisfied to live in a society where politicians have no interest in combating bigotry in politics because bigotry works; where the media, rather than condemning bigotry, promotes it because it sells; and where a college student is taught at orientation what to do about a bad meal or a leaky faucet, but not an incident of hate, hate—including Holocaust denial—has an open field.

No place in the world—including the United States—has a mission to empower its institutions to become effective combaters of intergroup hatred. We have armies for defense, schools for teaching, sanitation services for garbage. Our tax dollars are spent for road repair, tree trimming on highways, environmental clean-up. But more people throughout the history of the world have been harmed by intergroup hatred than by any other malady. No one would be satisfied with a school system that did not bother to teach children math or reading, because these are seen as essential skills for productive citizenship. Skills to reject intergroup hatred are just as essential to acquire. But we don't even have a vocabulary to speak about "communal literacy," let alone a societal mission to craft tools for our institutions to promote it. Would we rely on the goodwill, availablity, and unregulated expertise of nonprofit groups to teach our children, defend our shores, and repair our roads? As long as we're satisfied to do that about bigotry, all forms of hatred, including anti-Semitism and Holocaust denial, will continue to poison human relations.

We can, and we must, combat Holocaust denial as falsehood, as hatred, and as a form of politics. If we want to be effective, rather than just feel righteous or "correct," we have to have a sophisticated strategy. We have to work with other groups, building common lessons from the human tragedy of genocide. We have to exert political power, demanding that our institutions develop effective means to combat intergroup hatred. We must make demand that government create incentives for local institutions to fight bigotry on a day-in, day-out, unremarkable basis. Memory, or logic, or knowledge, or goodwill, by themselves, cannot conquer societal hate. Holocaust deniers count on that.

Appendix A

HOLOCAUST-DENYING AD PUBLISHED IN SOME COLLEGE NEWSPAPERS

THE HOLOCAUST CONTROVERSY: THE CASE FOR OPEN DEBATE

by Bradley R. Smith

The Contemporary Issue

No subject enrages campus Thought Police more than Holocaust Revisionism. We debate every other great historical issue as a matter of course, but influential pressure groups with private agendas have made the Holocaust an exception. Elitist dogma manipulated by special interest groups corrupts everything in academia. Students should be encouraged to investigate the Holocaust story the same way they are encouraged to investigate every other historical event. This isn't a radical point of view. The premises for it were worked out centuries ago during a little something called the Enlightenment.

The Historical Issue

Revisionists agree with establishment historians that the German National Socialist State singled out the Jewish people for special and cruel treatment. In addition to viewing Jews in the framework of traditional anti-Semitism, the Nazis also saw them as being an influential force behind international communism. During the Second World War, Jews were considered to be enemies of the State and a potential danger to the war effort, much like the Japanese were viewed in this country. Consequently, Jews were stripped of their rights, forced to live in ghettos, conscripted for labor, deprived of their property, deported from the countries of their birth and otherwise mistreated. Many tragically perished in the maelstrom.

Revisionists part company with establishment historians in that Revisionists deny that the German State had a policy to exterminate the Jewish people (or anyone else) by putting them to death in gas chambers or by killing them through abuse or neglect. Revisionists also maintain that the figure of 6 million Jewish deaths is an irresponsible exaggeration, and that no execution gas chambers existed in any camp in Europe which was under German control. Fumigation gas chambers did exist to delouse clothing and equipment to prevent disease at the camps. It is from this life-saving procedure that the myth of extermination gas chambers emerged.

Revisionists generally hold that the Allied governments decided to carry their wartime "black propaganda" of German monstrosity over into the postwar period. This was done for essentially three reasons. First, they felt it necessary to continue to justify the great sacrifices that were made in fighting two world wars. A second reason was that they wanted to divert attention from and to justify their own particularly brutal crimes against humanity which, apart from Soviet atrocities, involved massive incendiary bombings of the civilian populations of German and Japanese cities. The third and perhaps most important reason was that they needed justification for the postwar arrangements which, among other things, involved the annexation of large parts of Germany into Poland. These territories were not disputed borderlands but included huge parts of Germany proper. The millions of Germans living in these regions were to be dispossessed of their property and brutally expelled from their homelands. Many hundreds of thousands were to perish in the process. A similar fate was to befall the Sudeten Germans.

During the war and in the postwar era as well, Zionist organizations were deeply involved in creating and promulgating anti-German hate propaganda. There is little doubt that their purpose was to drum up world sympathy and political and financial support for Jewish causes, especially for the formation of the State of Israel. Today, while the political benefits of the Holocaust story have largely dissipated, the story still plays an important role in the ambitions of Zionists and others in the Jewish community. It is the leaders of these political and propaganda organizations who continue to work to sustain the Holocaust legend and the myth of German monstrosity during the Second World War.

For those who believe that the Nuremberg Trials revealed the truth about German war crimes, it is a bracing shock to discover that the then Chief Justice of the U.S. Supreme Court Harlan Fiske Stone, described the Nuremberg court as "a high-class lynching party for Germans".

The Photographs

We've all seen "The Photographs." Endlessly, Newsreel photos taken by U.S. and British photographers at the liberation of the German camps, and especially the awful scenes at Dachau, Buchenwald and Bergen-Belsen. Those films are typically presented in a way in which it is either stated or implied that the scenes resulted from deliberate policies on the part of the Germans. The photographs are real. The uses to which they have been put are base.

There was no German policy at any of those camps to deliberately kill the internees. In the last months of the war, while Soviet arms were advancing on Germany from the east, the British and U.S. air armies were destroying every major city in Germany with saturation bombing. Transportation, the food distribution system and medical and sanitation services all broke down. That was the purpose of the Allied bombing, which has been described as the most barbarous form of warfare in Europe since the Mongol invasions.

Millions of refugees fleeing the Soviet armies were pouring into Germany. The camps still under German control were overwhelmed with internees from the east. By early 1945 the inmate population was swept by malnutrition and by epidemics of typhus, typhoid, dysentery and chronic diarrhea. Even the mortuary systems broke down. When the press entered the camps with British and U.S. soldiers, they found the results of all that. They took "The Photographs."

Still, at camps such as Buchenwald, Dachau and Bergen-Belsen tens of thousands of relatively healthy internees were liberated. They were there in the camps when "The Photographs" were taken. There are newsreels of these internees walking through the camp streets laughing and talking. Others picture exuberant internees

102

throwing their caps in the air and cheering their liberators. It is only natural to ask why you haven't seen those particular films and photos while you've seen the others scores and even hundreds of times.

Documents

Spokesmen for the Holocaust Lobby like to assure us that there are "tons" of captured German documents which prove the Jewish genocide. When challenged on this, however, they can produce only a handful of documents, the authenticity or interpretation of which is always highly questionable. If pressed for reliable documentation, the Lobby will then reverse itself and claim that the Germans destroyed all the relevant documents to hide their evil deeds, or it will make the absurd claim that the Germans used a simplistic code language or whispered verbal orders for mass murder into each others' ears.

The truth appears to be, with regard to the alleged extermination of the European Jews, that there was no order, no plan, no budget, no weapon (that is, no so-called execution gas chamber) and no victim (that is, not a single autopsied body at any camp has been shown to have been gassed).

Eyewitness Testimony

As documentary "proofs" for the mass-murder of the European Jews fall by the wayside, Holocaust historians depend increasingly on "eyewitness" testimonies to support their theories. Many of these testimonies are ludicrously unreliable. History is filled with stories of masses of people claiming to be eyewitnesses to everything from witchcraft to flying saucers.

During and after the war there were "eyewitnesses" to mass murder in gas chambers at Buchenwald, Bergen-Belsen, Dachau and other camps in Germany proper. Today, virtually all recognized scholars dismiss this eyewitness testimony as false and agree that there were no extermination gas chambers in any camp in Germany proper.

Establishment historians, however, still claim that extermination gas chambers existed at Auschwitz and at other camps in

Poland. The eyewitness testimony and the evidence for this claim is, in reality, qualitatively no different than the false testimony and evidence for the alleged gas chambers at the camps in Germany proper.

During the war crimes trials many "eyewitnesses" testified that Germans made soap out of human fat and lamp shades from human skin. Allied prosecutors even produced evidence to support those charges. Today, scholars agree that the testimony was false and the evidence fraudulent.

With regard to confessions by Germans at the war crimes trials, it is now well documented that many were obtained through coercion, intimidation and even physical torture.

Auschwitz

British historian David Irving, perhaps the most widely read historian writing in English, has called the Auschwitz death-camp story a "sinking ship" and states that there were "no gas chambers at Auschwitz . . ."

The Auschwitz State Museum has recently revised its half-century-old claim that 4 million humans were murdered there. The Museum now says maybe it was 1 million. But what documentary proof does the Museum provide to document the 1 million figure? None. Revisionist want to know where those 3 million souls have been the last 45 years. Were they part of the fabled Six Million?

The Leuchter Report contains the results of the first-ever forensic examination of the alleged gas chambers at Auschwitz. The Report is the work of America's leading execution hardware expert, Fred A. Leuchter. It concludes that no mass gassings ever did or ever could have taken place there in the so-called gas chambers. Fred Leuchter has called for an international commission of scientists, engineers and historians to investigate the Auschwitz gas chamber rumor.

Those who promote the Holocaust story are unable to explain why, during the war and postwar periods, the most prominent and powerful men of the time failed to mention gas chambers and the genocide of the Jews. When asked why this is so, the promoters reply with the absurd answer that those people did not realize the enormity of what had happened.

But is certain that if there had been "killing factories" in Poland murdering millions of civilians, then men such as Roosevelt, Truman, Churchill, Eisenhower and many others would have known about it and would have often and unambiguously mentioned it. They didn't! The promoters admit that only a tiny group of individuals believed the story at the time—many of whom worked for Jewish propaganda agencies. The rise of the Holocaust story reads more like the success story of a PR campaign than anything else.

Winston Churchill wrote the six volumes of his monumental work, The Second World War, without mentioning a program of mass-murder and genocide. Maybe it slipped his mind. Dwight D. Eisenhower in his memoir Crusade In Europe, also failed to mention gas chambers. Was the weapon used to murder millions of Jews unworthy of a passing reference? Was our future president being insensitive to Jews?

Political Correctness and Holocaust Revisionism

Many people, when they first hear Holocaust Revisionist arguments, find themselves bewildered. The arguments appear to make sense but "How is it possible?" The whole world believes the Holocaust story. It is just not plausible that so great a conspiracy to suppress the truth could have functioned for half a century.

To understand how it could very well have happened, one needs only to reflect on the intellectual and political orthodoxies of medieval Europe, or those of Nazi Germany or the Communist-bloc countries. In all of these societies the great majority of scholars were caught up in the existing political culture. Committed to a prevailing ideology and its interpretation of reality, these scholars and intellectuals felt it was their right, and even their duty, to protect every aspect of that ideology. They did so by oppressing the evil dissidents who expressed "offensive" or "dangerous" ideas. In every one of those societies, scholars became Thought Police.

In our own society, in the debate over the question of political correctness, there are those who deliberately attempt to trivialize the issues. They claim that there is no real problem with freedom of speech on our campuses, and that all that is involved with PC are a few rules which would defend minorities from those who would hurt their feelings. There is, of course, a deeper and more serious aspect to the problem. On American campuses today there is a wide range of ideas and viewpoints that are forbidden to be discussed openly. Even obvious facts and realities, when they are politically unacceptable, are denied and suppressed. One can learn much about the psychology and methodology of Thought Police by watching how they react when just one of their taboos is broken and Holocaust Revisionism is given a public forum.

First they express outrage that such offensive and dangerous ideas were allowed to be expressed publicly. They avoid answering or debating these ideas, claiming that to do so would give them a forum and legitimacy. Then they make vicious personal attacks against the Revisionist heretic, calling him dirty political names such as "anti-Semite, "racist" or "neo-Nazi," and they even suggest that he is a potential mass murderer. They publicly accuse the Revisionist of lying, but they don't allow the heretic to hear the specific charge or to face his accusers so that he can answer this slander.

Next, the Thought Police set out to destroy the transgressor professionally and financially by "getting" him at his job or concocting a lawsuit against him. The courts are sometimes used to attack Revisionism. The Holocausters often deceptively claim that Revisionist scholarship has been proven false during a trial. The fact is that Revisionist arguments have never been evaluated or judged by the courts.

Moreover, the Holocausters accuse Revisionists of being hate filled people who are promoting a doctrine of hatred. But Revisionism is a scholarly process, not a doctrine or an ideology. If the Holocaust promoters really want to expose hatred, they should take a second look at their own doctrines, and a long look at themselves in the mirror. Anyone on campus who invites a Revisionist to speak is himself attacked as being insensitive. When a Revisionist does speak on campus he is often times shouted down and threatened. If he has books or other printed materials with him they might be "confiscated." All this goes on while the majority of faculty and university administrators sit dumbly by, allowing political activists to determine what can be said and what can be read on their campus.

Finally, the Thought Police try to "straighten out" that segment of academia or the media that allowed the Revisionists a forum in the first place.

It can be an instructive intellectual exercise to identify taboo subjects other than Holocaust Revisionism, which would evoke comparable responses from Thought Police on our campuses.

Recently, some administrators in academia have held that university administrations should take actions to rid the campus of ideas which are disruptive to the university. This is a very dangerous position for administrators to take. It is an open invitation to tyranny. It means that any militant group with "troops at the ready" can rid the campus of ideas it opposes and then impose its own orthodoxy. The cowardly administrator finds it much easier and safer to rid the campus of controversial ideas than to face down a group of screaming and snarling militants. But it is the duty of university administrators to insure that the university remains a free marketplace of ideas. When ideas cause disruptions, it is the disrupters who must be subdued, not the ideas.

Conclusion

The influence of Holocaust Revisionism is growing steadily both here and abroad. In the United States, Revisionism was launched in earnest in 1977 with the publication of the book *The Hoax of the Twentieth Century* by Arthur R. Butz. Professor Butz teaches electrical engineering and computer sciences at Northwestern University in Evanston, Illinois.

Those who take up the Revisionist cause represent a wide spectrum of political and philosophical positions. They are certainly not the scoundrels, liars and demons the Holocaust Lobby tried to make them out to be. The fact is, there are no demons in the real world. People are at their worst when they begin to see their opponents as an embodiment of evil, and then begin to demonize them. Such people are preparing to do something simply awful to their opponents. Their logic is that you an do anything you want to a demon.

But whatever the demonizers attempt, they are going to fail. Growing numbers of Revisionist sympathizers and supporters assure us that the political forces that promote and defend the Holocaust story as it stands today are going to have to accept the role that Revisionist scholarship is playing in revising Holocaust history and freeing it of fraud and falsehood. That's what scholars do. Scholars must not promote the censorship of ideas, and they must not attempt to oppress others who reach conclusions which differ from their own.

CODOH is a member of the National Coalition Against Censorship (NCAC), the National Association for College Activities (NACA), and the Free Press Association. CODOH has no affiliation whatever with any political organization or group.

CODOH speakers are available to address student organizations and other appropriate groups about the Holocaust controversy. For information contact: Bradley R. Smith

> Committee for Open Debate
> on the Holocaust

Appendix B

AJC LETTER TO COLLEGE AND UNIVERSITY PRESIDENTS ABOUT HOLOCAUST-DENYING ADS

Dear University or College President:

I write to alert you of an anti-Semitic ad that may be offered to your college newspapers from Bradley Smith, who purports to represent an organization known as the Committee for Open Debate on the Holocaust.

The ad, which has been printed in a few university papers, and which has been rejected by many others, suggests that the Holocaust is a hoax. The "Holocaust as hoax" idea is the standard view of neo-Nazi groups around the world today—that diabolical Jews have created this "great lie" in order to milk the world for sympathy. The concept is the latest addendum to the hateful conspiracies by Jews hypothesized in *The Protocols of the Elders of Zion.*

It is not surprising, therefore, that Mr. Smith is also associated with the anti-Semitic Institute for Historical Review (a Liberty Lobby offshoot). Before targeting universities, Mr. Smith geared his message to talk radio programs and neo-Nazi mailing lists (see enclosures).

Some student editors have decided to run the ad on a misguided understanding of the First Amendment, or a belief that the ad is not offensive. Mr. Smith has an absolute right under the Constitution to spread whatever lies and hate he wants. But the First Amendment does not require a newspaper to accept every ad any more than the right of Americans accused of crime to a lawyer obligates all lawyers to take every client.

The ad that calls the existence of the Holocaust into question is just as offensive as one that would question the existence of slavery, or advocate hate toward any group. The acceptance of such an ad not only tarnishes a newspaper's reputation for distinguishing between racist fiction and controversial debate, it also disrupts the harmony of the campus and causes palpable pain to Jewish students.

As part of our national program targeting bigotry on campus, the American Jewish Committee has met with over 100 university and college presidents around the country detailing plans to combat prejudice and improve intergroup relations. . . . One of the most important aspects of any anti-bigotry plan is the role of the president. The president must be visible, strong, and unequivocal in both upholding free speech rights and denouncing bigotry.

I respectfully suggest you contact the editor(s) of your student paper(s) to alert them to the possibility of the ad, and to advise them to exercise their First Amendment rights by refusing to run an ad for hate.

Very truly yours,
Kenneth S. Stern

A059 Sam Dickson: SHATTERING THE ICON OF ABRAHAM LINCOLN

A060 Soundtrack to the film: "DRESDEN: THE ASH WEDNESDAY APOCALYPSE"

A061 Ivor Benson and Donald Martin: SOUTH AFRICA IN MODERN HISTORY

A062 Dr. Ivo Omrcanin: TITO'S COMMUNISM: A JOINT BRITISH-ADL VENTURE

A063 Ed Dieckmann, Jr.: SENSITIVITY TRAINING AND THE NEW HISTORY: A TOOL FOR ADL "HOLOCAUST" INDOCTRINATION

A064 Ted O'Keefe: THE OSI-KGB CONNECTION

A065 Bradley Smith, Tom Marcellus, W.A. Carto, Mark Weber, et al.: DISCUSSION ON THE FUTURE OF REVISIONISM

The Eighth International Revisionist Conference—1987

A066 Ted O'Keefe: AUSTIN APP: A VOICE FOR JUSTICE

A067 Generalmajor Otto Ernst Remer: THE EVENTS OF JULY 20, 1944

A068 Alexander Berkis: LATVIA'S HALF-CENTURY ORDEAL UNDER SOVIET OCCUPATION

A069 Henri Roques: THE GERSTEIN 'CONFESSIONS' IN LIGHT OF THE ROQUES THESIS

A070 Dr. R. Clarence Lang: IMPOSED GUILT: PASTOR NIEMOELLER AND THE STUTTGART DECLARATION OF GERMAN GUILT

A071 Dr. Martin A. Larson/Dr. Robert Countess: (Side I) UPDATE ON THE DEAD SEA SCROLLS. (Side II) STUDENTS REACTIONS TO STUDY OF *THE HOAX OF THE TWENTIETH CENTURY* (Countess)

A072 Prof. Robert Faurisson: HOLOCAUST REVISIONISM IN EUROPE, 1983-1987

A073 Dr. Karl Otto Braun: THE SORGE-SMEDLEY SPY RING

A074 August Kapprott: A GERMAN-AMERICAN'S 50-YEAR STRUGGLE FOR JUSTICE AND HONOR

A075 Bradley Smith/Plenary: TALK-SHOW ANECDOTES AND TALKS FEATURING: Willis Carto, Mark Weber, Jurgen Neumann (for Ernst Zuendel), Fritz Berg (for Conrad Grieb), and Tom Marcellus

A093 Mark Weber/Ted O'Keefe: INTRODUCTION TO HOLOCAUST REVISIONISM.

A080 Dr. Robert Countess vs. Barry Farber

A080 Mark Weber: Revisionism Today

The Ninth International Revisionist Conference

A082 F. Rost van tonningen: THE VISION OF DR. M. ROST VAN TONNINGEN.

A083 Prof. Anthony Kubek: THE MORGENTHAU PLAN AND THE PROBLEM OF POLICY PERVERSION.

A084 Carlo Mattogno: THE FIRST GASSING AT AUSCHWITZ: GENESIS OF A MYTH.

A085 Lt. Gen. Hideo Miki: THOUGHTS ON THE MILITARY HISTORY OF THE OCCUPATION OF JAPAN.

A086 Victor Marchetti: THE CIA AND THE "MAKING" OF HISTORY.

A087 Fred Leuchter: THE MAKING OF *THE LEUCHTER REPORT.*

A088 David Irving: CHURCHILL AND U.S. ENTRY INTO WORLD WAR II.

A089 James Keegstra: CANADIAN CENSORSHIP AND THE KEEGSTRA CASE.

A090 Rev. Herman Otten: CHRISTIANS, CHRISTIANITY, AND THE HOLOCAUST STORY.

A091 Pro. Robert Faurisson: RECENT DEVELOPMENTS IN HOLOCAUST REVISIONISM IN FRANCE.

A092 Jerome Brentar: DEMJANJUK CASE UPDATE. Tom Marcellus: JDL ATTEMPTS TO CAUSE CANCELLATION OF THE 9th CONFERENCE.

Other Exciting Audio Tapes

A044 Noam Chomsky: THE MIDDLE EAST CRISIS AND THE THREAT OF NUCLEAR WAR (part one)

A045 Noam Chomsky: THE MIDDLE EAST CRISIS AND THE THREAT OF NUCLEAR WAR (part two)

A076 Bradley Smith on WMCA

A077 Bradley Smith on KHSL

A078-79 Briefing on the Zuendel Trial. (S12.00 for set of 2 tapes)

VHS
VIDEOTAPES

All of the following videos are available in American VHS (U.S. and Canada). Beta format is no longer supplied. Those videos indicated by a ✔ (check) mark are *also* available in European/Australian PAL format for an additional $10.00. American VHS (also known as VHS/NTSC) will not play on video machines designed for the PAL format. Some of these videos *do not* include English language subtitles, so please read the descriptions to know what to expect, or drop us a note if you're not sure.

V001 EPIC: THE STORY OF THE WAFFEN SS by Leon Degrelle. IHR-exclusive video-lecture taped at the General's home in Spain. An unapologetic and moving memoir of the history, philosophy and ideals of the unprecedented, all-volunteer, pan-European fighting force of which he was one of the most illustrious members. Professionally overdubbed English translation. Sound fair, picture fair. $49.00

V009 THE BIRTH OF A NATION (1915-U.S.A.). Directed by D.W. Griffith. With Lillian Gish. Henry B. Walthall, Mae Marsh. Perhaps the most famous silent film. Griffith's greatest film, a panoramic portrait of the civil war as seen from the South. With a 1930 sound prologue by D.W. Griffith (the only existing film interview with Griffith). Silent film with music score, correct projection speed. The most complete print known to exist. 175 minutes. (2 cassettes) $79.00

V011 HITLER: FEBRUARY 10th, 1933. The battle for Germany was not yet decided when Adolf Hitler, the newly appointed Chancellor, rose in the Berlin Sports Palace to deliver what was perhaps the most important speech of his career. Chancellor for only one week, the German leader stood beside a table surrounded by watchful SA and SS men. Faced with crucial upcoming elections on March 5, Hitler displayed the full, awesome charisma of his spellbinding oratory to condemn his political enemies and exhort his jubilant audience, and the millions listening on radio throughout Germany, to support the National Socialist Party. The Fuehrer, introduced by Minister Josef Goebbels is shown in an original National Socialist Party election film. B&W, 30 minutes, sound with English subtitles. $40.00 ✔

V012 PRE-WAR GERMAN FEATURETTES Four short films about life in Germany between the World Wars. *Yesterday and Today* is a comparison of the prosperity under National Socialism compared with the

despair and moral distress of Weimar Germany. *Three Years of Adolf Hitler*, an early work of NS filmmaking, this feature highlights scenes of Hitler's speeches and colorful rallies of the period. *Honor of Work* is virtually without commentary. This rare film demonstrates the joy of the German worker after years of Weimar unemployment. *Becoming an Army* on the night of March 7th, 1936 a shrill alarm awakes the peacefully sleeping soldiers at a barracks just east of the Rhine. This is not a drill! The soldiers are being led to liberate the Rhineland from the French. 4 short films, B&W, 60 minutes, sound with English subtitles, excellent visual quality. $60.00 ✔

V013 GERMAN INVASION OF POLAND This is the German version of the Polish conflict which precipitated the Second. World War. Shown is the peacetime bombardment of the Silesian town of Beuthen by Polish artillery; the persecution of ethnic Germans by Poles in the Corridor; the Waffen SS attack on the Post Office in Danzig; aircraft sorties; the naval bombardment of a Polish fort by the warship *Schleswig-Holstein;* the ferocious land battles of Radom and Kutno; and clips of Adolf Hitler at the front, conferring with his generals and relaxing with the German troops. Here captured on film is the birth of the legendary *Blitzkrieg.* B&W, 60 minutes, sound with English subtitles. $60.00 ✔

V014 DER FELDZUG IN POLAND (The Polish Campaign) A foreign language film for *Auslands Deutsche* (German emigres) produced by the NS Government. This is the German viewpoint of what happened during the war with Poland. B&W, 37 minutes, in English, $45.00 ✔

V015 SIEG IM WESTEN (Victory In The West) One of history's greatest victories is depicted in this documentary of the six week *Blitzkrieg* of Holland, France and Belgium. Authentic battle footage, both German and captured Allied footage, is combined to make this one of the most spectacular war films ever made. Battle scenes, often filmed at the peril of the cameraman's life, highlight this front line thriller: aerial combat between a Heinkel III and a hapless British Spitfire; French tanks clash with German panzers; and infantrymen brave a hail of machinegun fire to assault the formidable Magnot Line. Film score by Herbert Windt. B&W with English subtitles, picture quality good, sound quality varies. 120 minutes. $60.00 ✔

V016 THE SOVIET PARADISE A unique picture of life inside the Soviet Union, unrestrained by Soviet censors, depicting what life was really like after 20 years of Communist rule. The wretched peasants and workers starving and the desecrated churches, giving mute evidence of the anti-Christian pogroms, form a dismal picture of the Soviet paradise. B & W, 14 minutes, sound with English subtitles, a few jumps occur in the original German soundtrack, $30.00 ✔

V017 THE BALTIC TRAGEDY Fifteen short films and newsreels assembled from American, German, Latvian and Soviet sources, tell the tragic story of Latvia, Lithuania and Estonia from the years 1940-49. Invaded by the Soviet Union in 1940, these countries became the scene of some of the fiercest fighting of the Second World War when German troops began their offensive in "Operation Barbarossa" in 1941. Sold out by the Americans and the English to Stalin at Yalta, the plight of the Baltic States is an indictment against the selective human rights policies of those countries and a stern warning of the results of those misapplied policies. The video leads off with *My Latvia* which shows how this proud nation was sold out to the Soviets by traitors; then a series of German newsreels depicting the offensive on the Eastern front; Soviet atrocities against Baltic civilians perpetrated by Jewish NKVD members; violent air and land battles; Estonian Waffen SS members, battling for Western civilization at Narva; and the Army Group Courland which repulsed six Soviet offensives and was

111

A085 Lt. Gen. Hideo Miki: THOUGHTS ON THE MILITARY HISTORY OF THE OCCUPATION OF JAPAN.

A086 Victor Marchetti: THE CIA AND THE "MAKING" OF HISTORY.

A087 Fred Leuchter: THE MAKING OF *THE LEUCHTER REPORT*.

A088 David Irving: CHURCHILL AND U.S. ENTRY INTO WORLD WAR II.

A089 James Keegstra: CANADIAN CENSORSHIP AND THE KEEGSTRA CASE.

A090 Rev. Herman Otten: CHRISTIANS, CHRISTIANITY, AND THE HOLOCAUST STORY:

A091 Pro. Robert Faurisson: RECENT DEVELOPMENTS IN HOLOCAUST REVISIONISM IN FRANCE.

A092 Jerome Brentar: DEMJANJUK CASE UPDATE.

Tom Marcellus: JDL ATTEMPTS TO CAUSE CANCELLATION OF THE 9th CONFERENCE.

Other Exciting Audio Tapes, $9.95 each

A044 Noam Chomsky: THE MIDDLE EAST CRISIS AND THE THREAT OF NUCLEAR WAR (part one)

A045 Noam Chomsky: THE MIDDLE EAST CRISIS AND THE THREAT OF NUCLEAR WAR (part two)

A076 Bradley Smith on WMCA

A077 Bradley Smith on KHSL

A078-79 Briefing on the Zuendel Trial. ($12.00 for set of 2 tapes)

A080 Mark Weber: Revisionism Today

A093 Mark Weber/Ted O'Keefe: INTRODUCTION TO HOLOCAUST REVISIONISM.

MILITARY MUSIC
ON AUDIO CASSETTES $9.95 EACH

A200 GERMAN ARMY MARCHES Vol. I
A201 GERMAN ARMY MARCHES Vol. II
A202 GERMAN ARMY MARCHES Vol. III
A203 GERMAN ARMY MARCHES Vol. IV
A204 GERMAN ARMY MARCHES Vol. V
A205 GERMAN NAVY MARCHES Vol. I
A206 GERMAN NAVY MARCHES Vol. II
A207 PANZER MARCHES Vol. I
A208 LUFTWAFFE MARCHES Vol. I
A209 KAVALLERIE MARCHES Vol. I
A210 STORMTROOPER MARCHES Vol. I
A211 STORMTROOPER MARCHES Vol. II

VHS
VIDEOTAPES

All of the following videos are available in American VHS (U.S. and Canada). Beta format is no longer supported. Those videos indicated by a ✓ (check) mark are *also* available in European/Australian PAL format for an additional $10.00. American VHS (also known as VHS/NTSC) will not play on video machines designed for the PAL format. Some of these videos *do not* include English language subtitles, so please read the descriptions to know what to expect, or drop us a note if you're not sure.

V001 EPIC: THE STORY OF THE WAFFEN SS by Leon Degrelle. IHR-exclusive video-lecture taped at the General's home in Spain. An unapologetic and moving memoir of the history, philosophy and ideals of the unprecedented, all-volunteer, pan-European fighting force of which he was one of the most illustrious members. Professionally overdubbed English translation. Sound good, picture fair, $49.00

V009 THE BIRTH OF A NATION (1915-U.S.A.). Directed by D.W. Griffith. With Lillian Gish, Henry B. Walthall, Mae Marsh. Perhaps the most famous silent film. Griffith's greatest film, a panoramic portrait of the civil war as seen from the South. With a 1930 sound prologue by D.W. Griffith (the only existing film interview with Griffith). Silent film with music score, correct projection speed. This version is from the most complete print known to exist. 175 minutes. (2 cassettes) $79.00

V011 HITLER: FEBRUARY 10th, 1933. The battle for Germany was not yet decided when Adolf Hitler, the newly appointed Chancellor, rose in the Berlin Sports Palace to deliver what was perhaps the most important speech of his career. Chancellor for only one week, the German leader stood beside a table surrounded by watchful SA and SS men. Faced with crucial upcoming elections on March 5, Hitler displayed the full, awesome charisma of his spellbinding oratory to condemn his political enemies and exhort his jubilant audience, and the millions listening on radio throughout Germany, to support the National Socialist Party. The Fuehrer, introduced by Minister Josef Goebbels is shown in an original National Socialist Party election film. B&W, 30 minutes, sound with English subtitles. $40.00 ✓

V012 PRE-WAR GERMAN FEATURETTES Four short films about life in Germany between the World Wars. *Yesterday and Today* is a comparison of the prosperity under National Socialism compared with the despair and moral distress of Weimar Germany. *Three Years of Adolf Hitler*, an early work of NS filmmaking, this feature highlights scenes of Hitler's speeches and colorful rallies of the period. *Honor of Work* is virtually without commentary. This rare film demonstrates the joy of the German worker after years of Weimar unemployment. *Becoming an Army* on the night of March 7th, 1936 a shrill alarm awakes the peacefully sleeping soldiers at a barracks just east of the Rhine. This is not a drill! The soldiers are being led to liberate the Rhineland from the French. 4 short films, B&W, 60 minutes, sound with English subtitles, excellent visual quality. $60.00 ✓

V013 GERMAN INVASION OF POLAND This is the German version of the Polish conflict which precipitated the Second World War. Shown is the peacetime bombardment of the Silesian town of Beuthen by Polish artillery; the persecution of ethnic Germans by Poles in the Corridor; the Waffen SS attack on the Post Office in Danzig; aircraft sorties; the naval bombardment of a Polish fort by the warship *Schleswig-Holstein*; the ferocious land battles of Radom and Kutno; and clips of Adolf Hitler at the front, conferring with his generals and relaxing with the German troops. Here captured on film is the birth of the legendary *Blitzkrieg*. B&W, 60 minutes, sound with English subtitles, $60.00 ✓

V014 DER FELDZUG IN POLAND (The Polish Campaign) A foreign language film for *Auslands Deutsche* (German emigres) produced by the NS Government. This is the German viewpoint of what happened during the war with Poland. B&W, 37 minutes, sound English. $45.00 ✓

V015 SIEG IM WESTEN (Victory In The West) One of history's greatest victories is depicted in this documentary of the six week *Blitzkrieg* of Holland, France and Belgium. Authentic battle footage, both German and captured Allied footage, is combined to make this one of the most spectacular war films ever made. Battle scenes, often

filmed at the peril of the cameraman's life, highlight this front line thriller: aerial combat between a Heinkel III and a hapless British Spitfire; French tanks clash with German panzers; and infantrymen brave a hail of machinegun fire to assault the formidable Maginot Line. Film score by Herbert Windt, B&W, sound with English subtitles, picture quality good, sound quality varies, 120 minutes, $60.00 ✓

V016 THE SOVIET PARADISE A unique picture of life inside the Soviet Union, unrestrained by Soviet censors, depicting what life was really like after 20 years of Communist rule. The wretched peasants and workers starving and the desecrated churches, giving mute evidence of the anti-Christian pogroms, form a dismal picture of the Soviet paradise. B & W, 14 minutes, sound with English subtitles, a few jumps occur in the original German soundtrack, $30.00 ✓

V017 THE BALTIC TRAGEDY Fifteen short films and newsreels assembled from American, German, Latvian and Estonian sources, tell the tragic story of Latvia, Lithuania and Estonia from the years 1940-49. Invaded by the Soviet Union in 1940, these countries became the scene of some of the fiercest fighting of the Second World War when German troops began their offensive in "Operation Barbarossa" in 1941. Sold out by the Americans and the English to Stalin at Yalta, the plight of the Baltic States is an indictment against the selective human rights policies of those countries and a stern warning of the results of those misapplied policies. The video leads off with *My Latvia* which shows how this proud nation was sold out to the Soviets by traitors; then a series of German newsreels depicting the offensive on the Eastern front; Soviet atrocities against Baltic civilians perpetrated by Jewish NKVD members; violent air and land battles: Estonian Waffen SS members, battling for Western civilization at Narva; and the Army Group Courland which repulsed six Soviet offensives and was undefeated in the war. An English-narrated, Swedish-made film of "Operation Keelhaul," the forcible repatriation of Baltic men to certain death in the gulags of the U.S.S.R. Finally, *The Homeless*, narrated by Henry Fonda, examines life in a West German camp for displaced Baltic citizens unable to return to their homes for fear of the Communists. This film, instead of criticizing the Soviet Union, is rather an apologetic token to the suffering of these brave people, many of whom later found refuge in the U.S. 15 segments, B&W, 148 minutes, sound with English subtitles. $89.00 — Now $79.00 ✓

V018 THE BATTLE OF KHARKOV In May 1942, three Soviet armies collided with a German force which was launching its own offensive eastward. Captured in breathtaking detail is the massed Soviet attack and its repulsion by German, Romanian, Italian and Hungarian troops. Bombers blanket a forest filled with Soviet units. German panzers and infantry advance with the support of screaming Stukas. Blazing tank duels, artillery

Appendix C

Transcript of Montel Williams TV Talk Show on Holocaust Denial, April 30, 1992

(REPRINTED WITH PERMISSION OF MONTEL WILLIAMS SHOW.)

Man's Voice. Montel Williams's show April 30th . . .

Montel Williams. No matter how many times we see the footage, it shocks us. During the Holocaust an estimated 6 million Jews died under the regime of Adolf Hitler. They died from starvation, disease, and gassing. But there are some who say that these pictures are not real, that much of what is known about the Holocaust is fiction and not fact. One person who questions the existence of the Holocaust is Mr. Mark Weber.

Mark is a Holocaust revisionist. He is the editor and spokesman for the Institute for Historical Review. And also joining us is Mr. David Cole, another revisionist. He is a member of the Committee for Open Debate on the Holocaust. David was recently under the attack, or under attack, by members of the Jewish Defense League while he was speaking on the subject, because David is Jewish.

Thank you very much, gentlemen, for being here. We appreciate your coming. [applause]

We have all seen the specials, the news clips, the footage. Everyone around the world believes that the Holocaust took place. Why do you think it didn't?

Mark Weber. Well, Montel, it's very important to understand that no one says that those pictures are not real as you indicate at the beginning of the program. The pictures are very real, they're very horrible, they're very tragic, and we've all seen them. We've all

113

heard that 6 million Jews died in the second World War during the Holocaust. But it's very important to understand what these pictures show and what they don't show. The people, these pictures were taken at the Belson, Bergen-Belson concentration camp at the end of the war by the British when they liberated the camp. The people shown in these pictures, and it's a very, very terrible pictures, nobody denies that, nobody says it didn't happen, nobody says it's not true. These people were victims of starvation and disease, they died in the last weeks of the war. They died in the last weeks of the war, as, in fact, indirect victims of the war. British doctors who were at the camp themselves at the time the camp was liberated, and many inmates who were at the camp there and elsewhere, have also confirmed the conditions at Belsen, although certainly not a country club, were relatively good until the final weeks and months of the war. And that was because, in the final weeks and months of the war, all of Germany, all of Europe was in complete chaos. All the railroads were ruined, it was impossible to supply food, it was impossible to supply water. And particularly at Bergen Belson, thousands and thousands and thousands of Jews were evacuated from camps further to the east because the Soviets were coming in. And sent into this and other camps which were enormously overcrowded, and these people died in large numbers by disease and starvation. But if the policy of the Germany government had been to exterminate these people, they would not have, they would have long since been dead, and these pictures would not have been taken. In fact, the German government policy during the war was a very grim one. It was a very harsh one and so forth. As I said, again, no one denies those pictures. But those people were not victims of a program or policy of extermination. And that's what Holocaust revisionists say.

Montel Williams. Well, let's go back a little bit in history, so we can kind of bring everybody up to speed. Because I asked for a history lesson myself. I've done some reading on World War II and knew a few things. But just, 1933 was when Hitler became the führer, 1933 was also when Dachau opened, 1938 Hitler entered Vienna, making it part of the Third Reich, 1939 Germany invades Poland. We go on, in 1940 the Nazis invade Holland, Belgium, France, Luxembourg. In 1941 they invade Russia; 1941 the first death camp was opened; and 1942 the final solution was discussed

114

openly. And that final solution was a solution that included the extermination of the Jews. Is that not correct?

Mark Weber. You've raised a lot of very, very good points. There was, we know from German documents, we know from German officials during the war, they did talk about something they called the final solution to the Jewish question. There are German documents that talk about this. But in this thousands, millions, tons of German documents seized at the end of the war that deal with Jewish policy, there is not a single document, not a single piece of paper which talks about or confirms or even discusses an extermination policy.

Montel Williams. Yeah, but Mark, but wait. Hitler also knew that if, let's say he didn't win this war, and someone ever found a document that stated that, life would be real tough for him and everyone else.

Mark Weber. We know, we have German documents which show exactly what the policy was. And these documents are in fact, very, very important. What the German officials meant by the final solution policy was, before the end of 1941, was a policy of forced or, forced expulsion from Europe by forced emigration if necessary and need be. After 1941 and in 1942, this policy changed to one of forced, of deporting Jews, uprooting them and sending them to the east. And that meant first to ghettos and camps in Poland; and then later, throughout the war, they were sent to the occupied Soviet territories. That's what the German officials during the war said and meant by this final solution of the Jewish question.

Now at Nuremberg, this, of course this whole issue came up at Nuremberg. All of the German defendants at the big Nuremberg trial, 1945, 1946, all said that they had no knowledge during the war of any extermination program—

Montel Williams. Wait a minute, if I had been a German, if I had been a German guard at one of the camps, Dachau, Auschwitz, and somebody said, "Did you participate in the murder of a million people?" I would have said, "No, it was you. The homeboy did it. It wasn't me." And I would have said, "No, I never saw this before." I would have lied and said anything I could have said to prove that I wasn't involved.

Mark Weber. That's very reasonable. But what these . . . had to say, is also consistent from the documents that we have and what we know about. And it's also consistent with everything we know about the policy from many other sources.

Montel Williams. Well now David, I mean, I would think that there are enough older Jewish people in this country, people who are survivors, people whose families lived through the Holocaust, who would right now be willing to do exactly what happened here a couple of weeks ago, and that's attack you. Because you are Jewish. And to step forward and say this would be like myself stepping forward and saying that the United States government never brought slaves to this country.

David Cole. But now if you were to say that, couldn't people then make a case to show that there was, in fact, slavery? I am not trying to aggravate anyone, anybody, but I know that I am gravely aggravating people, to the point where they will actually physically come up and attack me. But I think it raises many interesting issues, specifically the role of truth in society. What happens when you have eyewitnesses and yet you have other evidence, physical evidence, forensic evidence, the evidence of documents, and intercepted transmissions.

You make a point, Montel. You make a grave assumption, a leap of faith when you say, well the reason we don't have these documents showing, where the Germans discuss what they did, is because Hitler didn't want them around, I guess, had them burned or something, because he knew that it would get him in trouble. But, that's making an assumption. Now other people might say, "We don't have the documents because there aren't any. Because they never existed."

Montel Williams. But what about all the things that you hear about gas chambers and all those things. The mass graves, graves with, with thousands—

David Cole. Well now no one doubts, no one doubts mass graves, no one doubts that there were bodies in this camp. But let me just for the record state, I don't doubt that it was an incredibly horrible thing that happened to the Jews of Europe. Something that should not be thought of in any lighter sense specifically because we doubt that there were gas chambers. These people were taken out of their villages, split up from their families and put into camps and made to work as forced labor and this is a horrible situation. And people died from disease and starvation and just plain being

116

worked to death. It is not that we are trying to sugarcoat what happened. But it's been many years after the fact and it's time that we brought the fact in, parallel to the actual history of what happened.

Montel Williams. Yes ma'am.

Question. The fact still remains, yes, that 6 million Jews were killed. And whether or not the documentation shows that it was the intent to completely get rid of Jews, it, it doesn't matter whether or not the intent was there. Because it happened. Six million Jews were murdered. [applause]

Montel Williams. . . . for both David and Mark, that's a very important issue. Because both of you dispute the fact that 6 million Jews died.

David Cole. If I could make a point, now she said the fact that 6 million Jews died. However, in 1988 the Auschwitz, the site of Auschwitz, where people can go and tour the gas chambers, they lowered their figure from 4 million dead to 1 million dead. So that was 3 million taken out of the equation over night. Where did these 3 million go? Were they never there in the first place? Were they in the camps and did they survive? And if you can lose 3 million people over night, whose to say that 1 million remaining figure is not also wrong?

Montel Williams. Now let me ask you this question. Weren't so many figures ascertained after the fact because they went back and did censuses after?

Mark Weber. The source of the famous 6 million figure is an affidavit by one of the, by somebody who was brought in at the Nuremberg trial in 1945–46. Even Raoul Hilberg, who is considered one of the major figures in the Holocaust, Holocaust historians, professor at the University of Vermont. He concedes himself that the 6 million figure is based upon crude calculations, it is only highly dubious. And he says we must re-examine this whole question of 6 million.

Look, it's very interesting, Montel. People have heard over and over about 6 million Jews dying in Europe during the Second World War. How many people in this audience know how many Germans died during the Second World War? How many Americans died during the Second World War? How many Chinese died during the Second World War? In America, as time goes by, the more time passes, the more there's emphasis on the fate of one particular people during the Second World War, almost to the exclusion of everyone else.

Montel Williams. Now that is, Mark, that is—

Mark Weber. Let me make another point. I mean, right now in Washington, D.C., a federal government agency, a taxpayer funded agency of the federal government, the United States Holocaust Memorial Council is organizing and building an enormous museum in Washington, D.C. There is no comparable museum in Washington, D.C. to the victims of slavery. There is no comparable museum in Washington, D.C. to the fate of the Indians, or any other people. But there is an enormous museum being built, under U.S., federal government auspices, the fate of only one particular people in one other place.

How many Chinese died during the Second World War? According to the *Encyclopedia Britannica* the number of civilians, Chinese civilians alone, who died during the Second World War is more than 20 million. Over 20 million. Who knows it? Who even cares?

Montel Williams. Are we saying that therefore we should not believe what happened to the Jewish people because these other things were admitted? Or should we stop and say that we believe what happened?

Mark Weber. Montel, it's right and proper to memorialize the dead. The dead of all wars, the dead of all genocide or all mistreatment, whatever it happens to be. But what is not right, is to take the fate of one particular people, and in effect, make a kind of political football out of it.

David Cole. I would like to also interject, speaking as a Jew, the Holocaust is an extremely important thing, especially to American and Israeli Jews, because most American Jews tend to be secularized, and the Holocaust and the shared history of persecution has tended to take the place of the religion of Jews. Now I'm Jewish, I'm also an atheist. I don't buy many things, I don't buy concepts of mysticism, spirituality and especially myths. And I have read both sides of the issue extensively, and I'm not looking to hurt anybody but I do have to say, from my own point of view, that the evidence saying that there were no gas chambers is a lot stronger than any of the evidence that can be presented saying there was.

Montel Williams. Well let's stop there and take a break. And when we come back, we'll find out, like David said, is it myth or is it truth? We'll find out when we come back. [applause, commercial]

We're talking about the Holocaust and whether or not it happened or it didn't happen. You had a question, sir.

Question. This is a remark to Dave's earlier statements. He said that they weren't really being prosecuted, persecuted. My point is, they were, the Jews were selected specifically to be annihilated. I think that's more important, and the fact that they were selectively chosen out of various groups to be annihilated. And secondly, I do have to agree with you to a degree that, what happened in Cambodia with Khmer Rouge wasn't played up as much as the issue of the Jews. But that still doesn't lessen the fact that the Holocaust occurred.

Montel Williams. And you both say that it didn't occur.

Mark Weber. Montel, we don't say the Holocaust didn't occur. That's really too simplistic. You know the Holocaust—

Montel Williams. Well what is a revisionist then? Okay, then make it simple enough . . . Mark, before you go. Because you're talking a little heady, I want you to make sure everybody can understand what it is you're talking about. What is it that a revisionist wants there to be shown in history?

Mark Weber. Revisionists say three essential things: we say first and foremost there was no policy or program to exterminate the Jews of Europe during the Second World War. Okay, so the—

Montel Williams. Stop right there for a second. Don't go too quick. Which refutes exactly what the gentleman just asked you, because he said that the policy was, they were picked out and isolated to be annihilated.

Mark Weber. That's certainly true.

Montel Williams. You're saying that's not true?

Mark Weber. They were, they were selectively persecuted, they were picked out, they were put in ghettos, they were put in camps, they were a victim group. But there was not a policy or program to exterminate them.

Montel Williams. Wait a minute, wait. I want you, you're getting ready to run real quick, and I want to slow you down so we can get every point out of what you're saying.

So if they were selected individually as a group, to be put into ghettos and to be starved to death, what was the key? Whether or not it was a gas chamber or not, they were starved to death.

Mark Weber. No, no, no. Montel, look, I mean during the Second World War, as you well know, as everyone in California, I think, knows, the west coast Japanese were also selected, they were rounded up, they were—

Montel Williams. They were fed.

Mark Weber. Sure, well, yes. Europe was not, Europe during the Second World War was not the United States during the Second World War. There was a lot of food in the United States, there were peace, essentially peacetime conditions. War didn't come here. Certainly the Japanese were not treated anywhere near as bad as the Jews. But the point is simply that they were selectively persecuted, and that's true. That was certainly true with the Jews.

David Cole. And I just want to also, I . . . say that I'd like to call you on what you said, "so what if there were no gas chambers, if they were starved to death." Hey if you, if we even make that much of a point, we've refuted a lot of what is in the history books that say there are gas chambers. Now, if all of a sudden the story is going to change and it's that the genocide was through starving them to death, well that makes a great big difference because then all that you've read in your history has been wrong. We're not prepared to deviate at all from the facts that are presented to us. And if the facts were ever to show that they were starved to death, we would reflect that.

Montel Williams. Okay now the second point, you said there were three points. That was the first point.

Mark Weber. Right.

Montel Williams. Second.

Mark Weber. The second point, Montel, is that we dispute the claims made over and over about gas chambers and gassings. That's the weapon of extermination, supposedly. It's very important to realize in this context that the Holocaust story, the gassing story has changed dramatically over the years. At the big Nuremberg trial of 1945–46, it was claimed that people were gassed at Dachau, at Buchenwald, and at various camps in Germany proper as well. Right after the war it was claimed, not that people were gassed at Auschwitz, but that they were electrocuted to death.

Montel Williams. And then later we found out that all the gas chambers were in Poland. Give me the third point.

Mark Weber. The point is that the evidence for supposedly gassing in some camps has just been done away with. It's a maybe.

Montel Williams. All right.

Mark Weber. Okay the third point is, we say that no, no, nothing like 6 million Jews in Europe died during the Second World War. And it's very important in this . . . also to realize that every, the Jew, every Jewish person in the Second World War who died of whatever cause, is considered "a victim of the Holocaust." That is, Jews who died even in Allied bombing attacks, Jews who died for whatever reason were considered victims of the Holocaust.

Montel Williams. So you're saying all 6 million is a compilation figure of every Jewish person who died during the war?

Mark Weber. Look, even a number of prominent Holocaust historians have conceded the 6 million figure is essentially symbolic in nature. It's repeated over and over, and it's not necessarily. All sorts of other things can change, and the 6 million figure will stay the same.

Montel Williams. Okay. Yes ma'am.

Question. Well I have two things to say. First of all, a death is a death. These people have died. I don't understand why you want to [applause]. What do you have to gain by questioning the facts in history? What is it, what's your purpose in all of this?

Montel Williams. Is what, let me ask this question. Is knowing the truth about what happened in your past important to you?

Question. Well to me, death is death. They have all died there. It was hurtful to many people. Why is, we have to question whether somebody set forth to gas chamber people or whatever? What do you have to gain?

David Cole. But you see, that is a philosophically based question, not a factual question. We know that there were camps we had for the Japanese. What if somebody came along and said we then cut up the Japanese and fed them to crocodiles. It is important for us to know what did happen and didn't happen. And if you're not interested in truth in history, fine. To some of us who are interested in what really happened, in the use of truth, the governmental use of truth, how truth can be changed, how truth can be altered, that does matter. A death is a death of course. But if we say the German people set up gas chambers, you ought to be willing to prove it and ready to prove it.

Montel Williams. But now wait, before you even jump in Mark Weber. David, but isn't it very important, also to know, that if, if the plan was, if the plan was to annihilate a race of people, if that was the plan, genocide of a race of people, does it then matter if there were gas chambers or if it was starvation? This lady is making a very interesting point. The point is death is death, and they set out to kill people.

David Cole. Maybe it's a fine line. I'm not arguing it with you, that maybe it's a fine line. But then why do we get all the flack when we then try to deny that there were gas chambers based on the facts available? If it is such a fine line, if it just don't matter at all, then we ought to be able to say, well here's some evidence showing that there are no gas chambers. And everybody would say, oh fine. But it was death, and we would say sure, it was death. All the same. And all the same thing about the idea of there being a final solution. Show us the evidence that there was the idea of a genocide of all the Jews. And if you show it to us, and if it passes at least my own personal skepticism when looking at things, then I will be the first person to say "I'm David the dunce. Just kick me out of the studio." But I want to see the evidence first.

Montel Williams. Yes sir.

Question. Two questions.

Montel Williams. Make it one, because we've got to go to break.

Question. Okay. How many Jews did the Germans have their hands on during the war that they could have exterminated, theoretically?

Mark Weber. That's a very good question. You know, I believe that the total number of Jews in Europe who died under German control or access control during the Second World War is probably in the neighborhood of a million, a million and a half. I don't think that it, that the Germans even had under their control 6 million Jews during the Second World War. This is confirmed, I think, by a report that was issued by the International Labor Office in, and by various, there's a number of reasons why I say that.

Montel Williams. Okay, we have to take a break. But when we come back, we're going to meet some survivors of the Holocaust, and they'll tell us what they saw. And whether or not what they're saying, both Mark and David, is true or false. We'll be back in just a second. [commercial]

We've been talking about the Holocaust with revisionist Mark Weber and Mr. David Cole. But joining us right now are Dr. Michael Thaler. Michael is the president of the Holocaust Center of Northern California. Michael is also a survivor who lost more than 60 members of his family in the Holocaust. Also joining us are Ernest and Anna Hollander. They are both survivors, Anna's entire family was wiped out in Auschwitz.

Now, before we even go any further in the discussion, Ernest, could you take us back to that day in 1944, when your family arrived at Auschwitz?

Ernest Hollander. Yeah, sure. First of all, I'd like to make an opening statement. That I watched before on the television, the revisionists, what they said, and I feel it's completely wrong, completely not true. Because I've been there, and I saw what happened. And I came tonight with pain and agony to tell you all these stories. But I also feel very bad, I feel sorry for these people, who after 50 years, still claiming there was not a Holocaust. They try to hide behind the truth.

Montel Williams. Well why don't you tell us some of the truth, Ernest. Let us know what the—

Ernest Hollander. This is the truth. In 1939, when Hitler occupied Czechoslovakia, the part of, where I lived, the Carpathian mountains, they give to the Hungarian government. And as they took over the government, right away they fired every Jew, from state, city and county jobs. A Jew couldn't hold anywhere a job, a government job. Well it didn't go too long where they started taking all their properties. And before the year was over, we have to wear yellow stars. Jews couldn't get out on the street any more regular. Just certain times, shopping, stuff like that.

In 1942, they said that every Jew have to have a Hungarian citizenship papers. Now we had close to three-quarters of a million Jews living in the Carpathian mountains. More than half didn't have Hungarian citizenship papers. We were lucky, my father was born under Austrian-Hungarian regime, and were able to get our citizenship papers.

Montel Williams. That's before the war. I want you to bring us up. . . . during the war, 1942.

Ernest Hollander. That was 1941, end of '41.

Montel Williams. Okay, end of '41. But bring us up to the point where, we know the historical things that took place. But we need to know whether or not the Holocaust, itself, took place. What happened in 1944? What did you see with your own eyes when you arrived at Auschwitz?

Ernest Hollander. In 1944, I had eight brothers and sisters, 4 brothers, 4 sisters. My father and mother, we arrived finally to Auschwitz, where right away they took away my mother and three little sisters and they killed them. They killed them in the crematoriums, in the gas chambers. The rest of the family went to work, to labor camps, where my father was working in a railroad station, and working in a saw mill where he cut off his left arm. The blade somehow cut his hand, they put him against the wall, they shot him right away. They never kept somebody in the camp if he couldn't earn his piece of bread and little hot soup.

Montel Williams. Now when you say they took your mother and your three younger sisters away, right there on the spot, and they took them away to the gas chamber, right? This was in Auschwitz. How do you know that that's exactly where they took them to the gas chamber?

Ernest Hollander. Because we stayed two days in Auschwitz, and some people who worked in the crematoriums, some people who worked in the gas chambers, they tell us. That they saw all these people who Dr. Mengele, the angel of death, send them to the labs, they went straight into the gas chambers, and into the crematoriums.

Montel Williams. Now, Dr. Thaler, you know a lot, I mean a lot about the history of the Holocaust. You've heard what both these gentlemen have to say. Do you think that they're right? Or is it, is it even worth the discussion that we're having today?

Michael Thaler. Well, I think that the discussion today is merely to allow those people, the vast majority, of course, who don't really know what happened, an opportunity to really find out what the truth is. And what you just heard is a tissue of lies. It's basically a combination of half truths, fantasy, and downright falsehood. And you know, I can begin taking it apart very easily.

Montel Williams. Let's start from the very beginning. The claim is that there were no gas chambers.

Michael Thaler. Right.

Montel Williams. There was no plan to annihilate the Jews. Start with the gas chambers, and tell me why that's not true.

Michael Thaler. All right. Well, I'll start with the most recent evidence, though it's been 50 years. The most recent evidence produced by the young historians in Germany, German historians working with German evidence, German documents, have shown in the last five years that the entire program, including the gas chambers, originated from a program which they, the Nazis called, the euthanasia program, which is typical of the terminology that they used. They always inverted the real meaning.

Euthanasia, you know, is going to be an initiative on the California ballot on euthanasia, and euthanasia literally means mercy killing. And the way we talk about euthanasia, it means at the request and at the desire of the patient, when they want to end their life, okay? The Nazis used that term just the opposite, to kill people, to murder, to mass murder, people whom they no longer desired to be alive, because they were useless to them, they couldn't work, they were blind, they were deaf. They even killed soldiers who came back from the front on this program. Now—

Montel Williams. But that, we get that. But that doesn't tell me about gas chambers.

Michael Thaler. Okay. Well—

Montel Williams. Tell me about gas chambers.

Michael Thaler. Okay. In order to institute this program, throughout Germany there were installations set up with gas chambers, which were disguised as shower rooms, in places like Hadamar, Grafeneck, Brandenburg, Sonnerstein, Hartheim, and so on, where they developed this entire program where they took up to 80,000 German children and people who were, as I said, useless to the Reich, and simply gassed them with the excuse of taking them to the showers, and then cremated them. And by 1941, August 1941, there was such an outcry in Germany from the bishops and from mistakes that they made by sending two urns to one family, you know for one child, that they terminated the program.

And at that point, they took the staff of this entire program, took them to the killing camps, Sobibór, Belzec, Treblinka, and many of those people became the commanders and the leading people both in the construction of the gas chambers and in the use of the gas chambers. They also had experimented with the Zyklon-B gasses during that euthanasia program. And so—

Montel Williams. There is physical proof of that—

Michael Thaler. There is physical evidence, and there is also strong documentation brought out by the German historians themselves, and this was the beginning of that program, which was then later applied to the destruction of the Jews.

Montel Williams. Yes sir.

Question. I just, want to comment and question directed to you two on the end. It seems like you're running around—

Montel Williams. Mark and David Cole.

Question. Mark and David, you seem like you're running around in two ways. One, the gas chambers, you say that prove it, there weren't any. Well *Inside the Third Reich* proves, um talks about it. There are personal experiences that talk about it, that should be enough. And that they have proof of them being there. Second, is that you say 6 million, that's, well maybe it's less, or whatever. Maybe it is, maybe it was a million, so what? That's a million people. I mean that's a lot. [applause]

Montel Williams. Go ahead, David Cole.

David Cole. We are not trying to downplay the seriousness that anybody died. But you just said, for example, we ought to have enough evidence. That's enough, case closed, that's enough. Forget about your questions. And let me say one thing, and let me present something to you. How, for example, do you come back at the two forensic studies that have been done, at the supposed gas chambers buildings at Auschwitz and Majdanek, which prove forensically, and the first one was conducted by a man from Boston named Fred Leuchter. Fred Leuchter had built execution equipment for American prisons, and he was very good at it, and he was recommended for that job. But the second forensic report was done by the people who run Auschwitz, the people who run the Auschwitz museum, and it proves that there could not have been cyanide gassings in those chambers. How do you come back at that?

Montel Williams. All right, we'll find out how we come back to that as soon as we take a break. We'll take a break, we'll be back right after this.

[film footage—Germany]

We've been talking about the Holocaust with revisionists and survivors. And for both Mark and David, if we were to presuppose that the Holocaust did not take place, and we were to presuppose that there were no gas chambers, there were no mass burials and no mass gassings, then what we are saying is that someone had a conspiracy to mislead the entire world. Why, for 50 years, would Jewish people want to have conspired to mislead the entire world?

David Cole. You see, now, you're reading something into that. You're saying they want to conspire. If, in fact, this was a conspiracy, propaganda set up, written by people, presented by people it was the Soviet government, the British government, and the American government at Nuremberg after the war. The reason that this thing, because most war propaganda ends up dying "x" number of years after the actual war. One of the reasons, however, that this particular issue has grown in importance since the war, is because the Jewish people have taken it as a very personal issue. It is very important in Israel, it was very important to the founding of Israel. This does not make them conspirators, it doesn't make them bad people at all. It's an issue that they take very personally. And in the Western world, Jews are usually very successful. And I'm speaking as a Jew. And I'm not trying to say that they in any way do anything wrong to become successful. But what matters to Jews can often times be reflected in Western society. If you were to go to Asia, though, this, the Jewish Holocaust wouldn't matter one way or another. Because there are not all that many Jews left in any positions of influence in a country like Cambodia.

Montel Williams. Dr. Thaler, you wait. Dr. Thaler is like churning in his seat. What, what did you want to say?

Michael Thaler. Well, first of all, I think it's already false to call these people revisionists. As the Department of History in Duke, the, all the professors of history in Duke wrote in response to one of their ads in the campus newspaper, "These people are not revisionists. They don't revise. They are deniers. They're basically denying the truth. Rather than revising the truth." [applause]

Montel Williams. And Dr. Thaler, let me ask, I'm going to let you finish your point. But then there is also the point that they are questioning the history. And we know for a fact, let me finish my point, we know for a fact, that history in this country, and the books that we see in this country, is written incorrectly in a number of ways. [applause cheers] . . . go ahead.

Michael Thaler. But every single point where he gets close to the actual data, the actual information, the actual fact, it's falsehood. For instance, this issue about this man Leuchter, Fred or Frank Leuchter, Jr., who I just heard quoted as a foremost engineer, you know, with gas chambers—

David Cole. I didn't say the word engineer.

Michael Thaler. Okay. He, you noticed this—

David Cole. I know why you didn't. But Fred Leuchter might not have been a licensed engineer, but did he not have the job of building gas chambers and other execution equipment for major American prisons? Was he not profiled on *Prime Time Live* and the *Atlantic Monthly?*

Michael Thaler. He had nothing to do—

David Cole. As an expert.

Michael Thaler. He had nothing to do, no.

Montel Williams. But David let him finish.

Michael Thaler. As a matter of fact, this is a lie. The fact is the man masqueraded as an engineer, a builder of these chambers, and then he was arraigned in Massachusetts for practicing engineering without a license. He's not registered as an engineer. The only scientific training he ever had was a B.A. in history. He was hired by another—

Montel Williams. Okay, so wait, wait, wait. Okay, okay. So Dr. Thaler we've refuted the fact that this man had . . . qualifications.

Michael Thaler. Okay. The question boils down whether there was Zyklon-B gas used or not. So, in 1988, for a fee of $35,000 he went to Birkenau and he scraped the walls and he did some hocus-pocus, and he came out 50 years later with the statement that there was no gas. And the court in Canada, in which this was tried, threw it out and declared him a non-expert.

Montel Williams. Wait a second sir, we can't hear you up there.

Michael Thaler. Okay? This is a matter of record.

Montel Williams. All right, Dr. Thaler, just stop there for a second. Ma'am you've been trying to get in, go ahead.

Anna Hollander. I am the living proof of this. I was age of 13 when they took me to Auschwitz with my family. I'm the only one who survived. And I was invited not too far from the gas chamber.

And we knew exactly then, they brought in Jews, and they burned them. We smelled, we breathed that air, we smelled that air, and we knew, we used to say to each other, you see, they are burning the Jews. I was not too far from the crematorium.

Montel Williams. When it happened?

Anna Hollander. When it happened, and I was 13 years of age at that time. My whole family was wiped out.

Montel Williams. Yes, sir, yes.

Question. The Holocaust is big business. Because Germany is so far, has given the Jews, I think, at least $200 billion. So it's big business. Some of you are still getting $1,000 a month, and a lot of people don't know this. And then, people don't realize who brought the slaves to America. They were Jewish ships. [applause]

Montel Williams. Wait, wait, wait a minute, that's a whole 'nother thing. Let's take a break. Because with the issue that we're talking about today is, whether or not there was Holocaust. We'll talk about slavery and who brought them here later. We'll be back after this. [commercial]

We've been talking about the Holocaust with revisionists and survivors. And you wanted to make a statement.

Question. Yes, I'd like to ask a question that's specific in nature, directed towards David, over there. We have all seen the pictures that were shown just recently, before the show, of the gas chambers, of the metal gates and everything like that. If you say there were no gas chambers, what were those specific pictures?

David Cole. The pictures of what? Now we saw pictures of a mass grave, we saw pictures of dead bodies, and we saw pictures of a crematorium. Did you see pictures of a gas chamber? Because I think you were smoking something before the show. We did not see any pictures of gas chambers.

Montel Williams. Wait, wait, wait, David. We don't have to accuse the guy of being on drugs. But he saw what I have seen in several specials across the country. And in those specials they showed me the same . . .

David Cole. But I specifically made the point earlier, no one doubts that there is a building, for example, that you can go to look at Auschwitz and take the tour of and say well here's the gas chamber. They also will tell you something like when the Jews died they all died pressed up against the door. However the door to the so-called chamber opens in. Now the Germans are not stupid people. And if they were going to build a room where hundreds of people would die pressed up against the door, don't you think they would make the door to open out? [applause]

Montel Williams. Okay. Let him finish his question.

Ernest Hollander. Mr. Montel, I'm sitting on pins and needles. I must answer the question. He said there was no Holocaust, there was no crematoriums and no gas chambers. Now, he said there was no gas chambers. Eichman's right hand, who the notorious Eichmann was the master builder of Auschwitz, of the crematoriums, and the gas chambers, his right hand, he had figured out that to kill a Jew cost three-quarters of a cent. Then they came out with the Zyklon gas that it cost only a half a cent. So they saved a penny, a quarter of a cent by mass killing. And he felt so bad about it, that he smuggled out some papers to the Swedish government. And the Germans had, very good, very good bookkeeping.

Montel Williams. But you see, Ernest. If these are things, these are points when we go through this, and historically, wait a second Dr. Thaler. When we go through this historically, there's no way for us to know what he was thinking, whether he smuggled this or that. The only thing that we can know is, whether or not there is fact. And let this gentlemen ask, finish his question, he's going to finish it very quickly.

Question. What were the metal chambers that we saw with the metal gates coming out, and the dead bodies inside all burnt up?

David Cole. Well now there were crematoria there, and they did cremate bodies. And we feel, for example, that the building at Auschwitz that you go through, that is said to be the gas chamber, was in fact, the morgue. And you can actually see where walls have been knocked down, where they used to be separating the place into different rooms.

One other real quick thing, if I may. A point about this Zyklon-B gas that I'd like to make. Now the nature of the Zyklon-B is very important. The Germans said the Zyklon-B was there to disinfect prisoners and their clothes, to try and cut down on the typhoid epidemic, which we all admit was going on in the camps. If this gas were there, not to do that, but to kill Jews, how come there was just as much gas in the camps that were never set to function as execution camps, as there are in camps like Auschwitz,

130

and camps that were supposedly meant to function as execution camps?

Montel Williams. Dr. Thaler, why don't you answer that.

Michael Thaler. Look, it's absurd. This whole discussion is crazy. We can't come in with the mountains of documentation and eye witness reports and case records that clearly establish the truth of what went on with the gas chambers and with the killing squads. I just want to state that my name is Michael Thaler, and I am willing to mortgage my home and put up $50,000 to anyone who comes in with acceptable evidence, acceptable by scholarly historian standards, that there was no gas chambers. Okay? End of discussion. I'm not going to continue this with these people.

Montel Williams. All right. Yes sir.

Question. Yes, I have a comment.

Montel Williams. Make it very quick, because we gotta go to commercial.

Question. First of all, I have the greatest sympathy for all innocent people who die in war. But the Jewish experience is not unique. I happen to be of Ukrainian descent, and 7 million of my people were murdered. And a disproportionate number of the perpetrators of these crimes in the Ukraine, the Ukrainian famine happen to be Jews. Trotsky, Beria, Dzerzhinsky, and I'd like to know when I'm going to get my reparations for my murdered relatives?

Montel Williams. That's also another issue. We'll take a break and we'll answer that when we come back. We'll take a break. [commercial]

You had a question, sir.

Question. Yes. I am a Holocaust survivor, and I'm the only one left from a family of seven. I would like to reply to the gentlemen that said the Ukrainians, 7 million Ukrainians were killed. The Ukrainians were the biggest collaborators with the Germans. They were hired and worked in the concentration camps to help exterminate the Jews.

Montel Williams. Well that's all, do me a favor. Let's not go back and forth from one . . . let's answer the question about the Holocaust. You were there—

Question. I also, I also would like to tell you, that the lady made a remark, my wife, she was 14 years old when she and her mother were taken to Auschwitz. And when her mother was ill and she couldn't work any longer, they took her to the crematorium and burned her. Now these are facts. And my wife is alive, and she is here and she has told me those things.

Montel Williams. They burned her, they burned her alive?

Question. They burned her, they burned her, that's right.

Montel Williams. Because she could not work?

Question. Because she could not work. She was too weak to work.

Montel Williams. I think, before you go, and I say this, David, this is the point. And this is a Jewish gentlemen, you are Jewish. Here's a man who has lived his whole life knowing, having these feelings, knowing what took place in his life. I have to ask you this, because it's coming, to me, do you dislike yourself because you are Jewish and you have turned the other way?

David Cole. Now see that's just plain silly. Two things real quick. First as an atheist, and people all over the world everyday claim to see God, I am also willing, therefore, to believe that people can mislead themselves very easily. But secondly, I would also like to say, that I want people to understand what my peculiar position is. Which is: I hear eyewitnesses and then I hear other forensic and factual evidence. What am I supposed to do? Would you like me then to just jump to the conclusion, go along with the flow? What if everybody did that about every subject? I have serious questions that I would like to be addressed. No one has yet addressed my question about Zyklon-B gas. No one has yet addressed my question about—

Montel Williams. Because you're also asking an audience that's not authorities on Zyklon-B gas. Go ahead Anna.

David Cole. Well they should be.

Anna Hollander. I want to tell David one thing. He should have been where I was. He would have seen what life was all about. [applause] How we was—we used to get up every morning, 3 o'clock in the morning, they used to put us in a line. And they used to call us, they used to pick from each day from us to go to those gas chambers. Day by day. We lived with that, we dreamt with that, and we slept with that.

Question. Well I'd like to ask the revisionists, I've heard that you don't believe that there were gas chambers. Do you believe that genocide did indeed take place? And what exactly is your definition of genocide?

Mark Weber. If you mean by genocide, the kind of treatment that was meted out to the American Indians or the blacks, then there was genocide. And there was a policy kind of genocide against the Jews in Europe during the Second World War. I would say yes. But the Holocaust is defined rather differently. It's defined as the systematic extermination of 6 million Jews. I do not think that there is evidence for that. The word Holocaust itself is a more or less modern creation. It wasn't used during the war, it wasn't talked about at Nuremberg, it didn't come into popular usage until the 1960s or '70s.

Montel Williams. Go ahead, Dr. Thaler.

Michael Thaler. I just want to straighten out a few things, okay, from our own personal experience. Again, I am not prepared to discuss this here with these gentlemen who are frauds. The point I am making now is this. I want to make one point: first of all there were 7 million Jews just in the area of Poland and Russia alone. There were fewer than 1 million Jews in the rest of Europe. So when the Germans occupied Poland and part of Russia, they were stuck with all these millions of Jews. The majority of those Jews never got to concentration camps.

I heard a glib reference to ghettos. Well I came from one of those ghettos. I came from a ghetto, and by the way there were hundreds of ghettos, not just one or two. I came from one of those ghettos in the Ukraine. And we started out with 11,000 people in 1941, when the Red Army came back in 1944, there were 306 left. Nobody went to concentration camps, we were taken out and shot and I myself watched the last 2,500 Jews of my town machine gunned to death. . . .

Montel Williams. We've got to take a break, Dr. Thaler. You know, you saw it. We'll be back in just a second. [commercial]

We've been talking about the Holocaust with revisionists and survivors. Anna, you wanted to make one final point.

Ann Hollander. Yeah, I would like to make one point. I came here for one reason. To tell the world that this Holocaust happened, and I'm a proof, I'm a living proof. I'm here to tell you that never again. We should watch out for another Holocaust to whom it ever happened, it should never happen. No race, no human should let, have to kill people.

Montel Williams. We are, we gotta go, join us again on the next Montel Williams show. [applause]

Appendix D

A Sampling of Holocaust-Denying Books, Booklets, and Pamphlets, and of Articles from the Journal of Historical Review

BOOKS, BOOKLETS, PAMPHLETS

APP, Austin, A STRAIGHT LOOK AT THE THIRD REICH: HITLER AND NATIONAL SOCIALISM, HOW RIGHT? HOW WRONG?

APP, Austin, HITLER-HIMMLER ORDER ON JEWS UNCOVERED

APP, Austin, NO TIME FOR SILENCE

APP, Austin, THE SIX MILLION SWINDLE

ARETZ, Emil, HEXENEINMALEINS EINER LÜGE

ARNOUF, Ream, THE LIE OF THE EXISTENCE OF THE GAS CHAMBERS

BARNES, Harry Elmer, BLASTING THE HISTORICAL BLACKOUT

BARNES, Harry Elmer, THE BARNES TRILOGY

BAUER, Gen. Hans, HITLER AT MY SIDE

BENNETT, John, YOUR RIGHTS 1990

BRENNER, Lenni, ZIONISM IN THE AGE OF THE DICTATORS: A REAPPRAISAL

BRITISH NATIONAL PARTY, HOLOCAUST NEWS

BRITISH PEOPLE'S PARTY, FAILURE AT NUREMBERG

BROWN, S.E.D., THE MYTH OF THE SIX MILLION

BURG, J.G. (a/k/a Joseph Ginsburg), ANNE FRANK—DAS TAGE-BUNCH

BURG, J.G. (a/k/a Joseph Ginsburg), HOLOCAUST DES SCHLECHTEN GEWISSENS UNTER HEXAGRAMM REGIE

BURG, J.G. (a/k/a Joseph Ginsburg), MAIDANEK IN ALLE EWIGKEIT?

BURG, J.G. (a/k/a Joseph Ginsburg), NS-VERBRECHEN: PROZESSE

BURG, J.G. (a/k/a Joseph Ginsburg), SCHULD UND SCHICKSAL

BURG, J.G. (a/k/a Joseph Ginsburg), SUNDENBOCKE

BURG, J.G. (a/k/a Joseph Ginsburg), TERROR UND TERROR

BUTLER, Eric, CENSORED HISTORY

BUTLER, Eric, RELEASING REALITY, SOCIAL CREDIT AND THE KINGDOM OF GOD

BUTZ, Arthur, THE HOAX OF THE TWENTIETH CENTURY

CAWTHRON, Edward, THE BIG LIE

CHERSI, Andrea, IL CASO FAURISSON

CHOMSKY, Noam, Introduction to Faurisson's TREATISE IN DEFENSE AGAINST THOSE WHO ACCUSE ME OF FALSIFYING HISTORY

CHRISTIE, Doug, THE ZUNDEL TRIAL AND FREE SPEECH

CHRISTOPHERHSEN, Thies, INQUISITIONSPROZESSE HEUTE—HEXENPROZESSE DER NEUZEIT

CHRISTOPHERSEN, Theis, AUSCHWITZ—AN EYEWITNESS REPORT

CHRISTOPHERSEN, Theis, DIE AUSCHWITZ LÜGE

COHN-BENDIT, Jean-Gabriel; DELOCROIX, Eric, KARNOOUCH, Claude, MONTEIL, Vincent, TRISTANI, Jean-Louis, INTOLERABLE INTOLERANCE

COLLINS, Doug, THOUGHT CRIMES: THE KEEGSTRA CASE

COMMITTEE FOR OPEN DEBATE ON THE HOLOCAUST: THE HOLOCAUST: LET'S HEAR BOTH SIDES (pamphlet)

CONNORS, Dr. Michael F., DEALING IN HATE: THE DEVELOPMENT OF ANTI-GERMAN PROPAGANDA

DEGRELLE, Leon, CAMPAIGN IN RUSSIA: THE WAFFEN SS ON THE EASTERN FRONT

DEGRELLE, Leon, EPIC: THE STORY OF THE WAFFEN SS

DEGRELLE, Leon, HITLER: BORN AT VERSAILLES

136

DEGRELLE, Leon, LETTER TO THE POPE ON HIS VISIT TO AUSCHWITZ

DIWALD, Hellmut, GESCHICHTE DER DEUTSCHEN

ECOCHACA, J. EL MITO D'EL SEIS MILLION

EL-SHAMALI, Dr. Khaled, "BURNING OF THE JEWS IN THE NAZI CHAMBERS IS THE LIE OF THE 20TH CENTURY IN ORDER TO LEGITIMIZE THE NEW NAZISM," El Istiglal (Independence)

EL-SHAMALI, Dr. Khaled, "HOW DID ZIONIST PROPAGANDA CLOUD SCIENCE AND MIND? A FIRST QUIET TRAVEL THROUGH THE CLIMATE OF FEAR," El Istiglal (Independence)

FAURISSON, Robert, "JEWISH SOAP," in ANNALS OF REVISIONIST HISTORY

FAURISSON, Robert (& S. Thion), VERITE HISTORIQUE OU VERITE POLITIQUE? LE DOSSIER DE L'AFFAIRE FAURISSON: LA QUESTION DE CHAMBRES A GAZ

FAURISSON, Robert, A PROMINENT FALSE WITNESS: ELIE WEISEL (pamphlet)

FAURISSON, Robert, FAURISSON ON THE HOLOCAUST

FAURISSON, Robert, "HOW THE BRITISH OBTAINED THE CONFESSION OF RUDOLPH HESS, THE COMMANDANT OF AUSCHWITZ," in ANNALS OF FAURISSON

FAURISSON, Robert, INTOLERABLE INTOLERANCE

FAURISSON, Robert, IS THE DIARY OF ANNE FRANK GENUINE?

FAURISSON, Robert, THE PROBLEM OF THE GAS CHAMBERS (pamphlet)

FAURISSON, Robert, THE RUMOR OF AUSCHWITZ

FAURISSON, Robert, TREATISE IN DEFENSE AGAINST THOSE WHO ACCUSE ME OF FALSIFYING HISTORY

FAURRISON, Robert, RESPONSE A PEIRRAE VIDAL-NAQUET

FAURRISON, Robert, THE PROBLEM OF THE GAS CHAMBERS (pamphlet)

FELDERER, Ditlieb, ANNE FRANK'S DIARY—A HOAX

FELDERER, Ditlieb, AUSCHWITZ EXIT

FIKENTSCHER, H., SECH MILLIONEN JUDEN: VERGAST-VERBRANNT

FORNI, A. (editor), IL CASO RASSINIER

FRIEDRICH, Christof, NAZI HORRORS: FACT, FICTION AND PROPAGANDA

GRENFELL, Capt. Russell, UNCONDITIONAL HATRED

GRIMSTAD, William (editor), THE SIX MILLION RECONSIDERED

GRIMSTAD, William, ANTIZION

HANKINS, Frank, HOW MANY JEWS WERE KILLED BY THE NAZIS?

HARWOOD, Richard, (true name VERRALL, Richard) DID SIX MILLION REALLY DIE? (Also sold under title SIX MILLION LOST AND FOUND.)

HARWOOD, Richard, (true name VERRALL, Richard) NUREMBERG AND OTHER WAR CRIMES TRIALS—A NEW LOOK

HESS, Frau Ilse, PRISONER OF PEACE

HOFFMAN, Michael A. II, THE GREAT HOLOCAUST TRIAL

HOGGAN, David, DER ERZWUNGENE KRIEG (WAR BY COMPULSION)

HOGGAN, David, THE FORCED WAR: THE ORIGINS AND ORIGINATORS OF WORLD WAR II

HOGGAN, David, THE FORCED WAR: WHEN PEACEFUL REVISION FAILED

HOGGAN, David, THE MYTH OF THE NEW HISTORY

HOGGAN, David, THE MYTH OF THE SIX MILLION

HUNECKE, Karl, ADOLF HITLER, BEGRÜNDER ISRAEL

HUSSEIN, Ahmad, PALESTINE MY HOMELAND

IHR, WORLDWIDE GROWTH AND IMPACT OF "HOLOCAUST" REVISIONISM (booklet)

IRVING, David, CHURCHILL'S WAR

IRVING, David, GORING: A BIOGRAPHY

IRVING, David, HITLER'S WAR

IRVING, David, THE DESTRUCTION OF DRESDEN

IRVING, David, THE WAR BETWEEN THE GENERALS: INSIDE THE ALLIED HIGH COMMAND

IRVING, David, THE WAR PATH

KERN, Erich, DIE TRAGODIE DER JUDEN: SCHICKSAL ZWISCHEN WAHRHEIT UND PROPAGANDA

"LA GUERRE SOCIALE," DE L'EXPLOITATION DANS LES CAMPS A L'EXPOITATION DES CAMPS

"LE CITOYEN," L'INCROYABLE AFFAIRE FAURISSON: LES PETITS

SUPPLEMENTS AU GUIDE DES DROITS DES VICTIMES NO. 1

LENSKI, Robert, THE HOLOCAUST ON TRIAL; THE CASE OF ERNST ZUNDEL

LEUCHTER, Fred, INSIDE THE AUSCHWITZ "GAS CHAMBERS" (pamphlet)

LEUCHTER, Fred, THE LEUCHTER REPORT

MALZ, Heinrich, THE BIG SWINDLE OF THE SIX MILLION

MARCELLUS, Tom, THE TRADITION OF HISTORICAL REVISIONISM (pamphlet)

MARTIN, James, AMERICAN LIBERALISM AND WORLD POLITICS 1931–1941

MARTIN, James, REVISIONIST VIEWPOINTS

MARTIN, James, THE MAN WHO INVENTED "GENOCIDE:" THE PUBLIC CAREER AND CONSEQUENCES OF RAPHAEL LEMKIN

MATTERN, Horst, JESUS, DIE BIBEL, UND DIE 6,000,000 JUDEN LUGE

MCCALDEN, David, EXILES FROM HISTORY

MCLAUGHLIN, Michael, DEATH OF A CITY

MORRIS, Warren B., Jr., THE REVISIONIST HISTORIANS AND JEWISH WAR GUILT

NICOLL, Rev. Peter H., BRITAIN'S BLUNDER

O'KEEFE, Theodore J., THE "LIBERATION OF THE CAMPS:" FACTS VS. LIES (pamphlet)

PLEVRIS, Kostas, O MYTHOS (THE MYTH)

PLO see EL-SHAMALI and ARNOUF (El Istiglal is a PLO Magazine, as is the publication of the Palestine Red Crescent Society)

PORTER, Carlos W., MADE IN RUSSIA: THE HOLOCAUST

PORTER, Carlos W., NOT GUILTY AT NUREMBERG: THE GERMAN DEFENSE CASE

RASSINIER, Paul, DEBUNKING THE GENOCIDE MYTH

RASSINIER, Paul, L'OPERATION "VICAIRE"

RASSINIER, Paul, LES RESPONSABLES DE LA SECOND GUERRE MONDIALE

RASSINIER, Paul, PASSAGE DE LA LIGNE

RASSINIER, Paul, THE DRAMA OF THE EUROPEAN JEWS (LE DRAME DES JUIFS EUROPEENS)

RASSINIER, Paul, THE HOLOCAUST STORY AND THE LIES OF ULYSSES (LE MENSONGE D'ULYSSE)

RASSINIER, Paul, THE REAL EICHMANN TRIAL (LE VERITABLE PROCES EICHMANN)

RASSINIER, Paul, ULYSSEE TRAHI PAR LES SIENS

REYNOUARD, Vincent, "IN PRISON FOR TELLING THE TRUTH" (leaflet)

ROEDER, Manfred, DIE AUSCHWITZ LUEGE (THE AUSCHWITZ LIE)

ROQUES, Henri, THE "CONFESSIONS" OF KURT GERSTEIN

ROSS, Malcolm, WEB OF DECEIT

ROTH, Heinz, ANNE FRANKS TAGEBUCH: DER GROSSE SCHWINDEL

ROTH, Heinz, PORQUE NOS MIENTEN? O ACASO HITLER TENIA RAZÓN? (WHY DO THEY LIE TO US? PERHAPS HITLER WAS RIGHT?)

ROTHE, Wolf Dieter, DIE ENDLOSUNG DER JUDENFRAGE, BAND I, ZUEGEN

SANNING, Walter N., THE DISSOLUTION OF EASTERN EUROPEAN JEWRY

SCHEIDL, Franz J, GESCHICHTE DER VERFEMUNG DEUTSCHLANDS

SERRANO, Miguel, (Introduction to) FIN DE UNA MENTIRA: CAMARAS DE GAS: HOLOCAUST—INFORME LEUCHTER

SMITH, Bradley, "THE CASE FOR TEACHING HOLOCAUST REVISIONISM IN OUR COLLEGES AND HIGH SCHOOLS" (pamphlet)

SMITH, Bradley, CONFESSIONS OF A HOLOCAUST REVISIONIST

SOLODAR, Tsesary, MAGGOTS HAVE GONE WILD

STAEGLICH, Wilhelm, and Udo Walendy, NS-BEWALTIGUNG: DEUTSCH SCHREIBTISCHTATER

140

STAEGLICH, Wilhelm, DIE WESTDEUTSCHE JUSTIZ UND DIE SOGENNANTEN NS-GEWALTVERBRECHEN

STAEGLICH, Wilhelm, INSTITUTE FUR ZEITGESCHICHTE: EINE SCHWINDELFIRMA?

STAEGLICH, Wilhelm, THE AUSCHWITZ MYTH (DER AUSCHWITZ MYTHOS)

STIMELY, Keith, IHR'S 1981 REVISIONIST BIBLIOGRAPHY

TAYLOR, A.J.P., THE COURSE OF GERMAN HISTORY

TAYLOR, A.J.P., THE ORIGINS OF THE SECOND WORLD WAR

THION, Serge (& R. Faurisson,), VERITE HISTORIQUE OU VERITE POLITIQUE? LE DOSSIER DE L'AFFAIRE FAURISSON: LA QUESTION DE CHAMBRES A GAZ

THION, Serge, HISTORICAL TRUTH OR POLITICAL TRUTH?

THOMPSON, H.K., DOENITZ AT NUREMBERG

TUDJMAN, Franjo, BESPUCA—POVJESNE ZBILJNOSTI (WASTELANDS—HISTORICAL TRUTH)

UNO, Masami, IF YOU UNDERSTAND JUDEA, YOU UNDERSTAND JAPAN

VAN DE BERGHE, Giel, DE UITBUITING VAN DE HOLOCAUST (THE EXPLOITATION OF THE HOLOCAUST)

VARY, Colin, THE VICTIMS

VEALE, Frederick J.P., THE VEALE FILE

VERBEKE, Siegfried, AMERICAN EXPERT DESTROYS THE GAS CHAMBER LEGEND (pamphlet)

VERBEKE, Siefried, THE SIX MILLION HOLOCAUST (pamphlet)

VON OVEN, Wilhelm, MIT GOEBBELS BIS ZUM ENDE (republished as FINALE FURIOSO in Germany)

WAEGENER, Otto, HITLER: MEMOIRS OF A CONFIDANTE

WALENDY, Udo, and Wilhelm STAEGLICH, NS-BEWALTIGUNG: DEUTSCH SCHREIBTISCHTATER

WALENDY, Udo, AUSCHWITZ IM IG-FARBEN PROZESS: "HOLOCAUST"-DOKUMENTE?

WALENDY, Udo, BEHORDEN CONTRA HISTORIKER

WALENDY, Udo, BILD "DOKUMENTE" FUR DIE GESCHICHTSSCHREIBUNG?

WALENDY, Udo, DER MODERNE INDEX

WALENDY, Udo, FAKED ATROCITIES

WALENDY, Udo, FORGED WAR CRIMES MALIGN THE GER-
MAN NATION

WALENDY, Udo, HOLOCAUST NUN UNTERIRDISCH?

WALENDY, Udo, THE METHODS OF RE-EDUCATION

WALENDY, Udo, THE TRANSFER AGREEMENT AND THE BOY-
COTT FEVER, 1933

WALENDY, Udo, TRUTH FOR GERMANY

WEBER, Charles A., THE "HOLOCAUST"—120 QUESTIONS AND
ANSWERS

WEBER, Mark, AUSCHWITZ: MYTHS AND FACTS (pamphlet)

WEBER, Mark, SIMON WIESENTHAL: BOGUS "NAZI HUNTER
(pamphlet)

WEBER, Mark, THE FINAL SOLUTION: LEGEND AND REALITY

WEBER, Mark, THE HOLOCAUST: LET'S HEAR BOTH SIDES
(pamphlet)

WECKERT, Ingrid, FEUERZEICHEN: DIE REICHSKRISTALL-
NACHT

WECKERT, Ingrid, FLASHPOINT—KRISTNALLACHT 1938: IN-
STIGATORS, VICTIMS AND BENEFICIARIES

WECKERT, Ingrid, REICH CRYSTAL NIGHT: INCITERS AND IN-
CENDIARIES, VICTIMS AND BENEFICIARIES

ZÜNDEL, Ernst, DID SIX MILLION DIE?

(Author Unknown), DER AUSCHWITZ-BETRUG

(Author Unknown), THE JUST FIGHT OF THE NAZIS AGAINST
COMMUNISM AND JUDAISM

ARTICLES IN THE JOURNAL OF HISTORICAL
REVIEW

ADAMS, Henry M., "David Irving, Goring: A Biography," JHR, Vol. 9
#4.

ATELIER, Robert, "Stephen Green, Taking Sides: America's Secret Relations With A Militant Israel," JHR, Vol. 7 #3.

BARNES, Harry Elmer, "The Public Stake in Revisionism," JHR, Vol. 1
#3.

BARNES, Harry Elmer, "Winston Spencer Churchill: a Tribute," JHR,
Vol. 1 #2.

BECK, Philip, "The Burning of Saint Malo," JHR, Vol. 2 #4.

BENNETT, John, "In the Matter of Robert Faurisson," JHR, Vol. 1 #2.

BENNETT, John, "Orwell's 1984: Was Orwell Right?," JHR, Vol. 6 #1.

BENNETT, John, "The Holocaust Debate," JHR, Vol. 2 #1.

BENSON, Ivor, "Iran: Some Angles on the Islamic Revolution," JHR, Vol. 9 #2.

BENSON, Ivor, "Russia 1917–1918: A Key to the Riddle of an Age of Conflict", JHR, Vol. 10 #3.

BENSON, Ivor, "The Siege of South Africa," JHR, Vol. 7 #1.

BERG, Friedrich P., "The Diesel Gas Chambers: Myth Within A Myth," JHR, Vol. 5 #1.

BERG, Friedrich P., "The German Delousing Chambers," JHR, Vol. 7 #1.

BERG, Friedrich P., "Typhus and the Jews," JHR, Vol. 8 #4.

BERKIS, Alexander V., "Soviet Russia's Persecution of Latvia, 1918 to the Present," JHR, Vol. 8 #1.

BLACK, Robert C., "Politics, Prejudice and Procedure: The Impeachment Trial of Andrew Johnson," JHR, Vol. 7 #2.

BRANDON, Lewis (true name McCALDEN, DAVID), "The Big Lie Technique in the Sandbox," JHR, Vol. 2 #1.

BRANDON, Lewis (true name McCALDEN, DAVID), "The Mendacity of Zion," JHR, Vol. 1 #2.

BRAUN, Karl Otto, "American Policy Toward Europe: The Fateful Change," JHR, Vol. 5 #s 2,3,4.

BUCHNER, Reinhard K., "The Problem of Cremator Hours and Incineration Time," JHR, Vol. 2 #3.

BUTZ, Arthur, "Letters to the 'New Statesman,' " JHR, Vol. 1 #2.

BUTZ, Arthur, "The Faurisson Affair," JHR, Vol. 1 #4.

BUTZ, Arthur, "The International 'Holocaust' Controversy," JHR, Vol. 1 #1.

BUTZ, Arthur, "Jack Eisner, "The Survivor; Moshe Mizrahi, Director, War and Love," JHR, Vol. 7 #4.

CARTO, Willis A. "Toward History," JHR, Vol. 5 #1.

CHAPMAN, Robert J., "A Challenge to Thought Control: The Historiography of Leon Degrelle," JHR, Vol. 6 #2.

CHOMSKY, Noam, "All Denials of Free Speech Undercut a Democratic Society," JHR, Vol. 7 #1.

CHRISTOPHERSEN, Thies, "Reflections on Auschwitz and West German Justice," JHR, Vol. 6 #1.

CLIVE, Robert, "Robert E. Herzstein, Roosevelt and Hitler," JHR, Vol. 10 #3.

CLIVE, Robert, Alfred M. de Zayas, "The Wehrmacht War Crimes Bureau," JHR, Vol. 10 #2.

COBDEN, John, "Lessons from Dachau," JHR, Vol. 9 #4.

COUNTESS, Robert H., "Thomas Franklin, An American in Exile: The Story of Arthur Rudolph," JHR, Vol. 8 #2.

DESJARDINS, Dan, "Critique of John S. Conway's Review of Walter Sanning's Dissolution of Eastern European Jewry, from The International History Review, August, 1985," JHR, Vol. 7 #3.

DIBERT, A., "Our Established Religion," JHR, Vol. 10 #2.

DICKSON, Sam, "Shattering the Icon of Abraham Lincoln," JHR, Vol. 7 #3.

EKNES, Enrique Ayant, "Crematoriums II and III of Birkenau: A Critical Study," JHR, Vol. 8 #3.

FAURISSON, Robert, "A Challenge to David Irving," JHR, Vol. 5 #s 2,3,4.

FAURISSON, Robert, "A Revised Preface to Auschwitz: A Judge Looks at the Evidence," JHR, Vol. 10 #2.

FAURISSON, Robert, "Auschwitz: Technique & Operation of the Gas Chambers - Part I," JHR, Vol. II #1.

FAURISSON, Robert, "Claude Lanzmann, Shoah (The Film)," JHR, Vol. 8 #1.

FAURISSON, Robert, "Confessions of SS Men who were at Auschwitz," JHR, Vol. 2 #2.

FAURISSON, Robert, "How the British Obtained the Confessions of Rudolf Hoss," JHR, Vol. 7 #4.

FAURISSON, Robert, "Letters to the 'New Statesman,' " JHR, Vol. 1 #2.

FAURISSON, Robert, "My Life as a Revisionist (September 1983 to September 1987)," JHR, Vol. 9 #1.

FAURISSON, Robert, "Response to a Paper Historian," JHR, Vol. 7 #1.

FAURISSON, Robert, "Revisionism On Trial: Developments in France, 1979–1983," JHR, Vol. 6 #2.

FAURISSON, Robert, "The Gas Chambers of Auschwitz Appear to be Inconceivable," JHR, Vol. 2 #4.

FAURISSON, Robert, "The Gas Chambers: Truth or Lie?" JHR, Vol. 2 #4.

FAURISSON, Robert, "The Mechanics of Gassing," JHR, Vol. 1 #1.

FAURISSON, Robert, "The Problem of the Gas Chambers," JHR, Vol. 1 #2.

FAURISSON, Robert, "The Zundel Trials (1985 and 1988)," JHR, Vol. 8 #4.

FAURRISON, Robert, "A Dry Chronicle of the Purge," JHR, Vol. 12, #1.

FELDERER, Ditlieb, "Auschwitz Notebook," JHR, Vol. 1 #1.

FELDERER, Ditlieb, "Auschwitz Notebook," JHR, Vol. 1 #2.

FELDERER, Ditlieb, "Auschwitz Notebook," JHR, Vol. 1 #3.

FELDERER, Ditlieb, "Auschwitz Notebook," JHR, Vol. 1 #4.

FELDERER, Ditlieb, and HARWOOD, Richard, "Human Soap," JHR, Vol. 1 #2.

FITZGIBBON, Louis, "Hidden Aspects of the Katyn Massacre," JHR, Vol. 1 #1.

FITZGIBBON, Louis, "Khatyn—Another Hoax," JHR, Vol. 1 #3.

FRANZ-WILLING, Georg, "Henry M. and Robin K. Adams, Rebel Patriot: A Biography of Franz von Papen," JHR, Vol. 8 #1.

FRANZ-WILLING, Georg, "The Origins of the Second World War," JHR, Vol. 7 #1.

FRIEDRICH, Leonhard, "Buchenwald and After," JHR, Vol. 2 #1.

GLEASON, K.C., "The Holocaust and the Failure of Allied and Jewish Responses," JHR, Vol. 5 #s 2,3,4.

GRIMSTAD, William, "Autopsying the Communist Cadaver," JHR, Vol. 10 #1.

GRIMSTAD, William, "Livia Rokach, Israel's Sacred Terrorism," JHR, Vol. 9 #2.

GRIMSTAD, William, "Nicholas Goodrick-Clarke, The Occult Roots of Nazism," JHR, Vol. II #1.

GRIMSTAD, William, "Roy Davies (Prod. by British Broadcasting Corp.)., Sacrifice at Pearl Harbor," JHR, Vol. 10 #1.

GRUBACH, Paul, "A Critique of the Charge of Anti-Semitism: The Moral and Political Legitimacy of Criticizing Jewry," JHR, Vol. 8 #2.

GRUBACH, Paul, "Jonathan Kaufman, Broken Alliance: The Turbulent Times Between Blacks and Jews in America," JHR, Vol. 10 #1.

GRUBACH, Paul, "Michael Curtis, Antisemitism in the Contemporary World," JHR, Vol. 9 #2.

HALL, Robert A., Jr., "C. Paul Vincent, The Politics of Hunger: The Allied Blocade of Germany, 1915–1919," JHR, Vol. 7 #2.

HALL, Robert A., Jr., "Carlo Mattogno, Il Rapporto Gerstein: Anatomia di un Falso," JHR, Vol. 7 #.

HALL, Robert A., Jr., "Deceptive Linguistic Structures in the Phrase 'The Holocaust,' JHR, Vol. 7 #4.

HALL, Robert A., Jr., "The Persecution of P.G. Wodehouse," JHR, Vol. 7 #3.

HALOW, Joseph, "Innocent in Dachau: The Trial and Punishment of Franz Kofler et al.," JHR, Vol. 9 #4.

HANSEN, Desmond, "The Enigma of Lawrence (Lawrence of Arabia)," JHR, Vol. 2 #3.

HARWOOD, Richard (true name VERRALL, Richard) and FELDERER, Ditlieb, "Human Soap," JHR, Vol. 1 #2.

HASEGAWA, Michiko, "A Postwar View of the Greater East Asia War," JHR, Vol. 6 #4.

HATTENHAUER, Darryl, "Ronald Reagan's Political and Cultural World View," JHR, Vol. 5, #s 2,3,4.

HAWKINS, James, "Felipe Fernandez-Armesto, The Spanish Armada," JHR, Vol. 10 #3.

HEIDE, Hans von der, "From the Allied Camps to the Revisionist Camp," JHR, Vol. 10 #2.

HESSELTINE, William B., "Atrocities, Then and Now," JHR, Vol. 9 #1.

HOFFMAN, Michael A., II, "The Psychology and Epistemology of 'Holocaust' Newspeak," JHR, Vol. 6 #4.

HOGGAN, David L., "Plato's Dialectic v. Hegel and Marx: An Evaluation of Five Revolutions," JHR, Vol. 6 #1.

HUMMEL, Jeffrey Rogers, "Not Just Japanese Americans: The Untold Story of U.S. Repression During 'The Good War,' " JHR, Vol. 7 #3.

IRVING, David, "Churchill and U.S. Entry into World War II," JHR, Vol. 9 #3.

IRVING, David, "Hitler's War: An Introduction to the New Edition," JHR, Vol. 10 #4.

IRVING, David, "On Contemporary History and Historiography," JHR, Vol. 5 #s 2,3,4.

IRVING, David, "The Trail of the Desert Fox: Rommel Revised," JHR, Vol. 10 #4.

JACKSON, Thomas, "Akira Kochi, Why I Survived the A-Bomb," JHR, Vol. 10 #1.

JOHN, Robert, "Behind the Balfour Declaration: Britain's Great War Pledge To Lord Rothschild," JHR, Vol. 6 #4.

JOHNSON, Edward, "Grace Halsell, Prophecy and Politics: Militant Evangelists on the Road to Nuclear War," JHR, Vol. 7 #4.

JORDAN, Rudolf, "Hitler, the Unemployed and Autarky," JHR, Vol. 5 #1.

KANOLD, Otto, with WEBER, Mark, "Letter From Berlin," JHR, Vol. 1 #2.

KEHL, Horst, "Holocaust Parmacology vs. Scientific Pharmacology," JHR, Vol. 2 #1.

KONKIN, Samuel Edward III, "J.N. Westwood, 'Russia Against Japan, 1904–05: A New Look at the Russo-Japanese War,' " JHR, Vol. 7 #3.

KONKIN, Samuel Edward III, "Palestine: Liberty and Justice," JHR, Vol. 1 #4.

KONKIN, Samuel Edward III, "Paul Buble, Marxism in the United States: Remapping the History of the American Left," JHR, Vol. 8 #2.

KUBEK, Prof. Anthony, "The Morgenthau Plan and the Problem of Policy Perversion," JHR, Vol. 9 #3.

KUESTERS, Elisabeth, "Encountering the Revisionists," JHR, Vol. 5 #s 2,3,4.

LANDWEHR, Richard, "The European Volunteer Movement in World War II," JHR, Vol. 2 #1.

LANG, Clarence R., "Imposed German Guilt: The Stuttgart Declaration of 1945," JHR, Vol. 8 #1.

LANG, Clarence R., "Friedrich Gollert Warschau unter Deutscher Herrschaft," JHR, Vol. 7 #4.

LANG, Clarence R., "Red Cross Humanitarianism In Greece, 1940–45," JHR, Vol. 9 #1.

LARSON, Martin A., "An Update on the Dead Sea Scrolls," JHR, Vol. 8 #1.

LASKA, Werner, "A U.S. Prison Guard's Story," JHR, Vol. 10 #2.

LAWSON, Richard, "National Socialism and Early British Socialism," JHR, Vol. 1 #4.

LEUCHTER, Fred A., & Faurisson, Robert, "The Second Leuchter Report," JHR, Vol. 10 #3.

LEUCHTER, Fred A., "The Leuchter Report: The How and the Why," JHR, Vol. 9 #2.

LEUCHTER, Fred A., "Witch Hunt in Boston," JHR, Vol. 10 #4.

LILIENTHAL, Alfred M., "Zionism and American Jews," JHR, Vol. 2 #2.

LINDBERGH, Charles A., "Hideki Tojo's Prison Diary - War and Peace: Two Historic Speeches," JHR, Vol. 12 #1.

LUTTON, Charles, "Review Article - Stalin's War: Victims and Accomplices," JHR, Vol. 5 #11.

LUTTON, Charles C., "The Miracle of Dunkirk Reconsidered," JHR, Vol. 2 #4.

LUTTON, Charles C., "Death From On High," JHR, Vol. 1 #3.

MARCHETTI, Victor, "Propaganda and Disinformation: How the CIA Manufactures History," JHR, Vol. 9 #3.

MARTIN, James J., "Raphael Lemkin and the Invention of 'Genocide,'" JHR, Vol. 2 #1.

MARTIN, James J., "A Good War It Wasn't," JHR, Vol. 10 #1.

MARTIN, James J., "Beyond Year Zero: The Pursuit of Peace Through War," JHR, Vol. 5, #s 2,3,4.

MARTIN, James J., "Knightley, Philip, 'The Second Oldest Profession: Spies and Spying in the Twentieth Century,' JHR, Vol. 8 #3.

MARTIN, James J., "Other Days, Other Ways: American Book Censorship 1918–1945," JHR, Vol. 10 #2.

MARTIN, James J., "The Pro-Red Orchestra Starts Tuning Up in the U.S.A. 1941," JHR, Vol. 6 #3.

MATTOGNO, Carlo, "Auschwitz: A Case of Plagiarism," JHR, Vol. 10 #1.

MATTOGNO, Carlo, "Jean Claude Pressac and the War Refugee Board Report," JHR, Vol. 10 #4.

MATTOGNO, Carlo, "The First Gassing at Auschwitz: Genesis of a Myth," JHR, Vol. 9 #2.

MATTOGNO, Carlo, "The Myth of the Extermination of the Jews: Part II," JHR, Vol. 8 #3.

MATTOGNO, Carlo, "The Myth of the Extermination of the Jews: Part I," JHR, Vol. 8 #2.

MATTOGNO, Carlo, "Two False Testimonies from Auschwitz," JHR, Vol. 10 #1.

MERRIAM, Ray, "The Malmedy Massacre and Trial," JHR, Vol. 2 #2.

MERSON, Martin, "On the Treadmill to Truth," JHR, Vol. 8 #2.

MIKI, Hideo, "Thoughts on the Military History of the Occupation of Japan," JHR, Vol. 9 #2.

MOROX, Valentyn, "Nationalism and Genocide: The Origin of the Artificial Famine of 1932–1933 in Ukraine," JHR, Vol. 6 #2.

NORDLING, Carl O., "The Jewish Establishment under Nazi Threat and Domination 1938–1945," JHR, Vol. 10 #2.

O'KEEFE, Theodore J., "Alan Abrams, Special Treatment: The Untold Story of Hitler's Third Race," JHR, Vol. 7 #1.

O'KEEFE, Theodore J., "Claude Lanzmann, Shoah (The Book)," JHR, Vol. 8 #1.

O'KEEFE, Theodore J., "Sara Nomberg-Przytyk, Auschwitz: True Tales from a Grotesque Land," JHR, Vol. 7 #3.

O'KEEFE, Theodore J., "Why Holocaust Revisionism?," JHR, Vol. 12, #1.

O'KEEFE, Theodore J., "Bradley R. Smith, Confessions of a Holocaust Revisionist," JHR, Vol. 8 #1.

O'KEEFE, Theodore J., "A Secret Report by Jan Karski," JHR, Vol. 7 #4.

O'KEEFE, Theodore J., "Carlos W. Porter, 'Made in Russia: The Holocaust,'" JHR, Vol. 9 #1.

O'KEEFE, Theodore J., "Irving on Churchill," JHR, Vol. 7 #4.

OPPENHEIMER, Peter H., "From the Spanish Civil War to the Fall of France: Luftwaffe Lessons Learned and Applied," JHR, Vol. 7 #2.

OPPENHEIMER, Peter H., "The Sudentendeutsche Landsmannschaft," JHR, Vol. 7 #3.

OTTEN, Herman, "Christianity, Truth and Fantasy: The Holocaust, Historical Revisionism and Christians Today," JHR, Vol. 9 #3.

PEEL, Peter H., "The Great Brown Scare: The Amerika-Deutscher Bund in the Thirties and the Hounding of Fritz Julius Kuhn," JHR, Vol. 7 #4.

PONSONBY, Aurther, "The Corpse Factory," JHR, Vol. 1 #2.

POULLADA, Major, "Nordhausen-Dora Case," JHR, Vol. II #1.

RASSINIER, Paul, "Rassinier to the 'Nation,' " JHR, Vol. 2 #4.

REILLY, Janet, "Art Spiegelman, Maus: A Survivor's Tale," JHR, Vol. 7 #4.

REMER, Otto Ernst, "My Role in Berlin on July 20, 1944," JHR, Vol. 8 #1.

RIES, John M., "Big Business and the Rise of Hitler," JHR, Vol. 8 #3.

RIES, John M., "Evan Burr Buckey, Hitler's Hometown: Linz, Austria, 1908–1945," JHR, Vol. 9 #3.

RIES, John M., "Francis R. Nicosia, The Third Reich and the Palestine Question," JHR, Vol. 8, #3.

RIES, John M., "Luc Rosenzweig and Bernard Cohen, Waldheim," JHR, Vol. 8 #2.

RIES, John M., "Rudy Koshar, Social Life, Local Politics, and Nazism: Marburg, 1880–1935," JHR, Vol. 9 #1.

RIGGENBACH, Jeff, "W.J. West, Editor, Orwell: The War Commentaries," JHR, Vol. 7 #3.

RONNETT, Alexander E. MD, BRADESCU, Faust, Ph.D., "The Legionary Movement in Romania," JHR, Vol. 7 #2.

ROQUES, Henri, "From the Gerstein Affair to the Roques Affair," JHR, Vol. 8 #1.

ROW, Robert, "Sir Oswald Mosley: Briton, Fascist, European," JHR, Vol. 5 #s 2,3,4.

SANNING, Walter N., "Soviet Scorched-Earth Warfare," JHR, Vol. 6 #1.

SELESHKO, M., "Vinnytsia—the Katyn of Ukraine," JHR, Vol. 1 #4.

SMITH, Bradley R., "Shoah: Abramham Bomba, the Barber," JHR, Vol. 7 #2.

SMITH, Dennis Nayland, "Ernst Topitsch, Stalin's War: A Radical New Theory of the Origins of the Second World War," JHR, Vol. 8 #2.

STAEGLICH, Wilheim, "Der Auschwitz Mythos: A Book and Its Fate," JHR, Vol. #1.

STAEGLICH, Wilhelm, "West German Justice and the So-Called National Socialist Violent Crimes," JHR, Vol. 2 #3.

STAEGLICH, Wilhelm, "Historians Wrangle over the Destruction of European Jewry," JHR, Vol. 7 #2.

STEIN, Howard F., "The Holocaust and the Myth of the Past as History," JHR, Vol. 1 #4.

STIMELY, Keith, "A Bibliography of Works on and Relating to Oswald Mosley and British Fascism," JHR, Vol. 5 #s 2,3,4.

STRANG, John P., "Richard Drinnon, Keeper of Concentration Camps: Dillon S. Meyer and American Racism," JHR, Vol. 8 #2.

TAYLOR, Samuel, "The Challenge of 'Multiculturalism' In How Americans View the Past and the Future," JHR, Vol. 12, #2.

THOMPSON, H. Keith, "John Phillips, It Happened in Our Lifetime," JHR, Vol. 7 #3.

THOMPSON, H. Keith, "Otto Ernst Remer, Verschworung and Verrat um Hitler: Urteil des Frontsoldaten," JHR, Vol. 8 #1.

THOMPSON, H. Keith, "Robert Harris, Selling Hitler," JHR, Vol. 7 #4.

TOLAND, John, "Living History," JHR, Vol. 2 #1.

TONNINGEN, Florence S. Rost van, "For Holland and for Europe: The Life and Death of Dr. M.M. Rost van Tonningen," JHR, Vol. 9 #4.

VERRALL, Richard (a/k/a HARWOOD, Richard), "Letters to the 'New Statesman,'" JHR, Vol. 1 #2.

WAINWRIGHT, Peter, "Fire in the Reichstag," JHR, Vol. 2 #2.

WALENDY, Udo, "The Fake Photograph Problem," JHR, Vol. 1 #1.

WARD, Arthur S. "John Keegan, The Second World War," JHR, Vol. 10 #3.

WARD, Arthur S., "Miron Dolot, Execution by Hunger: The Hidden Holocaust," JHR, Vol. 7 #2.

WARD, Arthur S., "Patrick Beesly, Room 40: British Naval Intelligence," JHR, Vol. 7 #1.

WARD, Arthur S., James Bacque, "Other Losses," JHR, Vol. 10 #2.

WEBER, Charles E., "Ingrid Weckert, Feuerzeichen: Die Reichskristallnacht: Anstifter und Brandstifter-Opfer und Nutziniesser," JHR, Vol. 8 #4.

WEBER, Mark, "An Open Letter to the Rev. Mark Herbener," JHR, Vol. 8 #2.

WEBER, Mark, "Buchenwald: Legend and Reality," JHR, Vol. 7 #4.

WEBER, Mark, "Hitler's Declaration of War Against the United States," JHR, Vol. 8 #4.

WEBER, Mark, "Joseph Sobran and Historical Revisionism," JHR, Vol. 7 #3.

WEBER, Mark, "My Role in the Zundel Trial," JHR, Vol. 9 #4.

WEBER, Mark, "Reviewing a Year of Progress," JHR, Vol. 10 #4.

WEBER, Mark, "Roosevelt's Secret Map Speech," JHR, Vol. 6 #1.

WEBER, Mark, "Simon Wiesenthal: Bogus Nazi Hunter," JHR, Vol. 9 #4.

WEBER, Mark, "Tell-tale Documents & Photos from Auschwitz," JHR, Vol. II #1.

WEBER, Mark, "The Boer War Remembered," JHR, Vol. 1 #3.

WEBER, Mark, "The Civil War Concentration Camps," JHR, Vol. 2 #2.

WEBER, Mark, "The Japanese Camps in California," JHR, Vol. 2 #1.

WEBER, Mark, "The Nuremberg Trials and the Holocaust," JHR, Vol. 12, #2.

WEBER, Mark, and ALLEN, Andrew, "Treblinka," JHR, Vol. 12, #2.

WECKERT, Ingrid, "Crystal Night 1938: The Great Anti-German Spectacle," JHR, Vol. 6 #2.

WESSERLE, Andreas, "Bombs on Britain," JHR, Vol. 2 #4.

WESSERLE, Andreas, "Allied War Crime Trials," JHR, Vol. 2 #2.

WESSERLE, Andreas, "Death and Rebirth: European Political Observations," JHR, Vol. 7 #4.

WHISKER, James B., "Karl Marx: Anti-Semite," JHR, Vol. 5 #1.

WIKOFF, Jack, "John W. Dower, War Without Mercy: Race and Power in the Pacific War," JHR, Vol. 7 #4.

WIKOFF, Jack, "Hollywood Goes to War: How Politics, Profits & Propaganda Shaped World War II Movies," JHR, Vol. 8 #1.

WIKOFF, Jack, "Neal Gabler, An Empire of Their Own: How the Jews Invented Hollywood," JHR, Vol. 9 #2.

WIKOFF, Jack, "Sam Keen, Faces of the Enemy," JHR, Vol. 10 #4.

WIKOFF, Jack, "Heckling Hitler: Caricatures of the Third Reich," JHR, Vol. 8 #2.

WILLIAMS, Robert H., "The End of the Romanoffs," JHR, Vol. 10 #2.

YOCKEY, Francis Parker, "On Propaganda in America," JHR, Vol. 10 #2.

ZIECHMANN, W.K. v U., "John D. Treadway, The Falcon and the Eagle: Montenegro and Austria, 1908–1914," JHR, Vol. 7 #2.

ENDNOTES

Introduction

1. This protest was briefly mentioned in the mainstream media, and highlighted in the far-right anti-Semitic press. It was not the only demonstration against the film, however.

For example, on June 18, 1979, a group called Concerned Parents of German Descent protested in front of the West German consulate in Toronto, Canada. Holding placards stating "ZIONIST EXTORTION" and "STOP ANTI-GERMAN HATE," the group not only targeted the film *Holocaust,* but also suggested that the West German government was an illegal entity established by the Allies as part of a plot by Zionists to extort money from the German people in reparation for a Holocaust that never occurred.

The anti-Semitic groups did more than write and protest about the movie—they conducted a write-in campaign to NBC stations, urging them to refrain from airing the "Zionist propaganda film," as it was neither "entertainment" nor "in the public interest," and as the Holocaust was "fiction," according to James Warner's Christian Defense League. "Over 300,000 gentile Americans died fighting for JEWISH RIGHTS," according to a letter Warner sent all NBC affiliates in January 1978. Writing that "it is a well known fact that CBS, NBC and ABC are owned and operated by Zionist Jews," Warner threatened that "CDL members in your community will also make sure LOCAL advertisers become aware of the pro-Zionist one sided stand of any station airing this program. A number of CDL members have also indicated their willingness to picket any station carrying this PROPAGANDA movie." (NBC answered Warner in a letter dated February 8, 1978. "We cannot help but regard [your] claims as anti-Semitic," the letter read. "Your threats to oppose the renewal of license of the stations carrying the program need not be dignified with comment." Thereafter, Warner advertised in the March

6, 1978, *Spotlight* for "Christian Attorneys . . . needed to file complaints against NBC affiliate stations airing 'Holocaust' propaganda film.")

Some protesters were people who held important positions. Gerald Domitrovic, a member of the Human Relations Board of Manhattan, Kansas, complained that the film *Holocaust* grossly misrepresented the number of Jews killed by the Nazis. He was asked to resign because of this statement and subsequent racist statements concerning blacks.

2. *Center for Democratic Renewal Weekly Update,* July 13, 1992; JTA, July 8, 1992, p. 4.

3. JTA, Nov. 2, 1992, p. 2, quoting poll conducted by Demoskopea and published in *L'Espresso.* See also *New York Times,* Nov. 5, 1992.

4. See IHR *Newsletter* #44, January 1987. "IHR CONFRONTS CONGRESS," the article reads, noting IHR's "official testimony to the Elementary, Secondary and Vocational Education subcommittee of the Education and Labor Committee of the House of Representatives on May 6 [1986, re] H. Con. Res. 121."

5. According to William H. Chafe, chairman of the history department at Duke University, "Scholarly revisionism is not concerned with the actuality of events, but only with interpretations of their causes and consequences" (quoted in the *Chronicle of Higher Education* 38 [Dec. 11, 1991]: 10). For example, a revisionist student of the Civil War might claim that some generally unappreciated societal forces helped determine the war's course in a certain manner. If someone claimed that the Civil War did not take place at all, but was rather a hoax, he or she would be a denier, not a revisionist.

6. IHR *Newsletter* #74, July/August 1990. Many right-wing anti-Semitic publications routinely promote Holocaust denial among their litany of anti-Semitic vitriol. James Warner's Christian Defense League and Ed Field's *The Truth at Last* (formerly the *Thunderbolt*) are two of the most prolific producers of denial material. But compared to the IHR, both pale in quality, quantity, and subterfuge; only the IHR tries to hide its overt joy at hating Jews.

7. Deniers also exploit the fact that some people erroneously believe that Dachau was an extermination camp rather than a concentration camp. When Dachau was liberated, many GIs were shown a gas chamber, and told that people were killed there. Historians believe that that chamber was not used. If witnesses could be wrong about what they saw in one camp, the deniers argue, why not in the others? Deniers ignore the fact that the same scholars who determined that Dachau had no active gas chambers determined that Auschwitz and others in Poland did. As historian Deborah Lipstadt notes: "In the early 60s, scholars who studied the Holocaust put the lie to that notion. They said 'This is not true. There may have been a gas chamber there, but it was never used to annihilate thousands of people.' The point to be made, the one that I make very strongly all the time, was, sure there were mistakes, and are mistakes even today, in certain aspects of Holocaust research—and that's why we're all studying it, that why we're all trying to understand better, what happened. To get a better handle on it" (interview with Deborah Lipstadt, 1992). (Quotes from Lipstadt throughout this book, unless noted otherwise, are from this interview.)

8. Some deniers (such as engineer William B. Lindsey, who has spoken at annual conferences of the Institute for Historical Review) claim not only that no one was ever killed by Zyklon-B, but that the Nazis used the gas to save Jews. "Survivors," Lindsey said, "who recall the fumigation chambers as deadly gas chambers probably have the pesticide to thank for the fact that they lived to tell the tale."

9. One Holocaust denier, Michael A. Hoffman II, has taken on the issue of slavery. Hoffman, who was once associated with Willis Carto and the Institute for Historical Review, now publishes a newsletter called the *Researcher* under the imprint Wiswell Ruffin House. His book, *They Were White and They Were Slaves—The Untold History of the Enslavement of Whites in Early America,* treats such topics as "A Holocaust Against the White Poor," "White Slaves Treated Worse than Blacks," and "Dutch Jews and the White Slave Trade."

10. Quotes from Gerry Gable throughout this book are from an interview the author conducted with him in 1992.

11. According to Dawidowicz, in the 1960s "even the neo-Nazis in Germany were circumspect . . . not daring to deny the facts of mass murder altogether but simply minimizing them" (Lucy Dawidowicz, "Lies About the Holocaust," *Commentary,* December 1980).

12. *Ibid.*

13. According to Dawidowicz, Hoggan's work also appeared in Germany in 1961. An American, Hoggan's work had first been a "Harvard doctoral dissertation done in 1948, but it was revised, expanded, and Nazified in the ensuing years" (Dawidowicz, "Lies About the Holocaust").

14. David McCalden, a leading Holocaust denier who worked with Carto to establish the IHR, said, "Carto wants a national socialist dictatorship in the United States" (*Los Angeles Times,* May 3, 1981). Carto wrote that "Hitler's defeat was the defeat of Europe. And of America" (see Linda Gordon Kuzmack, *The Hate Business: Anti-Semitism in America* [New York: Franklin Watts, 1993]).

15. The Liberty Lobby is America's largest anti-Semitic organization. It publishes a weekly paper, *Spotlight,* with a circulation of approximately 100,000.

16. Lucy S. Dawidowicz, in one of the first major articles about Holocaust denial, demonstrated the technique frequently used by deniers to distort history through half truths and quotes taken out of context. In "Lies About the Holocaust," she used *The Myth of the Six Million* as an example: "Benedikt Kautsky, an Austrian socialist, had been interned in Buchenwald and was later a slave laborer in Auschwitz. In his memoirs, *Teufel und Verdammie,* Kautsky wrote:

I should now like briefly to refer to the gas chambers. Though I did not see them myself, they have been described to me by so many trustworthy people that I have no hesitation in reproducing their testimony.

The neo-Nazis cite Kautsky, with the appropriate bibliographical references including the correct page number, but falsify the passage so that he appears to corroborate their claim that there were no gas chambers."

17. Dawidowicz wrote: "The first—and still the only—revisionist work on

World War II by a reputable historian was A.J.P. Taylor's mischievous book, *The Origins of the Second World War* (1961). There Taylor argued that Hitler had not planned a general war, that the conflict, far from being premeditated, was 'a mistake, the result on both sides of diplomatic blunders' " ("Lies About the Holocaust").

Years later Warren B. Morris, whose doctorate Dawidowicz termed "from Oklahoma State University on a minor 19th-century German diplomat," wrote *The Revisionist Historians and German War Guilt.* "Morris," Dawidowicz wrote, "set himself the task of determining who was right—the 'revisionists' or the 'traditionalists'—on such matters as the *Destruction of the European Jews,* aspects of Hitler's foreign policy, and the legitimacy of the Nuremberg trials.

"He rejected Butz et al., but noted that 'Even if the "revisionists" ' had failed 'to prove their most important arguments,' he wrote, 'by forcing historians to reconsider their evaluation of Nazi policy toward Jews,' they have 'indeed done a very valuable service to scholarship.'

". . . The June 1980 issue of the *American Historical Review,* the journal of the American Historical Association, the preeminent professional organization of American historians, published a respectful review of Morris' book" *(ibid.).*

18. See Samuel Rabinove, "Skokie and the First Amendment," *Keeping Posted,* February 1979, p. 20.

19. Other anti-Semitic groups are marketing similar material as well. For only $20, one can buy a "Holocaust Pack," described as follows: "This four (4) tape university level course is meant for beginners as well as the advanced student of this newly formed religion. Why did the holocaust figure start off as twelve (12) million and then end up cut in half to six (6) million? Where did Hitler get the six (6) million to kill when he only had six hundred thousand (600,000) in his grasp? Where are the six (6) million skeletons buried? Where are all the ashes? If four (4) million were killed at Auschwitz, the remains should be buried nearby. *Bones, ashes or something.* The jews claimed in the Jewish Encyclopedia that there were some fifteen (15) million jews in 1938, and in 1947 they claimed they had upped their number to eighteen (18) million. *IMPOSSIBLE!* If Hitler killed six (6) million jews between 1938 & 1945 that means the jews would have had to give birth to nine (9) million babies in less than eight (8) years! And we are supposed to believe they did all this while being worked to death *and gassed* all at the same time. Come on, *give me a break. Hey I MAY LOOK TIRED, BUT I'M NOT ASLEEP. Send for your set today and lets settle this matter once and for all."*

20. Quotes from Leonard Zeskind throughout are from an interview the author conducted with him in 1992.

21. Gerry Gable, editor of *Searchlight,* notes that "Money doesn't seem to be a problem" for Holocaust deniers who are busy meeting with each other, and traveling all over the world.

"I think the movements in Europe now are self-supporting," Gable says. "We're looking at something very carefully—the laundering of money that's received legally, and it's being laundered on to the more illicit groups. . . . In Scandinavia, Germany, Poland, they're robbing, big ones. In Sweden, 6–7 million dollars worth in a year. Also lots of small robberies in what was East Germany,

Poland, all the East European area, racketeering, skinheads trading ecstasy and LSD and this kind of stuff."

22. Historian Debrorah Lipstadt comments: "When I first started to work on this, people would look at me like I said I was working on flat earth theorists. We thought it would go away. Give it a little time, and it will go away. It hasn't gone away, and it's not going to go away. And I think we have to understand that. I don't think we have to run out and panic, and say, oh my God, the sky is falling. But we have to recognize that it is a very real thing, and that it's aiming at the college campus, because these are young and susceptible kids."

23. In a second report, Leuchter claims to have visited Dachau, Mauthausen and Hartheim Castle. Denying the gas chambers at Hartheim Castle, Leuchter targets the Nazi "euthanasia" program, which was a first test of the Nazi gassing of people, in this case the mentally handicapped, who were deemed unworthy of life.

Chapter 1

1. The *Denver Post* of March 10, 1991 reported: "Dorothy Groteluschen was an English teacher. She was giving a lesson on the placement of adjective clauses, and read from a textbook that said: 'The photographs that she [Margaret Bourke White] took near the end of the war of the Nazi prison camp at Buchenwald serve as a grim memorial to the victims of the Holocaust.'

"Court documents say Groteluschen told students, 'Now there is a reminder of the Holocaust even in the grammar book,' adding that there is historical disagreement about the Holocaust. 'Some say Holocaust, some say holohoax.'

". . . Her defense was 'I have for years automatically exposed my students to the other side of controversial issues, such as evolution and abortion. . . . [The Holocaust is] a taboo topic, and I did not realize how taboo the topic was . . . No reputable historian today is going to say that nothing happened. . . . What the argument is over is the six million deaths.' "

2. "Swindlers of the Crematoria" argued that "Some of the propaganda claims devoted to supporting the 6 million figure, which is not provable from any reliable source, are absurd. . . . The truth is more likely that the Jews said to have been exterminated, and truthfully no longer to be found in central Europe . . . found new homes for themselves in Israel and especially in the United States."

3. Groteluschen was initially reprimanded by the district for her expressions, which were termed "highly offensive to Jews and to others and are not adequately supported by fact." She was also removed from her job as department head. In 1988, however, an arbitrator ruled that she should be reinstated and given back pay. The Aurora Board of Education rejected that ruling, but ultimately settled. According to news reports the district was more concerned with the cost of litigation than holding to principle. The Institute for Historical Review commented: "Within two weeks [after the complaint] the boys in the white yarmulkes were riding to the rescue" (IHR *Newsletter,* April 1991).

4. The *Jewish Advocate* reported, on Jan. 18, 1991: "As of January 1, Illinois

law mandates the teaching of the Holocaust in the public schools. Although some other states, notably New Jersey, have vigorously encouraged Holocaust education where teachers volunteered, Illinois became the first to mandate it.

"The law reads in part: 'Holocaust Study. Every public elementary school and high school shall include in its curriculum a unit of instruction studying the events of the Nazi atrocities of 1933 to 1945. This period in world history is known as the Holocaust, during which 6,000,000 Jews and millions of non-Jews were exterminated. The studying of this material is a reaffirmation of the commitment of free peoples from all nations to never again permit the occurrence of another Holocaust.'

"... A father and mother have ordered their daughter, a good student, not to attend class while *Night* [Elie Wiesel's classic book about the Holocaust] is being taught and discussed.... The parents—and those who back them—have sent more than 6,000 letters to the parents of the school district, all communications-media outlets, public officials of community and state, and teachers—calling the Holocaust a 'myth.' They charge the school and the teachers with 'political intimidation' in 'perpetuating a fraudulent tale' of gas chambers and other horrors, since 'it can be adequately demonstrated that there were no gas chambers at Auschwitz.'

"The parents charge the Holocaust story was Allied war propaganda, 'perpetuated by the Jews' after the war."

5. "Holocaust Revisionism Scandal Unfolds at Indiana University," JTA, Feb. 23, 1990, p. 1. See also Deborah E. Lipstadt, "Deniers, Relativists, and Pseudo-Scholarship," *Dimensions* 6 (1991): 6.

6. IHR *Newsletter* #81, July/August 1991, p. 8. Even some nonprofessors have been distributing Holocaust-denying material. At the University of Texas, James Braezeeale, a physician at the student health center for over a quarter of a century, has been distributing the IHR's *Journal of Historical Review* (IHR *Newsletter* #88, July/August 1992).

7. Dawidowicz, "Lies About the Holocaust," p. 34. As Yale psychiatrist Walter Reich wrote in the May 3, 1981, *Washington Post*, "If the revisionist are successful in rendering the Holocaust just another matter of debate, then no piece of history is safe . . . all human experience is conveniently subject to ideological interpretation or wishful negation, and we become nothing more than what we believe."

8. Actually, an uproar about Holocaust denial had occurred in campus papers before Smith targeted them. As Jerry Stanley notes in *Midstream,* April 1988, pp. 22–23, "In December, 1984, Joe Fields, a self-proclaimed anti-Zionist at Harbor College, endorsed the Holocaust-as-myth idea in the Harbor College *Hawk,* triggering a vote of censure from the trustees and dismissal of the newspaper's faculty advisor."

Campus papers that ran Smith's ad either as an ad or in editorial form included Duke, Cornell, Howard, Michigan, Northwestern, and Rutgers. Among those who declined to run the ad were UCLA, Berkeley, Harvard, Yale, Brown, University of Pennsylvania, and the University of Wisconsin. (Howard refused to run a second ad after being informed of Smith's real purposes.)

This ad campaign was not the first for the deniers. The Institute for Historical

Review submitted an advertisement for one of its books in the Winter 1984 edition of the *German Quarterly,* the periodical of the American Association of Teachers of German. The AATG's executive council thereafter passed a resolution rejecting "material that is anti-Semitic or that can be construed as an apology for Nazism," and tightened its procedures for accepting advertisements.

The IHR has also used its prestigious-sounding name and slick-looking *Journal of Historical Review* to trick other historical associations into giving IHR their mailing lists. In 1983, both the American Historical Association and *Central European History* (a journal published at Emory University) mistakenly allowed the IHR access to their mailing lists, as had the *Journal of Modern History* and the University of Chicago Press two years earlier. (The Organization of American Historians also provided the IHR with its mailing list in 1980. Unlike the other associations, OAH apparently did not regret doing so, believing that it should not censor its mailing lists, that its members could tell truth from fiction, and that it would be a service for its members to see this "trash." As one member wrote in the OAH *Newsletter,* 8:2 [1980]: "The *JHR* arrived shortly after the end of my class [on the Christian Resistance in Nazi Germany] and I circulated it to members of the class as proof that the Holocaust revisionist movement is alive and well. [Earlier the class had found it hard to believe that there were people who denied the Holocaust happened.] I think it was important for my students to know about and to know the flaws in the *JHR* logic.")

9. Interestingly, there seems to be internal disagreement among some revisionists, who are not willing to "debate" their differences of opinion. Michael Hoffman, who used to work with the Institute for Historical Review, and now publishes his own *Researcher,* wrote: " 'Holocaust' revisionists have refused to debate Charles Provan of the *Christian News.* I was astonished when Friedrich P. Berg, the distinguished engineer and revisionist technical expert, announced that he would not debate Provan unless he made "two small" grammatical concessions to Berg.

"I first became curious about revisionist claims and indignant toward the official line, when I learned that orthodox historians refused to debate the revisionists. What do they fear? What are they trying to hide? Refusal to debate suggests a lack of confidence in one's ability to win a free debate. All of these thoughts went through my mind all the time and frankly they also come up when one learns that a leading revisionist and member of the IHR Advisory Board refused to debate unless his learned opponent concedes in advance that he doesn't understand the English language!

"For years the IHR was spoiling for a debate with all comers. Most recently they challenged attorney Alan Dershowitz and made much of his refusal. Yet nothing is being made of Fritz Berg's refusal to debate Charles Provan.

"I have studied Provan's research on the gas vans at some length and while I am not a technical expert, in lieu of what might have been a very cogent debate rejoinder from Fritz Berg, I am compelled to state that as a result of Provan's work, I believe . . . that the Jews were very likely exterminated at Treblinka and Chelmno, though I continued to doubt that Auschwitz and the centers in the "Old Reich" were anything more than labor camps.

"Revisionists have a golden opportunity in Charles Provan. They can debate him in their own forums and either defeat his propositions or incorporate those that are valid, thus strengthening their position; or they may proceed as they have, very much like their opponents in the functionalist and intentionalist schools of 'Holocaust' historiography, jealously guarding an inflexibly fixed turf against revision, a process which disqualifies them as revisionists" (*Researcher* 3 [1992]).

10. Yehuda Bauer, the head of Hebrew University's Holocaust history department, has said that the technology for making soap from human fat was not known during World War II, but that rumors of Nazis making soap were widespread, and had even been circulated during World War I, regarding British troops. Bauer said that the Nazis were not displeased that the camp inmates believed the soap story.

Professor Raoul Hilberg noted that "There were all kinds of rumors" that turned out to be untrue, including one that Jews were given deadly injections before deportation, or were killed by electrocution, or were gassed in trains.

Hilberg has also said that in Gdansk, Poland, a receipe for rendering soap and pictures of people cut into pieces were found at the Stutthof camp, "but we don't know that the bodies were of Jews, or that the pictures and the recipe went together" (JTA, Apr. 24, 1990, p. 4).

11. From an Institute for Historical Review flier for Bill Grimstad's *The Six Million Reconsidered.*

12. *Chronicle of Higher Education* 38 (Jan. 8, 1992): 6.

13. At Duke University, where *the Chronicle* published Smith's ad, all the members of the Duke history department joined in running another ad, stating: *"The Chronicle* editors make a serious error when they confuse Holocaust deniers with historical revisionists. Whatever one thinks of the right of *The Chronicle* to accept this advertisement, as historians we deplore this effort to use the language of 'scholarship' to distort and obliterate an event which to our everlasting shame did occur. We urge all members of the Duke community to treat such advertisements with the contempt they deserve."

14. College newspapers are, and should be, editorially independent entities. Yet they speak in the "name" of a university. It is essential that if a paper prints something hateful, other voices on campus, especially the leadership, must also be heard, and heard forcefully. When the University of Georgia's *The Red and Black* ran Bradley Smith's ad, President Charles B. Knapp issued a statement that was widely disseminated. "The First Amendment," the statement read in part, "guaranteed the editors' right to accept the ad: it also guaranteed their right to reject it. This ad, so full of misstatement of fact, is deeply offensive to the victims of the Holocaust and to the University of Georgia community. The Holocaust is as indisputable an historical fact as World War II. The acceptance and publication of this ad purveying such blatant falsehood has brought unnecessary pain and suffering to the Holocaust victims, their families and all caring people."

Another effective response is to hold a university-sponsored ceremony, such as a name-reading of Holocaust victims. 9,000 names were read at Northwestern University on Holocaust Remembrance Day in 1991. 150 volunteers read the names between 8 A.M. and 6:30 P.M.

15. Deniers have targeted American talk-radio programs since 1979. Lucy Dawidowicz wrote: "While I was writing this article, a man associated with the Larry King radio show, a national network program, called to ask if I would debate with Faurisson. When I replied indignantly that Faurisson should not be provided with a platform for his monomania, the man mildly inquired why I was against discussing 'controversial' matters on the radio. I in turn asked *him* if he thought the murder of the European Jews was a 'controversial' matter. Had it not been established to his satisfaction as a historical fact? 'I don't know,' he answered. 'I wasn't around at the time' " ("Lies About the Holocaust").

16. This was AJC's second successful effort to counter bigotry, including Holocaust denial, on the airwaves. In 1987 the AJC monitored local radio stations through its membership in over 30 chapters.

17. IHR *Newsletter,* April 1991. Also, in 1992, David Wayfied of Tisbury, Massachusetts, sued the town for raising his property taxes, which, he claimed, was due in part to retaliation for his efforts to have the local library add Holocaust-denying books to its collection (*Spotlight,* Aug. 17, 1992, p. 28).

18. *Journal of Historical Review,* Apr. 16, 1981, supplement.

19. Jerry Stanley, "History on Trial," *Midstream,* April 1988, p. 23.

20. Ron Csillag, "Witness for the Defense: The Neo-Nazis Were Saying the Holocaust Was a Hoax. Mel Mermelstein Set Them Straight," *Inside,* Winter 1989, p. 127. See also Mel Mermelstein, *By Bread Alone—The Story of A-4685* (Huntington Beach, Cal.: Auschwitz Study Group, 1979).

21. Oct. 10, 1981, p. A3.

22. Mermelstein also sued the Swedish Holocaust denier Ditlieb Felderer for the emotional distress suffered from Felderer's claim that Mermelstein "was peddling the exterminationist hoax." A Los Angeles jury awarded Mermelstein $5.2 million in damages (*New York Times,* Jan. 18, 1986, p. 11).

23. JTA, Aug. 11, 1991.

24. Buchanan wrote: "The problem is—diesel engines do not emit enough carbon monoxide to kill anybody. In 1988, 97 kids, trapped 400 feet underground in a Washington, D.C. tunnel while two locomotives spewed diesel exhaust in the car, emerged unharmed after 45 minutes. Demjanjuk's weapon of mass murder cannot kill."

"The problem is," wrote Mark Lasswell in *GQ* about Buchanan's claim, "diesel engines don't need to emit enough carbon monoxide to kill anybody; they emit more than enough nitrogen and carbon dioxide to kill with great efficiency. The net effect is the same because of a lack of oxygen." And as the *New Republic* pointed out, "carbon monoxide emitted by diesel engines is sufficient to asphyxiate people when they are crammed by the hundreds into thirteen-foot chambers. . . . Suffocation at Treblinka took as much as half an hour; Buchanan's comparison only proves that the children he describes had sufficient oxygen to survive whatever length of time they were trapped in the tunnel."

Buchanan has written about Hitler: "Though Hitler was indeed racist and anti-Semitic to the core, a man who without compunction committed murder and genocide, he was also an individual of great courage, a soldier's soldier in the Great War, a political organizer of the first rank, a leader steeped in the history of

Europe, who possessed oratorical powers that could awe even those who despised him. But Hitler's success was not based on his extraordinary gifts alone. His genius was an intuitive sense of the mushiness, the character flaws, the weakness masquerading as morality that was in the hearts of the statesmen who stood in his path." See Kenneth Stern, *Backgrounder: Patrick Joseph Buchanan* (New York: American Jewish Committee, 1990).

25. The American Party, founded by Alabama governor George Wallace for his presidential run in 1968, ran Tom Anderson for president in 1972. Anderson "repeatedly denied that Hitler exterminated six million Jews during the Holocaust," according to Linda Gordon Kuzmack, *The Hate Business: Anti-Semitism in America* (New York: Franklin Watts, 1993).

26. Quotes from Elizabeth Rickey throughout are from an interview the author conducted with her in 1992.

27. Jeffries had given a speech in Albany, New York, in 1991, in which he accused Jews of "control over the movies," which they used to "put together a system of destruction of black people," and as the driving force behind the African slave trade. See Kenneth Stern, *Dr. Jeffries and the Anti-Semitic Branch of the Afrocentrism Movement* (New York: American Jewish Committee, 1991).

28. Black soldiers—who were segregated in the military—took part in the liberation of some camps. As the United States Holocaust Memorial Museum notes, "African American GIs were present at and/or immediately after the liberation of Buchenwald concentration camp. These soldiers were reconnaissance and intelligence troops who were attached to the 183rd Engineer Combat Battalion. On the basis of documentary evidence in the National Archives, we can also say with certainty that [the] 761st Tank Battalion—an all-black unit—was involved in the liberation of Günskirchen, a subcamp of the Mauthausen concentration camp." US Holocaust Memorial Museum Statement of Evidence: Black Liberators, November 6, 1992.

"Liberators" is a military designation given to divisions (and the units attached thereto) that entered camps within the first 48 hours. Other black soldiers were in the camps in the days following liberation, and were also part of the liberation process (most camps were actually liberated when the guards fled at the sound of artillery and soldiers in the distance). Unfortunately, some controversy threatens to detract from the heroics of the all-black units. The documentary film *Liberators* claimed that the 761st entered Dachau and Buchenwald, an assertion that some members of the unit and experts refute. Both veterans and survivors insist upon accuracy in relating their stories—inaccuracies, such as these, only serve as grist for the propaganda mills of the deniers.

29. See Kenneth Stern, *Farrakhan and Jews in the 1990s* (New York: American Jewish Committee, 1992).

30. *Chicago Sun Times,* 1984.

31. The Nation of Islam has published a sophisticated piece of hate entitled *The Secret Relationship Between Blacks and Jews.* See Stern, *Farrakhan and Jews in the 1990s.*

32. *Amsterdam News,* Dec. 28, 1991.

Chapter 2

1. Quotes from Deborah Lipstadt are from an interview the author conducted with her in 1992.

2. Quotes from Zeskind throughout are from an interview the author conducted with him in 1992.

3. One exception to the trend is in Bulgaria. Even though Bulgaria was aligned with Nazi Germany, King Boris III was able to save Bulgaria's Jews from deportation to the death camps. The postwar communist government took credit for the rescue of Bulgaria's Jews. New publications are giving credit where it is due: to King Boris III. See *Antisemitism: World Report 1992* (London: Institute of Jewish Affairs, 1992), p. 45.

4. Quoted in Institute for Historical Review pamphlet advertising 10th conference.

5. Allyn Fischer, "How Many Died? Glasnot May Reveal Holocaust Secrets as Israeli Researchers Comb Soviet Files," *Jewish Week,* Dec. 8, 1989, p. 3.

6. According to the September 1982 IHR *Newsletter,* a German-language edition of a *Spotlight* report was translated by the IHR, and 40,000 copies were shipped to Germany. Tom Marcellus, IHR's director, when asked about the IHR's purpose in so doing, "replied that it appears that [Germany] would be a good market for revisionist material."

7. Holocaust-denying material can be found in neo-Nazi publications such as *Nationalzeitung, Neue Nation, Junge Freiheit,* and *Historiche Tatsachen* (*Antisemitism: World Report 1992,* p. 19).

8. In March 1992, a "European Revisionist Conference" was scheduled for Munich. According to *Spotlight,* the anti-Semitic weekly of the Liberty Lobby, "First the government cancelled the event. Then . . . it was suddenly OK again. But the museum where the conference was to take place broke its contract . . . Organizers were, however, able to obtain permission to hold a rally outside the museum." Speakers included the American Mark Weber of the Institute for Historical Review, the British David Irving, the French Robert Faurisson, and the American Fred Leuchter, who called the Munich police "very cooperative." According to *Spotlight,* the police "allowed the rally to continue for some two hours, breaking it up only after a few 'skinheads' showed up on one side of the crowd and began trading insults with a few protestors on the other side."

9. *Spotlight,* June 15, 1992. The article, "Britain Honors Genocidal Bomber," notes that the British erected a statue to Air Marshal Sir Arthur Harris. Anti-British animus is a mainstay of many deniers.

10. JTA, Aug. 18, 1992, p. 4.

11. *New York Times,* Nov. 3, 1991, p. 16.

12. JTA, Aug. 18, 1992, p. 4.

13. JTA, Sept. 1, 1992, p. 4.

14. *New York Times,* Oct. 25, 1992, p. 12.

15. Erich Kulka, "Another Face of Anti-Semitism: Denying the Shoah," p. 24. Nolte also has written, "Was not possibly the class murder of the Bolsheviks the predecessor of the racial murders?" *(ibid.)*

16. Gill Seidel, *The Holocaust Denial: Antisemitism, Racism and the New Right* (Leeds: Beyond The Pale Collective, 1986), pp. 122–123.

17. IHR *Newsletter* #69, November 1989, p. 3. The IHR *Newsletter* of June/July 1992 claims that all references to extermination camps were deleted from the latest edition of *Hitler's War*. Michael Hoffman's *Researcher*, however, claims that some references were left in, but notes that Irving's recent speeches claim that there were no extermination camps (*Researcher* 3:12 [1992]: 5).

18. IHR *Newsletter* #88, July/August 1992, p. 3.

19. See David A. Jodice, *United Germany and Jewish Concerns: Attitudes Toward Jews, Israel, and the Holocaust* (New York: American Jewish Committee, 1991).

20. Attacks by neo-Nazis on immigrants are becoming commonplace in Germany. The British publication *Searchlight* has monitored the neo-Nazis carefully. Below is an excerpt from *Searchlight*'s June 1992 issue, pp. 15–16, detailing neo-Nazi activities for April 1992:

1 April, DACHAU. A howling mob of fascist Republikaner members try physically to disrupt a visit by Polish president Lech Walesa to the site of the former Nazi concentration camp.

3 April, ERFURT. Marauding Nazi skinheads burn out car belonging to Vietnamese. POTSDAM. A fascist gang severely beats a Cuban in full view of passers-by. JENA. Fascists wreck car belonging to a Libyan tourist. On the same evening, 20 Nazis board a train and attack passengers. A 20-year-old woman is seriously injured.

4 April, DRESDEN. 1,000 Nazis, carrying Imperial war flags and giving Hitler salutes, march through the city centre after painting swastikas on the Lenin monument. . . . The march is loudly applauded by by-standers. The march breaks assurances given last year by Dresden mayor Wagner to the Jewish community that no further Nazi marches would be allowed.

6 April, STRUVENBERG in Brandenburg. Police find the body of a 35-year-old Bulgarian asylum seeker. His throat has been cut. He had disappeared on 27 March. On the same day Nazis launched three attacks on foreigners in town.

7 April, BONN. Death threats against Liberal politicians Burkhard Hirsch and Gerhardt Baum, addressed to "the Jews Baum and Hirsch."

8 April, BERLIN. Nazi skinheads seriously injure a 54-year-old man who dared to argue with them. FRANKFURT AN DER ODER. Fifty neo-Nazis, giving Nazi salutes and chanting "Heil Hitler," "Poles out," and "Germany for the Germans," demonstrate at German-Polish frontier crossing.

11 April, TREUENBRIETZEN, [former] East Berlin. Fifteen racists blitz refugee hostel, smashing windows and entry door as well as damaging a car. FRANKFURT AN DER ORDER. Fascists attack leftist youths in Mikado youth club.

12 April, BERLIN. Nazi boneheads run riot in [former] East Berlin,

hurling beer bottles at passersby and police. Three policemen injured.

14 April, BERLIN. Racist youths attack and badly injure three foreigners at [former] East Berlin's Warschauer Brü S-bahn station. WERNIGERODE. Monument to anti-fascist resistance fighters daubed and damaged.

17 April, BERLIN. Nazi youths board S-bahn train and set upon Lebanese refugee, assault him and try to hurl him out of the moving train.

18 April, WITTENBERG. Nazi skins rampage through Wittenberg, armed with baseball bats and axes and smashing the windows of a local pub. Six guests injured. GREIBEN. Shouting Nazi slogans, 40 fascist youths storm pub which had refused them entry and wound three guests. HALBERSTADT. Memorial to Jewish victims of Nazism daubed with swastikas and Reich eagles and badly damaged by neo-Nazis only a week after being unveiled. SCHWERIN. Nazis assault a Russian army officer and two relatives, one a pregnant woman.

19 April. SCHWERIN. Neo-Nazis run riot in local community of Jamel, prompting mayor Fritz Kalf to call for a local militia to be built for self-defense against fascists. He is denounced by the Meckleburg-West Pomerania Interior Minister "for taking the law into his hands." Police are now investigating him for possession of a shotgun.

20 April, DRESDEN. Sixty neo-Nazis arrested when about to stage a Hitler-birthday celebration in public. GRANSEE. Nazi skins and other Nazi youths, wielding axes and clubs, launch violent attacks on several local pubs. ORANIENBURG. Nazi skin troop marches through town, attacking young people. QUEDLINBURG. More than 100 Nazis attack passers-by and smash pub windows. Later they march through the town centre with swastika flags. MAGDEBURG. Neo-Nazis try to storm squatter house. BERLIN. Nazi arrested as he throws bag of excrement over memorial to Jews in city's Tiergarten area.

22 April, BERLIN. Fascist bomb attack on Turkish cemetery in the city's Tempelhof district. One person lightly injured.

24 April, BERLIN. Nguyen Van Tu, a 29-year-old Vietnamese guest-worker, dies after being stabbed by a racist in a crowded market place as people look on. The killer, a 21-year-old bonehead, is later arrested.

25 April, WERNIGERODE. More than 500 Nazi skins lay siege to house owned by autonome groups. Several people injured as autonomes fight back.

26 April, ESSEN. A refugee centre goes up in flames in racist arson attack. BERLIN. The historic Jewish cemetery in Weissensee is desecrated. More than 55 gravestones smashed.

28 April, BAUTZEN. Thirty-strong Nazi stormtroop wrecks and tries to set fire to "red-light" club after owner refuses to pay protection money.

21. JTA, June 19, 1992, p. 3.
22. JTA, Aug. 24, 1992, p. 3.

23. Both the National Front and the more significant neo-Nazi British National Party promote Holocaust denial. The BNP prints and distributes a publication entitled *Holocaust News.*

24. Interestingly, his *Convoy PQ17,* which claimed that the destruction by German U-boats of British ships bound for the Soviet Union was the fault of a "scatter" order by a Royal Navy captain resulted in a libel suit. The captain was awarded damages.

25. Despite the fact that historians have never accepted Irving's theories, he was provided respectful and thoughtful criticism. Philip Rubenstein notes that "serious historians Alan Bullock, Hugh Trevor-Roper, Eberdard Jackel and Martin Broszat all reviewed the book—and all dismissed its methods and conclusions. Gerald Fleming wrote *Hitler and the Final Solution,* an exhaustive repudiation of Irving's theory. And a panel of distinguished Germans discussed (and harshly criticized) the book on German national television." Philip Rubenstein, " 'The Leuchter Report' in the United Kingdom," printed in Shelly Shapiro et al., eds., *Truth Prevails: Demolishing Holocaust Denial—The End of "The Leuchter Report"* (New York: Beate Klarsfeld Foundation, 1991), p. 86.

26. Quotes from Gable throughout are from an interview the author conducted with him in 1992.

27. See IHR *Newsletter* #76, November 1990, p. 4.

28. Rubenstein, "Leuchter Report in the United Kingdom."

29. Even denier Michael Hoffman, who believes that Auschwitz was a myth, admits that "Jews were very likely exterminated at Treblinka and Chelmno" (*Researcher* 3:12 [1992]: 5).

30. Michael Winograd, "Elie Wiesel Ridiculed," *Southern Israelite,* Oct. 24, 1986.

31. *Searchlight,* June 1992, p. 17.

32. JTA, July 22, 1992, p. 3. The JTA story also notes that the journalist for the Italian magazine who interviewed Irving was Jewish, and that Irving said that "if he had known she [the journalist] was Jewish he would not have agreed to be interviewed by her."

33. A genetic disease associated with Ashkenazi Jews.

34. *London Jewish Chronicle,* Jan. 17, 1991, p. 1.

35. Kulka, "Another Face of Anti-Semitism," p. 18.

36. *Ibid.*

37. Werner Cohn, *The Hidden Alliances of Noam Chomsky* (New York: Americans for a Safe Israel, 1988), p. 4.

38. Paul Berman explains how Karl Marx took this phrase from Hegel, who in turn borrowed it from Shakespeare. It means "the underground process of revolution": "our old friend, our old mole who knows how to work underground in order to appear suddenly: the revolution" (Paul L. Berman, "Gas Chamber Games: Crackpot History and the Right to Lie," *Village Voice,* June 10–16, 1991, pp. 1, 42).

39. For example, a questionnaire asking whether people believed that Germans made soap out of Auschwitz victims was mailed to families in Belgium ("Neo-Nazi Questionnaire," JTA, May 31, 1987).

40. See Cohn, *Hidden Alliances,* p. 3, referring to *L'Express,* Sept. 4, 1987.

41. *Ibid.*

42. Pierre Guillaume, the force behind "The Old Mole," was "forced to close down his Revisionist bookstore in Paris after weeks of attacks and demonstrations by Jewish protestors," claims the IHR *Newsletter* #88, July/August 1992, p. 5.

43. The interview appeared in what the JTA terms "the far right-wing monthly *Le Choc du Mois* (Shock of the Month), a magazine linked to Jean-Marie Le Pen's extreme rightist National Front" (JTA, Apr. 19, 1991).

44. JTA, Apr. 19, 1991.

45. Quoted in "Revisionist Historian Suspended for One Year from Lyon University," JTA, July 20, 1990.

46. "Revisionist Professor Restored to Job," *Washington Jewish Week,* Mar. 21, 1991.

47. "Editor Is First in France to Receive Jail Term for Anti-Semitic Writings," JTA, May 20, 1990, p. 4.

48. Le Pen, who received nearly 20 percent of the vote in some parts of France, once "earned a living by selling German marching songs, tapes, videos, and such," notes *Searchlight* editor Gerry Gable. Gable also says that Le Pen's picture can be found on posters in many parts of France today.

49. Wistrich notes that Le Pen and these publications also "systematically attack Jewish politicians or journalists (the 'Judeo-cosmopolitan mediocratie'), insinuate dual loyalties at every opportunity and use the language of the pre-war fascist Right" (Robert S. Wistrich, *Anti-Semitism: The Longest Hatred* [New York: Pantheon Books, 1991], p. 139).

50. JTA, June 29, 1992; IHR *Newsletter* #88, July/August 1992, p. 5.

51. IHR *Newsletter* #88, July/August 1992, p. 5.

52. Jennifer Golub, *Austrian Attitudes Toward Jews, Israel and the Holocaust* (New York: American Jewish Committee, 1992).

53. See Stephen J. Roth, "Denial of the Holocaust: A Criminal Offense?" *Patterns of Prejudice* 23 (Summer 1989): 42.

54. *Ibid.*

55. *Antisemitism: World Report 1992,* p. 4.

56. See Fritz Karmasin, *Austrian Attitudes Toward Jews, Israel, and the Holocaust* (New York: American Jewish Committee, 1992).

57. IHR *Newsletter* #74, July/August 1990, p. 3.

58. *Antisemitism: World Report 1992,* p. 6.

59. On Oct. 3, 1992, Radio Islam announced that it would cease operating. The announcement came two days after a Stockholm jury found that anti-Semitism had been broadcast. There is some speculation that the decision to close the station (in operation since 1986) was intended to avoid a court order mandating closure, so that the station could be reopened at a later date. See *Searchlight,* November 1992, p. 22.

60. Gabriel Weimann and Conrad Winn, *Hate on Trial* (Oakville, Ont.: Mosaic Press, 1986), p. 25.

61. "2 French Rightists Barred by Swiss," *New York Times,* Dec. 7, 1986, p. 15.

62. *Antisemitism: World Report 1992*, p. 34.

63. IHR *Newsletter* #74, July/August 1990.

64. JTA, July 22, 1992, p. 3.

65. *Antisemitism: World Report 1992*, p. 25.

66. JTA, Nov. 2, 1992, p. 2, quoting poll conducted by Demoskopea and published in *L'Espresso.* See also *New York Times,* Nov. 5, 1992.

67. *London Jewish Chronicle,* Jan. 8, 1988.

68. IHR *Newsletter* #74, July/August 1990.

69. *Antisemitism: World Report 1992*, p. 29.

70. *Ibid.,* pp. 8, 21, 22, 26 and 27. See also JTA, Nov. 6, 1992, regarding a Dutch court's order that a Belgian publisher cease distributing Holocaust-denying material in the Netherlands.

71. *New York Times,* July 3, 1991, p. A8.

72. Randolph L. Braham, "A Changing Landscape of Memory: Eastern Europe and the U.S.S.R.," *Dimensions* 6:1 (1991): 21.

73. See "Revisionism in Croatia: Croatia's President Rejects 'Six Million' Story," JHR 12 (1992): 240. See also the *New Republic,* Nov. 25, 1991, pp. 16, 18; *Die Presse* (Vienna), Jan. 28, 1992. Holocaust denial in the form of rehabilitating Nazis is occuring in the other parts of the former Yugoslavia as well. More than 10,000 copies of *The Protocols of the Elders of Zion* have been distributed in Bosnia, and excerpts from the *Protocols* have been printed in *Tribuna,* a paper targeted to the youth of Slovenia (*Searchlight,* June 1992, p. 21). The printing of the *Protocols* is directly related to the agenda of outright Holocaust denial. Holocaust denial is a fitting addendum to the paranoid Jew-hatred of the *Protocols.*

74. *Antisemitism: World Report 1992*, p. 49. The *Protocols* are also a hot item in Hungary. Margaret Thatcher, the former British prime minister, asked British companies to give newsprint to newly independent Hungary. "When it arrived," *Searchlight* editor Gerry Gable recalls, "somebody wrote to us and said, 'the gift has arrived, it's in the printing works, and they're printing the *Protocols'.* And we got to Downing Street, and they intervened and stopped it."

75. *Antisemitism: World Report 1992*, p. 53.

76. *Politika,* a Prague weekly with a circulation of 2,000, regularly prints Holocaust-denying material (*Antisemitism: World Report 1992*, p. 46).

77. See also Zora Butorova and Martin Butora, *Wariness Toward Jews and "Postcommunist Panic" in Slovakia* (New York: American Jewish Committee, 1992).

78. Braham, "A Changing Landscape of Memory: Eastern Europe and the U.S.S.R," p. 16.

79. Wistrich, *Anti-Semitism,* p. 188.

80. Yehuda Bauer, " 'Revisionism'—The Repudiation of the Holocaust and Its Historical Significance," in Yisrael Gutman and Gideon Greif, eds., *The Historiography of the Holocaust Period* (Jerusalem: Yad Vashem, 1988).

81. Kulka, "Another Face of Anti-Semitism," p. 20.

82. *Antisemitism: World Report 1992*, p. 117.

83. Bauer, " 'Revisionism,' " p. 699.

84. *Antisemitism: World Report 1992*, p. 121.

85. *Ibid.,* p. 122.

86. JTA, June 16, 1992.

87. *Antisemitism: World Report 1992,* p. 124.

88. *Ibid.,* p. 126.

89. Bauer, " 'Revisionism,' " p. 702.

90. IHR *Newsletter* #88, July/August 1992, p. 6.

91. *Antisemitism: World Report 1992,* p. 89.

92. IHR *Newsletter* #90, November 1992.

93. Dawidowicz, "Lies About the Holocaust," p. 35.

94. "Air Time Given Revisionist Outrages Australian Jews," Feb. 26, 1990, p. 4.

95. Shelly Shapiro, "An Investigation," in Shapiro et al., *Truth Prevails,* p. 25. Shapiro also notes that "Bennett runs a tiny organization called the Australian Civil Liberties Union (ACLU) which was formed after he was expelled from the mainstream rights group, the Victoria Council for Civil Liberties (VCCL) for repeating anti-Holocaust lies on VCCL letterhead."

96. JTA, Oct. 9, 1990. For an analysis of Holocaust denial in Australia, see Paul L. Gardiner, "Profile: The League of Rights in Australia," *Without Prejudice* (Australian Institute of Jewish Affairs) 3 (June 1991): 46–48.

97. In the original, Dr. Morsey used the Arabic term for "sucking blood."

98. *An Nahar,* Nov. 8, 1982, quoted in Jeremy Jones, "Holocaust Revisionism in Australia," *Without Prejudice* (Australian Institute of Jewish Affairs) 4 (December 1991): 53.

99. Weimann and Winn, *Hate on Trial,* p. 26.

100. See David Bercson and Douglas Wetheimer, *A Trust Betrayed: The Keegstra Affair* (Toronto: Doubleday Canada Limited, 1985), p. 172.

101. Gil Kezwer, "Keegstra Is Found Guilty Again of Hatemongering Against Jews," JTA, July 13, 1992, p. 3. According to Bernie Farber, acting national director of the Canadian Jewish Congress, Keegstra has appealed this latest conviction, but not on constitutional grounds. See also Patrick Nagle, "Keegstra Threatens Another Appeal," *Calgary Herald,* July 11, 1992, p. B5.

102. Bram D. Eisenthal, "Canadian High Court Strikes Down Law Banning Revisionist Material," JTA, Aug. 28, 1992, p. 1.

103. See Sean Fine, "No 'Open Season' for Zundel, Jewish Congress Says," *Globe and Mail,* Aug. 29, 1992, p. A9; Peter Small, "Jewish Groups Demand New Criminal Charges Be Laid Over 'Falsehoods,' " *Toronto Star,* Aug. 28, 1992, p. A16; Patricia Chisholm, "Justice: The Right to Lie—The Supreme Court Acquits Ernst Zundel," *MacLeans,* Sept. 7, 1992; Paul Lungen, "CJC Seeks New Charges," *Canadian Jewish News,* Sept. 3, 1992, p. 1.

104. There have been attempts to prosecute other Canadian Holocaust deniers as well. Malcolm Ross, another teacher, also published material denying the Holocaust. Because his book, *Web of Deceit,* was not generally available, the prosecutors decided not to proceed with a case.

105. For example, Stephen Stiles, a member of government from the Conserv-

ative Party, was quoted in the press as saying that he was unaware of any "evidence" proving the persecution of Jews during the World War II. See Bercuson and Wetheimer, *A Trust Betrayed*, p. 140.

106. Irving was deported, and is now barred from Canada permanently ("Anti-Nazi Activist's Home Damaged by Suspicious Fire," JTA, Nov. 11, 1992 p. 3.; JTA, Nov. 16, 1992, p. 4).

107. Jennifer Golub, *Japanese Attitudes Toward Jews* (New York: American Jewish Committee, 1992).

108. Uno was set to deliver a series of seminars on this topic, as well as on "Jewish 'Responsibility' for the Persian Gulf War," until the Pacific Rim Institute of the American Jewish Committee intervened, and the lectures were canceled (Tom Tugend, "Japanese Righteous Gentile Honored in Native Land for Saving Thousands," JTA, Aug. 14, 1992, p. 3).

109. Golub, *Japanese Attitudes,* p. 6.; see also Tugend, "Japanese Righteous Gentile Honored."

110. IHR *Newsletter* #76, November 1990, p. 4.

111. William Grimstad's *Anti-Zion* and *The Six Million Reconsidered.* See *Antisemitism: World Report 1992,* p. 83.

112. Baroodi also claimed that the diary of Anne Frank was a fraud, and used as sources both Richard Harwood's (true name Richard Verrall) *Did Six Million Really Die?* and Theis Christophersens's *Die Auschwitz Lüge* (Kulka, "Another Face of Anti-Semitism," p. 22; see also Bauer, " 'Revisionism,' " p. 702).

113. *Ibid.,* p. 703.

114. *New York Times,* Oct. 8, 1977.

115. One of the earliest Palestinian references to Holocaust denial occurred at the United Nations. "In 1972," wrote Teressa Hendry approvingly in the December 1978 edition of the *National Educator,* "with little attendant publicity, a Palestinian Arab addressed the UN, charging that the Zionists financed Adolf Hitler and 'invented the big lie of the extermination of the six million Jews in Europe,' who were 'still very much alive,' he averred, in order to 'blackmail Germany for more than $18 billion in compensation.' He also asserted: 'The world Zionist propaganda machine keeps reminding the Gentiles of their responsibility for the alleged extermination of the six million Jews and suppresses the truth that was published in several Jewish periodicals, that Hitler was a Jew.' "

116. *Los Angeles Times,* Dec. 16, 1990. See also Jeremy Jones, "Holocaust Revisionism in Australia," p. 56.

117. For many years the IHR, like its cousin, the Liberty Lobby, has tried to ingratiate itself with the Arab world. While refusing to call what happened to Jews in World War II genocide, it liberally promotes the term to describe Israeli treatment of Palestinians. At the IHR's Third Revisionist Conference, Issah Nakhleh, described as "chairman of the Palestine-Arab Committee," was a highlighted speaker about "Zionist genocide." An IHR article noting the criticism of the Palestinian Red Crescent Society for printing Holocaust denial wondered if the Red Crescent would be expelled from the ICRC, thus allowing Israel "to strafe those Palestinian ambulances which roll up to collect the latest dead and wounded Arab youngsters on the West Bank and Gaza strip?" An IHR pamphlet advertis-

ing its tenth conference quotes Faurisson as saying: "Of course I am ready to go to jail. I don't mind. I am sure that I will convert first the guards, and then the prisoners, because seventy per cent of them are Arabs."

118. In IHR *Newsletter* #81, July/August 1991, an American resident of Saudi Arabia (identified only as "R.K.") wrote the IHR that "I am well aware of the role that myth, propaganda and the falsification of history have played in our disastrous policy towards Israel and the Arabs. Mainstream historians and journalists have given us such a bizarre version of recent Near East history that it is not difficult to believe that their statements about the Second World War are similarly full of distortions."

119. The IHR *Newsletter* #88, July/August, 1992, touts both speakers at the deniers' 1992 conference as "manifesting the IHR's growing international outreach." Zemzemi was described as a scholar, historian, and author who was expert in "Pan-Islamic resistance to Western and Zionist-fostered nationalism."

120. *Antisemitism: World Report 1992*, pp. 74, 76.

121. In fact, when a young college student was sentenced in France for posting Holocaust-denying material at colleges and universities in Nice, he explained the he was anti-Zionist and pro-Palestinian (JTA, June 29, 1992).

122. Undated letter from Thomas J. Marcellus on IHR stationary to "Dear History Enthusiast."

123. See *Spotlight,* Sept. 27, 1982, pp. 12–13.

124. IHR *Newsletter* #74, July/August 1990 notes: "Tear-gassing Christian clergymen and Arab infants, opening fire on the yacht of Jordan's King Hussein, defacing Jewish gravestones in a calculated attempt (à la Carpentras in France) by provocateurs to inspire further murderous fury against Arabs, imposing nugatory sentences on free-lance Arab-killers: these and similar acts, it becomes clear, are not aberrations but standard products of the mentality which rules Israel today. The Israelis, the quintessential Holocaust survivors and principal beneficiaries of the Holocaust lie, are rapidly becoming world pariahs, as more and more the Zionist leadership and rank and file come to embody the synthetic "Nazi" archetype—brutal, arrogant, reckless—which they have so long imputed to their enemies. Furthermore, the publication, at long last, of a Holocaust Revisionist study ("Burning of the Jews in the Nazi Chambers [*sic*] is the Lie of the Twentieth Century") in an official PLO magazine, *El-Istiglal* (13 and 20 December, 1989), demonstrates that the Palestinians, and thus the Arab and Islamic world, are at long last arming themselves against the most potent propaganda weapon in their oppressors' arsenal."

125. Chomsky claimed that his association with Faurisson was merely to promote the right to "free speech." But he did more than that. He circulated a petition calling Faurisson a "respected" professor, who performs "extensive independent historical research" leading to "findings." In his introduction to Faurisson's book, Chomsky wrote: "One can ask whether Faurisson is truly an anti-Semite or a Nazi. As I have said, I do not know his work very well. But from what I have read, in large part because of the nature of the attacks made against him, I do not see proof that would lead to such conclusions. I find no credible proof in the documents, published text or private correspondence, that I have read concern-

ing him. As far as I can judge, Faurisson is sort of a relatively apolitical liberal" (quoted in Paul Berman, "Gas Chamber Games," *Village Voice,* 26 [June 10–16, 1981]: 1, 37).

126. Chomsky, interestingly, wrote to discredit evidence of another genocide—that in Cambodia. As William Shawcross documents in his *The Quality of Mercy: Cambodia, Holocaust and Modern Conscience* (New York: Simon and Schuster, 1984), p. 55, Chomsky "fervently and frequently" dismissed claims of the Cambodian genocide as anti-Khmer Rouge "propaganda" from the "western media."

127. Nobel Prize winner Elie Wiesel, in referring to the horror of Serbian camps in 1992, called them "concentration camps," and, according to the Jewish Telegraphic Agency, "criticized the use of the words 'genocide' and 'Holocaust' to describe the 'ethnic cleansing' campaign being mounted by the Serbs in Bosnia" (JTA, Aug. 31, 1992, p. 3).

128. Jeffrey Yitzhak Santis, *Questions Often Asked About the Holocaust* (pamphlet), p. 2.

129. Brenner also writes frequently for the *Amsterdam News,* a New York publication targeted to African Americans. This paper, which promotes the anti-Semitic Rev. Al Sharpton, and defends the anti-Semitic CCNY professor Leonard Jeffries, used Brenner to diminish the claim that there is any serious anti-Semitism in the United States today.

130. As Paul Berman notes in his excellent "Gas Chamber Games," the strain of isolationism that a Harry Elmer Barnes produced (most recently echoed in the right-wing anti-interventionist protests regarding Iraq) was easily compatible with Holocaust denial: The Germans weren't so bad, weren't worth fighting—see, there really was no Holocaust, we should have stayed out.

Berman believes a similar delusion occurs on the left. "Historical materialism and Marxist philosophy suddenly seem useless for explaining the awful turn history has taken in various genocidal corners of the globe," Berman writes. "[Some] have resolved all philosophical difficulties raised by the existence of genocidal insanity by declaring genocide to be a false rumor. . . . With a single stroke all theoretical problems disappear. Irrational genocide makes the Marxist notion of historical progress look ridiculous?—it must not exist. Gas chambers are an affront to the materialist logic of Marx and Engels?—they must be a lie. Bad news?—poof!"

131. In the first use of a new European Community regulation allowing residents of one member state to sue residents of another, a Dutch court prohibited Siegfried Verbeke, a Belgian publisher, from distributing his Holocaust-denying pamphlets in the Netherlands (JTA, Nov. 6, 1992).

132. *Patterns of Prejudice* 23 (Summer 1989).

Chapter 3

1. Some of the less careful deniers spout anti-Semitic rantings that can be used to expose them. For example, the late David McCalden, once director of the IHR

and then head of his own "Truth Missions," wrote the following about a visit he paid to the Simon Wiesenthal Center for Holocaust Studies in Los Angeles (quoted from the anti-Semitic journal *Instauration*): "A sign on the door requires that all male visitors wear a yarmulka out of respect for the six million. A bin of yarmulkas by the door reminds me of those photographs of piles of shoes and eyeglasses from Auschwitz (Or was it Lublin? Or was it Birkenau?) I have seen the same pictures with various captions—photographs which prove that the original wearers of said shoe/eyeglasses were gassed, burned, or disappeared without leaving so much as a smidgen of ash or bone for forensic scientists to examine.

"I enter yarmulkaless. Fourteen years of Presbyterian aversion to idolatry and icons have left their mark. I wait for some Orthodox rabbi in a long black coat, black hat and 'dread locks' to challenge me. Fortunately, there is no rabbi, and I have free access to roam the displays. Everything seems pretty standard. There are the usual photos of deportations and camp liberations; a large wall map showing all the camp sites; some oil paintings by survivors. It's all so slick that a professional exhibition company must have been engaged to lay on the display. The photos and captions are quite artsy, some hanging in midair like merchandise descriptions in a department store showcase. The lighting is subdued.

"I pick up a phone and listen to a tape of Himmler's rambling speech at Posen on October 4, 1943. An interpreter is superimposed to translate it into English. The speech abounds in phrases like 'extermination of the Jews,' but I couldn't make head nor tail of it.

"Over now to a display case in the middle of the room. Besides a few camp artifacts such as stamps, passports, IDs, the case contains a most incongruous object: a tattered lampshade which appears to be made of parchment with ink etchings of rural, bucolic scenes. Could this be . . . ? I had always been under the impression that the 'lampshade' and 'soap' allegations were Soviet canards.

"Curiously, the lampshade appears to have been added to the showcase after the professional exhibition people had done their best—or worst. It just doesn't fit in with the other aesthetically arranged objects d'art. While all the other items have a permanent description plate, the lampshade has a plain typed slogan on a pressure-sensitive label. It reads: 'The Nazis even made lampshades out of human life itself.' Does this mean that the lampshade is really made out of human skin?

"A junior rabbi in a three-piece suit who is hovering nearby explains that it is a replica. If it had been genuine, it would have had to have been buried with the recitation of the Kaddish, the prayer for the Jewish dead. No, he couldn't tell where it came from. . . .

"Leaving the subterranean world of the Exterminationists, I step out into the smoggy haze of a Los Angeles Sunday afternoon. The acidic air out here tastes better than the Hassidic air down there—and there isn't a religious artifact in sight!"

2. Deborah E. Lipstadt, "Deniers, Relativists, and Pseudo-Scholarship," *Dimensions* (Anti-Defamation League) 6:1 (1991): 8.

3. Eric Zorn, "NU Is Wrestling Slippery Problem," *Chicago Tribune,* May 7, 1991, p. 1.

4. Gabriel Weimann and Conrad Winn, *Hate on Trial* (Oakville, Ont.: Mosaic Press, 1986), p. 24.

5. This quotation is from an interview the author conducted with Jim Davis in 1992.

6. See, *infra,* pp. 71-78 and correponding citations to Pressac's and others' refutations of Leuchter's claims about Auschwitz.

7. Hitler advocated extermination of the Jews *before* he wrote *Mein Kampf.* In a letter of Sept. 16, 1919, Hitler wrote that his type of anti-Semitism would go beyond pogroms; it would wipe out the Jews "root and branch" (C. C. Aronsfeld, "The Big-Lie Historians: Rewriting the Holocaust," *Australia/Israel Review,* April, p. 26). In *Mein Kampf,* he even wrote of gassing Jews: "If at the beginning of the War and during the war, twelve or fifteen thousand of these Hebrew corrupters of the people had been held under poison gas, as happened to hundreds of thousands of our very best German workers in the field, the sacrifice of millions at the front would not have been in vain." For analysis of Hitler's attitudes toward Jews, see Lucy S. Dawidowicz, *The War Against the Jews 1933–1945* (New York: Holt, Rinehart and Winston, 1975).

8. Quoted in Robert S. Wistrich, *Anti-Semitism: The Longest Hatred* (New York: Pantheon Books, 1991), p. 74.

9. Judith Bolton, "Holocaust Revisionism: Editing the Past," *Congress Monthly,* July/August 1992, p. 9.

10. Quoted in Wistrich, *Anti-Semitism,* pp. 75–76.

11. Jim Davis, "Revisionist Arguments," *Sun-Sentinel,* Apr. 26, 1992, p. 4E.

12. Quoted in Dorothy Rabinowitz, *About the Holocaust: What We Know and How We Know It* (New York: American Jewish Committee, 1980), p. 39.

13. David Germain, "They Say It Never Happened," *Syracuse Herald-Journal,* May 14, 1990, p. 5. (Germain notes: "Pressac claims that the actual figures by 1943 were only half those in Franck-Griksch's report. He concludes that Auschwitz guards inflated the figures to make the camp appear more efficient at killing Jews.")

14. Alan Bullock, a British historian, writing in the *New York Review of Books,* noted: "This [the lack of a Hitler-signed death warrant for Jews] is hardly surprising considering the monstrosity of the crimes being committed, the massacre of several million people. Elaborate precautions were taken to confine knowledge of the facts to as small a circle as possible, denials were issued which Mr. Irving himself characterizes as 'the purest humbug,' and the ghastly reality was camouflaged by a series of euphemisms . . . which were employed even between those who knew what was taking place."

15. Davis, "Revisionist Arguments," p. 4E. The Final Solution was the topic of a meeting coordinating various parts of the German government—SS and high state officials—at Wannsee, a Berlin suburb, on Jan. 20, 1942. For details, see Rabinowitz, *About the Holocaust,* p. 14. Rabinowitz also notes that "The minutes of the Wannsee Conference appear in German in Robert M. W. Kempner, *Eichmann und Komplizen* (Zürich, 1961), pp. 133–147. A translation in Dawidowicz, *Holocaust Reader,* pp. 73–82."

16. Helmut Krausnick, a German historian, studied the records of the *Ein-*

satzkommando and *Einsatzgruppen,* which were Nazi murder squads that killed people beyond those herded into the gas chambers. He wrote: "From 15 August 1941 the *Einsatzkommando* (according to its own 'general report') was also shooting Jewish children almost daily: for instance, in the operation carried out in Moletai and Utena on 29 August 1941, '1,460 Jewish children' were put to death in addition to 582 Jewish men and 1,731 Jewish women. Under the heading 'Executions up to 1 February 1942,' . . . the following figures were given: communists, 1,064; guerrillas, only 56; mentally unsound, 653; Poles, 44; Russian prisoners-of-war, 28; gypsies, 5; Armenians, 1; Jews, 136,421! These figures were reported by *Einsatzgruppe* A, which had already executed 229,052 Jews. *Einsatzgruppe* B reported 45,467 shootings by 14 November 1941; *Einsatzgruppe* C, 95,000 by the beginning of December 1941; and *Einsatzgruppe* D, 92,000 by 8 April 1942. To these figures must be added a further 363,211 shootings carried out during the months August to November, 1942 in the Ukraine, South Russia, and the province of Bialystock, as reported to Hitler by Himmler himself' (quoted in Martin Perry, "Denying the Holocaust: History as Myth and Delusion," *Encore American & Worldwide News Service,* September 1981).

17. Perry, "Denying the Holocaust" p. 32

18. Kulka, "Another Face of Anti-Semitism," p. 19.

19. According to the *Jerusalem Post* (International Edition), May 16, 1978: "In a sworn statement made in Nuremberg on November 26, 1945, by Dr. Wilhelm Hoettl, a *sturmbannfuehrer* (major) in the SS who was head of a department of German intelligence in Budapest. . . . Hoettl stated that he had met Adolf Eichmann in his Budapest flat in August 1944. Eichmann was in a pessimistic mood, as he had become convinced that the Germans were about to lose the war and that he would be sought by the Allies as a major war criminal, because he had 'millions of Jews on his conscience.'

"Eichmann told me that a short time previously he had made a report to SS chief Heinrich Himmler, who wanted to know the exact number of Jews killed. . . . In the various extermination camps about four million Jews had been killed, Eichmann said, and another two million were killed in other ways, mainly through shooting by the Einstazkommandos during the Russian campaign," Hoettl said.

"But Eichmann said Himmler had not been satisfied with the report, because he believed that, according to his own information, the number of Jews murdered must have exceeded six million."

20. *Sun-Sentinel,* Apr. 26, 1992, p. 4E.

21. Quotation from an interview author conducted with Shelly Shapiro in 1993.

22. Reprinted in Serge Klarsfeld, *The Holocaust and the Neo-Nazi Mythomania* (New York: Beate Klarsfeld Foundation, 1978), p. 145.

23. Quoted in Kulka, "Another Face of Anti-Semitism," p. 15.

24. Rudolf Höess, *The Autobiography of Rudolf Höess,* tr. Constantine Fitzgibbon (London: Pan Books, 1959), p. 15.

25. Deniers offer the lame suggestion that "High ranking defendants were

cynically assured that by 'voluntarily' accepting all responsibility themselves they would thereby protect their former subordinates from prosecution" (Mark Weber, "The Nuremberg Trials and the Holocaust," JHR 12 [1992]).

26. Lemkin has been credited for pursuing the enactment of the Genocide Convention in the United States.

27. Kulka, "Another Face of Anti-Semitism," p. 19.

28. *Ibid.*

29. See Bradley F. Smith [not to be confused with the Holocaust denier Bradley R. Smith], "Two Alibis for the Inhumanities—A.R. Butz's *The Hoax of the 20th Century* and David Irving's *Hitler's War*," *German Studies Review*, Oct. 1978, p. 327.

30. See Rudolf Vrba and Alan Bestic, *I Cannot Forgive* (New York: Bantham, 1964).

31. *Ibid.*, p. 21.

32. *Ibid.*

33. Davis, "Revisionist Arguments."

34. Auschwitz was not the only death camp. Why has it drawn the major focus of the deniers? Erich Kulka offers a theory: "Why was Auschwitz chosen? Jews had been similarly killed by gas in five other death camps! All traces of annihilation installations in Chelmno, Belzec, Treblinka, and Sobibor had been destroyed in time by the Nazis and are all but forgotten. The area of Auschwitz, however, with its undeniably recognizable ruins of four crematoria and gas chambers in Birkenau, together with the original crematorium in the main camp in Auschwitz, have been included in the State Museum Oswiecim Brzezinka with its damning documents and displayed proofs. The most shocking of all are the shoes of thousands of babies and children suffocated by the Zyklon B gas. Millions of tourists from all over the world visit them daily, see them and prove wrong revisionists, neo-fascists and terrorists of all shades and ways. Auschwitz has become an indestructible undeniable evidence and answer to all who try to clear Hitler and his helpers. The revisionists however are stepping up their fraudulent campaigns against the mass murder by gas in Auschwitz and spreading lies all over the world" (Kulka, "Another Face of Anti-Semitism," p. 26).

35. The camp was obviously not in the same condition as it was during World War II. As Erich Kulka notes: "One of the four crematoria in Birkenau with three gas chambers was destroyed by the prisoners during the insurrection on October 7, 1944. The three remaining crematoria with gas chambers were destroyed by dynamite by the SS immediately before the evacuation in January, 1945. The ruins of the underground gas chambers are apparent until today" ("Another Face of Anti-Semitism," p. 19).

36. See Arthur Goodman, "Leuchter: Exposed and Discredited by The Court," in Shelly Shapiro et al., eds., *Truth Prevails: Demolishing Holocaust Denial—The End of "The Leuchter Report"* (New York: Beate Klarsfeld Foundation, 1990), p. 78. and Charles R. Allen, Jr., "The Role of the Media in the Leuchter Matter," *ibid.*, p. 114. 37. See "Execution 'Engineer' Settles Criminal Case," *New York Times,* June 13, 1991; "Jewish Groups Hail Revisionist's Concession," *Jewish Exponent,* June 21, 1991. According to the Consent Decree itself,

filed in *Commonwealth of Massachusetts v. Fred A. Leuchter, Jr.*, Leuchter not only admitted that he had never been registered as a professional engineer, he agreed for the life of the decree not to use the title engineer, nor to "provide engineering opinions, specifically but not limited to [his Leuchter report]."

38. See Jean-Claude Pressac, "The Deficiencies and Inconsistencies of 'The Leuchter Report,' " Shapiro, *Truth Prevails,* p. 31. See also Davis, "Revisionist Arguments"; "Death Machine Builder Under Scrutiny for Nazi Gas Report," *Boston Globe,* Oct. 1, 1990, p. 13.

39. Shelly Shapiro, in a conversation with the author, notes that the book was published after "the Leuchter Report was used in the defense of a Nazi war criminal in Canada. An *Atlantic Monthly* article had described Leuchter as an expert in gas chambers, and a judge permitted his report to be read into the record of the trial."

40. The book also destroys Leuchter's claims to be an expert, and notes that his "research" was paid for by Ernst Zündel—the Canadian Holocaust denier who hired Leuchter to disprove the existence of gas chambers. Goodman ("Leuchter: Exposed," *ibid.,* pp. 77–78, citing trial records at 8962, 8972, 9072, 8973) quotes Leuchter's questioning under oath at the trial of Ernst Zündel:

Q: What formal education have you had?
A: I've had physics on the college level.
Q: All right. Do you consider yourself a physicist?
A: I do not.

Asked about his training in chemistry, Leuchter said:
A: I had basic chemistry on the college level.
Q: Basic chemistry on the college level?
A: Yes. I am certainly not a chemist.
Q: Have you done any university level work in toxicology?
A: No, I have not.
Q: Do you consider yourself a toxicologist?
A: I do not.
Q: Are you a professional engineer?
A: I am. I have been functioning as such for the last 24 years.
Q: What degree in engineering do you have?
A: I have a Bachelor of Arts.
Q: How do you function as an engineer if you don't have an engineering degree?
A: Well, I would question what an engineering degree is.

Judge Thomas did not allow Leuchter to express opinions as to the existence of the gas chambers, finding his competence to come to such conclusions wholly inadequate. See also David Bernstein, "Demolishing the Leuchter Lie," *Australian Institute of Jewish Affairs Briefing* no. 3, April 1991.

41. See Pressac, "Deficiencies," p. 41.

42. As Bernstein points out ("Demolishing the Leuchter Lie"), "Lice, Pressec points out, have a much higher resistance to hydrocyanic acid (HCN) than do

humans. Thus a HCN concentration of 0.3 g/m³ will kill a man instantaneously, while a much higher concentration (5.0 g/m³) has to be maintained for at least two hours and usually as long as six hours to be certain of eradicating lice. The dose used to exterminate humans at Birkenau varied between 12–20 g/m³ (that is, 40–70 times over the lethal concentration). This infallibly killed 1,000 people in less than five minutes, after which the chambers were ventilated and the cadavers removed. At the most, Pressac notes, the walls in the extermination chambers were in contact with the gas *for no more than 10 minutes a day*. In the delousing sheds, on the other hand, a minimum concentration of 5 g/m³ was used—but this remained in contact with the walls for up to 18 hours a day for up to two years. It is this long-term saturation over the course of several years which accounts for the relatively high concentration of cyanide in the samples from the delousing chambers, while the very brief exposure of the extermination chambers to the gas accounts for the negligible traces found from those chambers." (Bernstein relies on Pressac, "The Deficiencies," *ibid.,* p. 36.)

43. Pressac, "Deficiencies," p. 45.

44. Quoted in Arthur Goodman, "Leuchter: Exposed and Discredited by the Court," in Shapiro, *Truth Prevails,* p. 82 (citing trial record at 9254).

45. H. L. Silets, "Facts Written in Blood: The Zyklon B Trial of Bruno Tesch," in Shapiro, *Truth Prevails,* pp. 100–102. This article also quotes the Nuremberg testimony of Wilhelm Bahr, identified as "an ex-medical orderly and Unterscharfurher at Neuengamme concentration camp, who himself used Zyklon-B to gas two hundred prisoners of war:

Q: Is it correct that you have gassed 200 Russian prisoners of war with Blausauregas [Zyklon-B]?
A: Yes, on orders.
Q: Where did you do that?
A: In Neuengamme.
Q: On whose orders?
A: The local doctor, Dr. Von Bergmann.
Q: With what gas?
A: With prussic acid.
Q: How long did the Russians take to die?
A: I don't know; I only obeyed orders.
Q: How long did it take to gas the Russians?
A: I returned after two hours and they were all dead.
Q: For what purpose did you go away?
A: That was during lunch hour.
Q: You left for your lunch and came back afterwards?
A: Yes.
Q: Were they dead when you came back afterwards?
A: Yes
Q: Did you look at their bodies?
A: Yes, because I had to load them.

Q: Why did you apply the gas to the Russians?

A: I only had orders to pour the gas in and I do not know anything more about it (*ibid.,* p. 99).

46. Perry, "Denying the Holocaust," p. 28.

47. As Dr. Turid Karin Epstein wrote (in *Gannett Westchester Newspapers,* July 9, 1983): "[Holocaust deniers try to prove] scientifically, the mass extermination of Jews by gas was impossible. The 'proof' listed, without direct quotation even, is a German language technical magazine from 1933! Is it not an insult to German technical ingenuity to assume that they made progress, if one can call it that, in ten years?"

48. See extensive examination in Paul L. Berman, "Gas Chamber Games: Crackpot History and the Right to Lie," *Village Voice,* June 10–16, 1981, pp. 1, 38.

49. As Ian Barnes and Vivienne R.P. Barnes point out, "This phrase has been lifted verbatim from *Mein Kampf* [Jews' activities] 'a pestilence worse than Black Death.' " See "A 'Revisionist Historian' Manipulates Anne Frank's Diary," *Patterns of Prejudice* 15 (1981).

50. *Bible Researcher,* no. 106 (1979): 1.

51. Other deniers, including Richard Harwood, Arthur Butz, Robert Faurisson, and Alfred Lilienthal have also touched on the claim that Anne Frank's diary was a fraud. The IHR, however, promotes Felderer's work as the only "published work devoting itself exclusively to this trickery."

52. P. 19.

53. *Patterns of Prejudice,* Radical Round Up, p. 36. "On the basis of expert literary and graphological opinion accepted by the court [the teacher Otto Frank had sued] made three statements: (1) he completely retracted; (2) he offered apologies; (3) he declared himself 'convinced of the genuineness of the Diary' " (*ibid.,* p. 37).

Chapter 4

1. Regarding the Holocaust Museum, the national president of the German American National Congress wrote to President Reagan on Mar. 23, 1983, as follows: "I request this project be stopped. . . . At a time when so many of our fellow citizens are out of work . . . it does not seem proper to spend millions of tax dollars on these types of endeavors. . . . Further, this sets an alarming precedent for the use of federal tax money and buildings to perpetuate other dark moments in the history of each ethnic group that constitutes this great land. To cluster them all around Washington, D.C. would make our Capitol a veritable museum of horrors. . . . If such a Holocaust Museum is to be built, let it be done in Israel with the tax money of their citizens."

Sometimes, as in the Illinois case mentioned in chapter 3, deniers object. Sometimes, the opponents raise all these issues—for example, George Pape, president of the German-American Committee, objected to the New York City Board of Education's 1977 proposal for such a curriculum, stating "there is no real proof that the Holocaust actually did happen" (*New York Times*, Nov. 9, 1977).

2. Raoul Hilberg once spoke at a high school where some students surveyed thought the "Holocaust" was "A Jewish holiday" (cited, approvingly, in the *Christian Vanguard*, January 1978, p. 8).

3. As Leonard Zeskind of the Center for Democratic Renewal notes: "What the white supremacists, the neo-Nazi Klan type movement in the United States needs, requires, is some founding set of idea that will hold the various organizations together, serve as an ideological glue that would bind a Klan group that marches through the street and an Identity Church that holds bible camps and organizes around electoral issues and a skinhead group with their skinhead music and streetfighting. What will provide the glue that will hold these groups together? Increasingly, historical denial holds all these different type groups together, and helps mold them into a single movement."

4. A sample: "The Holocaust itself is really an edifice, a monument, so to speak, to the naive gullibility of the world in which even the most outrageous survivors' tales and falsest testimonies are totally believed without the slightest doubt or criticism" (from Mitchell Bard, "The Future of Anti-Semitism," *Near East Report*, June 15, 1992, p. 116).

5. For material on the Armenian genocide, see Richard G. Hovannisian, ed., *The Armenian Genocide in Perspective* (New Brunswick, N.J.: Transaction Books, 1986) and Henry Morgenthau, *Ambassador Morgenthau's Story* (Plandome, N.Y.: New Age Publishers, 1984).

6. See Vahé Oshagan, "The Impact of the Genocide on West Armenian Letters," in Hovannisian, ed., *Armenian Genocide*, p. 169. As with the Holocaust, the exact number of Armenians who were killed is not precisely attainable. As Leo Kuper notes in his "The Turkish Genocide of Armenians, 1915–1917," in *ibid.* p. 52, Richard Hovannisian puts the total population of Armenians in Turkey as between 1.5 and 2 million, while "the American Committee for Armenian and Syrian Relief [provides] a prewar Armenian population of 1.8 million. [Michael J. Arlen] writes that 'it is possible to say, not precisely but with a general respect for accuracy and plausibility, that in the course of the 1915–1916 massacres and deportations close to one million Armenians—more than half the Armenian population of Turkey—disappeared.' "

Robert Melson, in "Provocation or Nationalism: A Critical Inquiry Into The Armenian Genocide of 1915," *ibid.*, pp. 64–66, puts the figure of Armenians killed as approximately one million, which would be either "nearly half" or "more than half" of the population, depending on which population figures are used.

7. See Hovannisian, *Armenian Genocide*, pp. 5, 13.

8. Peter Sourian, "In This Genocide the Victims' Voices are Drowned Out," *Newsday*, April 23, 1990, p. 48.

9. See Kenneth Stern, *Loud Hawk: The United States vs. the American Indian Movement* (Norman, Oklahoma: University of Oklahoma Press, 1994.)

10. There was much to celebrate in the 500th anniversary of Columbus's trip to the New World. He did not "discover" America—there were people here when he arrived who, more correctly, "discovered" him.

11. Zohar Shavit, a professor of Jewish studies at Tel Aviv University, lived in West Germany between 1986 and 1988, and studied the textbooks and novels about World War II designed for 9- to 12-year-olds. The books say "There was a very terrible war in which Germany suffered. . . . It is Hitler who is to blame for the war; none of the Germans had anything to do with it . . . German children's literature doesn't deny the Holocaust, but it selectively banishes it from the consciousness. . . . In the books, one gets the impression that the Nazis hijacked Germany from the Germans. The message is clear: Nazis were not human beings but demons that did not have anything to do with humanity in general or Germany in particular."

12. The American Jewish Committee has met with over 100 university and college presidents, outlining the findings of its publication, Kenneth S. Stern, *Bigotry on Campus* (New York: American Jewish Committee, 1990).

13. In fact, as time goes on, the Holocaust deniers will need do nothing, for by trying to debate the "facts" of the Holocaust, they may be doing themselves a disservice; that is, drawing attention to something that most people are ignorant of.

14. Sourian, "In this Genocide."

15. Yoseff Goell, "The Tragedies of Other People: Israel and the Turkish Attempt to Play Down the Armenia Holocaust," *Jerusalem Post*, Oct. 26, 1989, p. 4.

16. *The Effort to Repeal Resolution 3379,* ed. Kenneth S. Stern (New York: American Jewish Committee 1991), p. 41. As Marvin Perry, an assistant professor of history at Baruch College, noted in an early article on Holocaust denial:

Jews have always been astonished at the utterly bizarre content of anti-Semitic myths; they have found it incomprehensible that to their tormentors these myths were unassailable truths. If Nazis, with immense dedication and moral indifference, could drive Jews into gas chambers believing that they were purging the world of an evil race of conspirators, we should not be too surprised that their spiritual descendants, with equal conviction and meanness of spirit, believe that the Jews fabricated a tale of mass murder (Marvin Perry, "Denying the Holocaust: History as Myth and Delusion," *Encore American & Worldwide News,* September 1981, p, 32).

17. "Anniversary of U.N. Repeal marked," JTA, Dec. 17, 1992, p. 2, quoting Israeli ambassador Gad Yaacobi.

18. Many historians have suggested that Hitler could have been more effectively opposed in the 1930s if the world had helped the anti-fascist forces during the Spanish Civil War.

ACKNOWLEDGMENTS

In writing this book, I discovered that there are only a handful of real experts on Holocaust denial, and fortunately for me, they were all friendly people generous with their time and help.

Deborah Lipstadt, Leonard Zeskind, Gerry Gable, Elizabeth Rickey, Alex Gross, Jim Davis, Shelly Shapiro, and Justus Rosenberg consented to lengthy interviews, freely sharing their insights and the fruits of their research. Shelly was especially helpful, going over the manuscript with a dedication and clarity that markedly improved the final product.

Thanks also to Mel Mermelstein for seeing something of value in this work, and to Susan Jerison, Michael Harrison, Bernie Farber, Sybil Milton, Peter Sourian, and Marjorie Dobkin for helping in their areas of expertise.

This book would not have been possible without the encouragement of my colleagues at the American Jewish Committe, the patience of my wife, Margie, or the joyous disposition of our infant son, Daniel.

K.S.S.

Index

Doctors' Plot, 40
Dora-Nordhausen, 30
Drama of the European Jews, The, 70
Dregger, MP A., 29
Dresden, 9, 27, 31, 50
Dubno, 64
Duke, David, 2, 7–8, 18–19, 21, 96
Dutch Jews, 80
Durafour, Michel, 35

East Germany, 90–91
East Timorese
  mass killings of, 55
Eastern Europe, 26, 38–42, 95–96
Eckville, 46
Edison, Thomas, 8
Editora Revisao, 43
Edizioni All'Insegna Del Vetro, 37
Egypt, 52
Eichmann, Adolf, 28, 63, 66
Eidgenoss, 37
Einsatzkommandos, 28
Einsatzgruppen, 56
Eisenhower, Dwight D., 31, 71
El Istiglal, 50
El-Shammali, Khaled, 50
Ellwanger, Siegried, 43
Erzerum, 86
Ethnic cleansing, 90
Eugenics
  interest in by deniers, 13, 21
Europe. See individual countries; See
    also Eastern Europe
European Society for Free Speech, 25
Euthanasia Order of 1939, 63
Evacuation
  as euphemism for extermination, 63
Executive Council of Australian Jews, 45
Extermination camps
  contrasted with concentration camps,
    3, 20, 71
  See also Auschwitz, Maidanek

Facing History and Ourselves, 84
"False News," 46–47
Farber, Barry, 14
Farrakhan, Louis, 19–20
Fascism
  rehabilitation of pre-World War II
    fascist governments, 26, 38, 40,
    41–42, 82, 95, 96

David Irving as self-described "mild
    fascist," 30
Faurisson, Robert, 8, 33, 34, 35, 44, 48,
    51–52, 53–54, 73–74, 78
F.D.R.: My Exploited Father-In-Law, 49
Felderer, Ditleib, 37, 46, 48, 79–80
Fin de Una Mentira: Camaras de Gas:
    Holocaust-Informe Leuchter, 43
Final Call, 19–20
Final Solution, 28, 55, 63–64, 78
Final Solution, The, 66
Finale Furioso. See Mit Goebbels bis zun
    Ende
First Amendment (to the U.S.
    Constitution). See Free Speech
Fischer, Arthur, 30
Focal Point Publications, 32
Fort Lauderdale Sun Sentinel, 61, 67
France
  Holocaust denial in, 33–35
  French fascists quoted in Russian
    press, 42
  outlawing of Holocaust denial in, 56
  See also Faurisson, Robert; Rassinier,
    Paul
Francke-Griksch, SS Major, 63
Frank, Anne. See Diary of Anne Frank
Frank, Hans, 68
Frank, Otto, 32, 81
Free speech
  academic freedom debate regarding
    Butz, 7, 11–12
  claims of deniers, 4–5, 59
  debating deniers, problems of, 5, 15,
    59–61
  in countries other than United States,
    46–48, 56–57
Front National. See National Front

Gable, Gerry, 6, 7, 25, 31, 41–42, 59, 97
Gack, 36
Gas chambers
  chamber at Dachau not used, 13, 20
  questioning existence of, 3, 9, 32,
    33–35, 36, 37, 44–45, 46, 48, 50, 51,
    60–61, 71–78, 85
  questioning of survivors' testimony
    regarding, 3
  See also Leuchter, Fred; Leuchter
    Report, The; Zyklon-B gas
Gaüzerre, Pier, 35

Holocaust Survivors and Friends in
Pursuit of Justice, 72
Homosexuals
as victims of Nazis, 90, 94
Horthy, Miklos, 41
*How Did Zionist Propaganda Cloud
Science and Mind? A First Quiet
Travel Through the Climate of Fear,*
50
Human soap, 3
Hunecke, Karl, 49
Hungary
Holocaust denial in, 40
Hungarian Jews, 65
Hussein, Ahmad, 49
Hussein, Saddam, 14
Huttenbach, Henry, 59

Iasi, 38
Ich Kan Nicht Vergeben, 71
Identity churches, 21
Il Candido, 38
Independence. See El Istiglal
Indiana-Purdue University, 11
In Prison for Telling the Truth, 35
Inquisition, 92
Institute for Historical Review (IHR),
2–4, 7, 8, 10, 12, 13, 16, 17, 19, 20,
21, 25, 26, 27, 28, 34, 35, 43, 44,
47–49, 51, 53, 56, 58, 85
Institute for Historical Review Newsletter,
11, 38–39, 44, 51, 53
Institute for Jewish Affairs, 40, 52
Interactive computer bulletin boards. *See*
Computer bulletin boards
International Association of Jewish
Lawyers and Jurists, 94
International Conference on the
Holocaust and Genocide (1982), 87
International Revisionist Conferences,
48, 49, 51, 52, 58
Internet, 85
Internment camps
Japanese-Americans in, 49
Intilli, 86
Iran, 34, 96
Irish Republic, The
Holocaust denial in, 38
Irving, David, 2, 9, 14, 27, 29–33, 37, 38,
44, 45, 46, 48, 62, 63
Islam. *See* Religious groups

Isolationism
of Harry Elmer Barnes, 6
of far-right, 56
Israel 1, 2, 4, 11, 33, 36, 45, 50–56,
85–86; *See also* Zionism
Italian
as language of denial material, 2, 37
Italians
belief that Holocaust did not occur, 2
Italy
comparisons of civilians killed to Jews
in Holocaust, 28
David Irving in, 32, 33, 37
Holocaust denial in, 37
Ivana Frankovska, 39

Jackson, Andrew, 88
Jackson, Robert, 66, 67
Jackson, Nigel, 45
Janklow, William, 88
Japan
comparison of civilians killed to Jews
in Holocaust, 28
Holocaust denial in, 49–50
Japanese-Americans
in internment camps, 49
Jeffries, Leonard, 19, 20
Jewish Telegraphic Agency, 34, 43
Jewish Week, 50
JG Burg Society, 29
John Paul II, Pope, 22
Johnson, Lyndon, 62
Johnson, Thomas T., 17
Jones, Jeremy, 45
Journal of Historical Review, 8, 26, 36,
53, 85
"Judeo-Nazis," 39
*Just Fight of the Nazis Againt
Communism and Judaism, The,* 43

Kassel, 25
Kawachi, Albert, 49
Keegstra, James, 46–47, 56
Kharput, 86
Khmer Rouge, 23, 90
Beate Klarsfeld Foundation, 61, 72
Kobori, Keiichiro, 48
Kohl, Helmut, 23
Korherr, Richard, 67
Korneyev, Lev, 41
Krausnick, Helmut, 67